# THE FABRICATION OF THE LATE-VICTORIAN
## *FEMME FATALE*

# The Fabrication of the Late-Victorian *Femme Fatale*

## *The Kiss of Death*

Rebecca Stott

*Lecturer in English*
*University of Leeds*

This title is published in the *Women's Studies at York/Macmillan Series*
*General Editors*: Haleh Afshar and Mary Maynard

First published 1992 by
THE MACMILLAN PRESS LTD
Houndmills, Basingstoke, Hampshire RG21 2XS
and London
Companies and representatives
throughout the world

ISBN 0–333–55612–7 hardcover

A catalogue record for this book is available
from the British Library.

Printed in Hong Kong

# Contents

# List of Plates

1 Philip Burne-Jones, *The Vampire* (ca. 1897).

2 Sketch Map of the Route to King Solomon's Mines. Reproduced from Rider Haggard, *King Solomon's Mines* illustrated by Walter Paget (1898).

3 'Sheba's Breasts' by Walter Paget. Reproduced from Rider Haggard, *King Solomon's Mines* (1898).

4 'She Took a Map and Placing Her Finger Upon Pekin, Said "There is the Place that Shall be Our Home."' Maurice Grieffenhagen (1905). Reproduced from Rider Haggard, *Ayesha: The Return of She*.

5 French Cartoon (1904) of the 'Yellow Peril' as seen in Europe. By permission of the British Library.

6 Sketch by Conrad. By permission of the Lilly Library, Indiana University, Bloomington.

7 Stanley Resisting Temptation'. From J. W. Buel, *Heroes of the Dark Continent* (1898).

8 Two Suffrage Posters: 'Franchise Villa' and 'Justice at the Door'. 'Franchise Villa' is reproduced by permission of the Museum of London and 'Justice at the Door' by permission of the Fawcett Collection.

9 Anti-Suffrage Posters: 'Votes for Women', 'Hear Some Plain Things' and 'We Want the Vote'. 'Votes for Women' is reproduced with the permission of the John Johnson Collection (Bodleian Library) and 'Hear Some Plain Things' and 'We want the Vote' with permission of Rosemary Hard's Collection.

# Preface

> There is no such thing as sexuality; what we have experienced and are experiencing is the fabrication of a 'sexuality', the construction of something called 'sexuality' through a set of representations – images, discourses, ways of picturing and describing – that propose and confirm, that make up this sexuality to which we are then referred and held in our lives, a whole sexual fix precisely . . . not a liberation but a myth, an ideology, the definition of a new mode of conformity . . . .[1]

This book concerns the 'fabrication' of a recurring fictional type of the late nineteenth century, a type of woman whom I have chosen to call the '*femme fatale*'. She is not unique to the nineteenth century, but she is fabricated, reconstructed in, and apparently necessary to, the cultural expressions of the closing years of the century. She is a powerful and threatening figure, bearing a sexuality that is perceived to be rapacious, or fatal to her male partners. The constructors of this type in these years rarely named her as *femme fatale*: there is a variety of names for her, from the 'wild woman' of Eliza Lynn Linton,[2] to the vampires of Bram Stoker. She appears time and time again in art, poetry and fiction either in her mythical forms or in contemporary guise: she can be prostitute, man-hunting aristocrat, vampire, African queen, native (black) woman or murderess. She crosses boundaries of class and race.

She is distinct from, yet related to, another familiar type of turn-of-the-century British writing: the New Woman. Unlike the New Woman, the *femme fatale* is mythically rooted and derives power from her association with figures such as Cleopatra, Salome, Judith, Helen, mermaids and sirens. She is characterised above all by her *effect upon men*: a *femme* cannot be *fatale* without a male being present, even where her fatalism is directed towards herself. The New Woman, in contrast, comes to refer to a new type of woman emerging from the changing social and economic conditions of the late nineteenth century: she is a woman who challenges dominant sexual morality, and who begins to enter new areas of employment and education. While she is often threatening, and sometimes sexually threatening, in her challenging of sexual norms, she does not carry the sexual fatalism of the *femme fatale* type.

In *The Romantic Agony*,[3] Mario Praz has traced a shift in the nine-teenth-century European text from a preoccupation in the first half of the nineteenth century with the *l'homme fatal* (the Byronic seducer) to a preoccupation in the second half of the century with the *femme fatale*. The *femme fatale* type can be found in the earlier nineteenth century, and indeed throughout literary periods and genres but, he argues, she is only formulated as a clear and recognisable 'type' in the late nineteenth century:

> During the first stage of Romanticism, up till about the middle of the nineteenth century, we meet with several Fatal Women in literature, but there is no established type of Fatal Woman in the way that there is an established type of Byronic hero.[4]

As this shift takes place, the gender of the vampire figure changes too, as we might expect: the vampire figure is predominantly female in the latter half of the nineteenth century.

Praz's work is valuably encyclopedic but he does not seem to need to ask why this particular phenomenon, this shift, occurs. His aim, he insists, is only to 'trace the course of certain currents' but his work leaves us with numerous challenging questions. Why does the *femme fatale* figure so prominently in the fiction of the *fin-de-siècle* (the closing decades of the nineteenth century)? What does she express? What is distinctive about British culture in these closing decades? Why is it that male authors of this period need to create a 'type' of fictional female who is sexually assertive, a figure who stimulates male sexual anxieties and who brings moral atrophy, degeneration, or even death to the male protagonists?

Michel Foucault's work, *The History of Sexuality*, Volume 1, a work of an entirely different kind, seemed to offer ways of answering these unresolved questions of Praz's work. Foucault says of the nineteenth century: 'In no other literary period, I think, has sex been so obviously the mainspring of works of the imagination'.[5] Foucault argues that although the received view of the nineteenth century is one of sexual repression, censorship and prohibition (what he terms 'The Repressive Hypothesis') these mechanisms of prohibition func-tioned to incite a whole range of sexual discourses rather than to silence them. He argues also that what is produced is not merely sexual discourse, but many sexual discourses, corresponding to the multiple mechanisms which acted to produce such discourses (in the areas of medicine, justice, pedagogy, science) in the nineteenth century:

> We are dealing less with a discourse on sex than with a multiplicity of discourses produced by a whole series of mechanisms operating in different institutions.[6]

For Foucault, as is implied in the above passage, the production of sexual discourses is not centralised, but dispersed. Power to produce such discourses comes from everywhere:

> power is not an institution, and not a structure; neither is it a certain strength we are endowed with; it is the name that one attributes to a complex strategical situation in society.[7]

Foucault's work is arguably the most important text in its field. It has influenced and informed a variety of twentieth-century studies of the construction of 'sexuality' in Western culture. Critics, however, have not found the work unproblematic. Feminist critics in particular, while acknowledging the importance of his work and of its analysis of the construction of sexuality, have taken issue with the lack of gender analysis in its formulations. Lynda Nead[8] is one such critic:

> The most serious problem of *The History of Sexuality* is the absence of any differentiation between male and female sexualities. Within dominant sexual codes the definition of sexuality was and still is gender specific.[9]

It was the conjunction of these two analyses of nineteenth-century 'sexuality' that began this investigation: that the late nineteenth century is characterised by the rise of the *femme fatale* (Praz) and that the same period saw the 'multiplication of mechanisms' (in science, pedagogy, psychiatry, medicine and criminal justice) for *producing* (not repressing) sexual discourses, an attempt to classify and to institutionalise such discourses (Foucault). This, Foucault claims, was the period in which 'sexuality' was 'constructed'. Was there to be a connection between the rise of the *femme fatale* and the historical process that Foucault tracks? Was the *femme fatale* a 'symptom' of a cultural 'condition' preoccupied with defining, classifying and, above all, constructing different types of 'sexuality'? Raymond Williams, in *The Long Revolution*, writes:

> it is with the discovery of patterns of a characteristic kind that any useful cultural analysis begins, and it is with the relationship between these patterns, which sometimes reveals unexpected identities and correspondence in hitherto separately considered activities, sometimes again reveals discontinuities of an unexpected kind, that general cultural analysis is concerned.[10]

Edward Said has written of representation:

> In any instance of at least a written language, there is no such thing as a delivered presence, but a *re-presence*, or a representation.[11]

If we are to imagine the 're-presentation' of the *femme fatale* as a kind of patterned woven image (the etymological root of the word 'text' is the latin *texere*: to weave) then my aim in this book is to examine the threads that make up that 'fabricated' image. These threads are of many kinds – discourses of many kinds that express differing cultural anxieties and preoccupations. It is the combination and interweaving of these threads that make up the *femme fatale* as a cultural 'sign'. In the process of examining this figure, much more began to emerge which seemed to be woven into a wider fabric – the complex fabric of late nineteenth-century culture. If we are to see each thread that makes up this figure as a 'discourse' (and the word discourse itself comes from *discurrere*: to run to and fro – like a shuttle carrying a thread), then such discourses are not unique to the image of the *femme fatale* but run into other areas of language, writing and representation.

I have been influenced in the course of my work by the words of Roland Barthes who warns, in 'The Death of the Author': 'In the multiplicity of writing . . . everything is to be disentangled, nothing deciphered . . . '.[12] Barthes' words and the post-structuralist poetics behind it, inform the methodology and approach of this book. My aim is not to furnish a final causal explanation as to why the *femme fatale* occurred as a cultural phenomenon of the *fin-de-siècle*, nor to close these texts, but to investigate channels of interaction between literature and ideology and to reveal the multiplicity of discourses mobilised to speak about sex and about the sexual woman in this period. The process of deconstructing or disentangling a fabricated representation such as the *femme fatale* is a politically important one. To disentangle the representation of sexual types is to come to understand the complex systems by which we are kept in place in our lives, by which models of unacceptable sexuality are held up to us and to which we are referred. Mrs Alving, from Henrick Ibsen's *Ghosts*, discovers the powers of 'unpicking' or disentangling as she challenges the prescriptive morality of Pastor Manders. She explains that such prescriptive morality:

> led me to examine your teachings critically. I only wanted to unravel one point in them; but as soon as I got that unravelled, the whole fabric came to pieces. And then I realised that it was only machine-made.[13]

I begin with a conception of literature not as a reflection of real life or ideology, but as one of the mechanisms which not only reinforce ideology but inscribe and produce it. As Nelly Furman has observed:

> In the last few years ... critical approaches influenced by structuralism and deconstruction have challenged the view that language is a stable, predictable medium, and have put into question the notion that writing merely 'represents' speech, thought or experience. Language, from a post-structuralist position, is not an empirical object but a structuring process; and questions concerning women and literature will be broached differently according to whether we apprehend language as a stable medium or a continuous process.[14]

And as Furman adds: 'in a post-structuralist world there is no place that is conceivable outside culture and safe from its ideology'.

Further questions arise: in an age in which 'sexuality' is constructed and when sexual discourses are being multiplied, in an age when science and medicine are preoccupied with the identification and definition of female sexuality in its various (constructed) forms, how does literature engage in this historical process? How does literature write about the sexually threatening female type: the *femme fatale*? What discourses does literature mobilise in writing about her and what does it share with non-literary discourses such as those used by 'scientists' engaged in defining femininity and sexuality?

In attempting to resist seeing literature as merely a reflection of dominant ideology and to examine the ways in which the construction of this threatening female type plays a part in the construction of theories about female sexuality, I have adopted a multidisciplinary approach. I am interested in searching for the circulating models of threatening womanhood in this period in other areas outside literature. I am interested in the different languages used to speak or write about female sexuality in the period. It was with the aim of maintaining the multiplicity of writing and of interacting discourses in individual texts that this book began: to resist closure and to resist reduction or simplification. The book offers ways of exploring its central question – why is the *femme fatale* so prominent in the literature and art of the closing decades of the nineteenth century? – but will not supply a single cause and effect solution to this question. The *femme fatale* is one of many 'symptoms' of this period; to study her and her significations is to explore the cultural mood and anxieties of this moment and to ask also how and why cultures need to set up types as threateningly 'Other'. To ask such questions is to cross boundaries of classification: 'racism' and 'sexism' become increasingly inadequate as terms. We must find new ways, and new concepts for the grey areas where such terms become imprecise, and there is an increasing number of writers working in this grey area, finding shapes and patterns. Gayatri Chakravorty Spivak, for example, is cautious about what she calls 'essentialist freezing' of the concepts of gender, race and class.[15] She writes about analysis which, when pushed far enough, causes these names, these concepts, 'to begin to show the ragged edges of their own limits as unitary determinants'.[16]

The boundaries of the book have excluded many other important writers of the *femme fatale*, the writers of the decadence for instance. The aim of this investigation is not encyclopedic. The investigation of literary works of this kind and the analysis of sexual discourses of the period outside literary works, necessitated a systematic and close reading of the material involved, an attempt to comprehend a complex system of patterns in depth. Karl Jaspers has addressed this dilemma:

> Comprehension in depth of a single instance will often enable us, phenomenologically, to apply this understanding in general to innumerable cases. Often what one has grasped is soon met again.

What is important in phenomenology is less the study of a large
number of instances than the intuitive and deep understanding of
a few individual cases.[17]

This book will attempt to disentangle a few particular instances of
the fabrication of the *femme fatale* and, by doing so, suggest the
existence of a larger whole, a cultural pattern from which the *femme
fatale* is textured.

# Acknowledgements

This book has passed through so many stages from its beginnings as a glimmer of an idea for a doctoral thesis through its large-scale revisions into a book, that over the years my debts to those who have supported and encouraged me have grown out of all proportions. I would like to thank in particular, however, Nicole Ward Jouve, Sara Chadwick, Geoff Wall, David Howard, Mickey Pepler, Treva Broughton, Mary Maynard, Haleh Afshar, Jacques Berthoud and Ted Chamberlin for inspiration, advice and models of scholarship. I would like to thank, too, my sister, Anne-Marie, and father, Roger Stott for quickening and nurturing my literary curiosity. Finally I tender grateful thanks to Paul Morrish and my son, Jacob, for putting up with the frustrations of its production for so long and for supporting my critical endeavours with enthusiasm and faith.

# 1

# Historical Perspectives

There has been a tendency in historical and literary research to allude to the period 1880–1900 as a distinct period in history, standing alone with its own peculiarities and idiosyncracies. It has been called variously the *fin-de-siècle* or the turn-of-the-century, frequently characterised by what historians have detected as a new mood in areas as diverse as the study of literature, imperial policy and the study of the history of sexuality. Recently, however, historians such as Ronald Robinson and John Gallagher,[1] historians of empire, have warned of the dangers of perceiving history as a series of turning-points and instead search for continuity between periods previously considered distinct. The tendency of current historical research (particularly in the area of imperialist studies) is to follow Robinson and Gallagher's lead: to emphasise continuities and to weaken the periodisation of the past. Are we justified in our allocation of boundary lines in the study of the turn-of-the-century? Is there a distinct change of mood, of national consciousness, in Great Britain in the 1880s and 1890s? And, if so, what form does it take?

The prominence of the *femme fatale* in the literature and art of this period appears to be culturally and historically specific. This would suggest that, as a recurring sign in literature and art, her emergence is perhaps linked to what historians have considered to be perceptible changes in the closing decades of the nineteenth century. That is not to say that there is a *causal* link between material, social and cultural changes of the late nineteenth century and the emergence of the *femme fatale* as a cultural phenomenon, but that she is one of many features which are specific to this period and which form a network of correspondences.

In *The Sense of an Ending*,[2] Frank Kermode has shown how we 'project our existential anxieties onto history'[3] and that 'our sense of epoch is gratified above all by the ends of centuries':[4]

Sometimes, indeed, it appears that we induce events to occur in accordance with this secular habit of mind . . . for most of us the

1

best known outbreak of *fin de siècle* phenomena occurred at the end of the nineteenth century; at any rate, it was in that century that the expression became current. Certainly there was a deal of apocalyptic feeling at the time, not least in the revival of imperial mythologies both in England and Germany, in the 'decadence' which became a literary category . . . in the utopian renovationism of some political sects and in the anarchism of others.[5]

The *fin-de-siècle*, he asserts, is to us the best-known period of apocalyptic thinking, but there have been others, other periods in history which carry with them a profound sense of an ending. We have it now, and it increases as we reach, not the end of a century but the end of a millennium: we, too, live in 'the mood of end-dominated crisis'.[6] 'Crisis', Kermode writes, 'is a way of thinking about one's moment, and not inherent in the moment itself'.[7]

In this chapter I will be examining what social, literary and imperial historians have considered to be the *zeitgeist* of the *fin-de-siècle* period, and at ways in which a national identity changes – the way in which Britain constructs itself in relation to its European competitors and perceives itself to be in a moment of crisis. The material changes in themselves are important but cannot be seen in isolation. To sense this change in mood we have to move from the myopic perspectives of more traditional 'discipline'-bound studies to a point where we can see the broader cultural patterns into which individual historical changes are woven. Standing back like this, we can see not only these patterns but how they are repeated in often unexpected ways. Much of what is impressionistic here will be returned to in the study of the discourses which emerge in the individual texts, and will be substantiated and consolidated there.

## CHANGES IN THE SECURITY OF EMPIRE

It is in this rapidly expanding field of study – the history of imperialism – that an important debate is going on about whether the late nineteenth century is distinct from other periods. This debate was spawned by the 'continuity thesis' set out by Robinson and Gallagher in an article of 1953 entitled 'The Imperialism of Free Trade'.[8] In this article Robinson and Gallagher challenged the received version of the nineteenth century as classified into a middle period of British aversion towards imperialism bounded on either side by periods of rapid colonial expansion. They argue that by perceiving imperialism as not merely the annexation of overseas territory but as the various ways by which an economically expanding society exerted its influence and protected its interests abroad, a basic continuity could be detected throughout the nineteenth century. This controversy has revitalised the study of imperialism, sharpened its definitions and challenged historians to be much more precise about the ways in which they consider the late nineteenth century in particular to be a distinct period.

The period from 1870 onwards has been labelled the period of 'new imperialism'. Disraeli's famous Crystal Palace speech is frequently taken to be the breakthrough of imperialism into public consciousness.[9] Disraeli asked England:

> Will you be a great country, an Imperial country, a country where your sons, when they rise, rise to permanent positions, and obtain not merely the esteem of their countrymen but the respect of the world?[10]

This period saw the rise of a 'conscious' policy of imperialism which by 1902 had added 4 750 000 squares miles of territory and 88 million people to the existing empire. While British imperial policy of the late nineteenth century appeared to be not just 'conscious' but fervently expansionist, historians have been in agreement that the motives behind such expansionism differ from the motives behind earlier imperialist policy. Even Robinson and Gallagher, while they are anxious to assert, in their book about the motives behind British involvement in the scramble for Africa, that the mid-Victorian period has much more continuity with the periods on either side, and are anxious to play down the distinctiveness of the late Victorian period, nevertheless outline a change in what they call 'the official mind':[11]

> Whereas the earlier Victorians could afford to concentrate on the extension of free trade, their successors were compelled to look above all to the preservation of what they held, since they were coming to suspect that Britain's power was not what it had been. The early Victorians had been playing from strength. The supremacy they had built in the world had been the work of confi-

4 *The Late Victorian* Femme Fatale

dence and faith in the future. The African empire of their succes-
sors was the product of fear lest this great heritage should be lost
in the time of trouble ahead.[12]

Historians of late Victorian imperial policy and empire consistently use words such as 'defensive', 'fearful', 'preservationist', to
describe the spirit of the age. What appears to be a period of rapid
and confident expansion, and annexation of territory, is animated by
fear of decline and loss of confidence. Paul Kennedy puts this even
more forcefully when he talks about a 'siege mentality' current in
late Victorian imperial policy:

> Late nineteenth-century imperialism, so far as the British were
> concerned, was increasingly an imperialism of fear, of
> Weltpolitische Angst and a growing 'seige' mentality (albeit su-
> perficially hidden behind a Kiplingesque assertiveness) – which
> makes it altogether different in form from the decades prior to
> 1870, when the empire's trade and territories were expanding in a
> power-political vacuum.[13]

The picture thus painted by historians is of a period of history
characterised by suspicion, intolerance and perceived vulnerability.
Britain had stretched itself out into the corners of the globe and
began to find its responsibilities, commitments and power difficult
to maintain. The emphasis became anxiously placed on
preservationism at all costs: the empire must not be seen to be
slipping away. This is a country nervous of the future, taking imperialist measures to avert decline, obsessed with security and with
safeguarding the routes to the East. The age saw 'the beginnings of
contraction and decline', but it also felt the effects of a changing
perception of itself as a nation, as a nation in decline, slipping from
power and fearful of the consequences:

> Over and over again [official calculations of policy behind impe-
> rial expansion in Africa] show an obsession with security, a fixa-
> tion on safeguarding the routes to the East. What stands out in
> this policy is its pessimism. It reflects a traumatic reaction from
> the hopes of mid-century; a resignation to a bleaker point; a
> defeatist gloss on the old texts of expansion.[14]

The spirit of this age, we might add, was not just pessimistic and
defeatist, but fatalistic.

Much late Victorian adventure fiction confirms this fatalism. In his study of this genre, Martin Green plots a change of mood in the late nineteenth-century adventure novel, which he describes as an 'anxiety of possession'.[15] The 'anxieties' expressed in this genre are to be seen in its recurring theme of regression, its persistent xenophobia and stress on the precariousness of civilisation. Patrick Brantlinger's study of the genre of what he calls 'imperial gothic' concurs with Green's assessment: that there is a strange mixture of nostalgia, nationalism and fear in these novels. 'Imperial gothic' is a genre peculiar to the late nineteenth century and combines imperialist themes with a fascination for the occult and the supernatural. Its principal features are a fear of individual regression or of the male protagonist out in the empire 'going native'; a fear of the invasion of civilisation by the forces of barbarism or demonism, and a nostalgia for the diminished opportunities for adventure and heroism in the modern world.[16] Such recurring themes can be seen to be symptomatic of (and conducive to) a change in the perceived security of empire, the weakening of Britain's imperial hegemony:

> the Imperial Gothic themes of regression, invasion, and the waning of adventure express the narrowing vistas of the British Empire at the time of its greatest extent, in the moment before its fall.[17]

What, then, were the factors that contributed to this change of national self-identity? If we are not content with merely attributing it to 'number magic', the sense of a closing century, then what are the material conditions that contributed to both a declining empire and the crisis-consciousness accompanying it?

## SOCIAL PROBLEMS

Historians have tested various hypotheses about the causes of the so-called 'new imperialism' (the sudden rash of annexations in the closing decades of the century) and have asked why British power should be in decline at this point. One of the explanations is to attribute these changes to a shift in the balance of power in Europe. Britain was no longer the supreme industrial power in the west. In 1873 a crash in the Vienna money market heralded the beginning of a depression which affected the whole of Western Europe. Its symptoms were surplus production, low prices, poor investment opportunities and widespread unemployment. There were changes taking place in European industry, too, which cut down Britain's lead in commerce:

> By the final quarter of the nineteenth century . . . a fundamental change had taken place: the transfer of industrial technology to the United States, Imperial Germany, later Russia and Japan, had created new centres of economic and strategic power where previously none had existed. British industry was no longer supreme, its commerce was hit by rival manufacturers and foreign tariffs, its naval supremacy was ebbing away, its empire was much more vulnerable.[18]

By 1885 the situation seemed serious enough for the Government to set up a Royal Commission to investigate the 'Depression of Trade and Industry'. The members of the commission were divided over what they believed to be the causes and what they advocated as solutions to the economic decline. Many believed the problem was caused by foreign competition. A minority advocated a system of imperialist preference: imperial colonies must be worked up into safe markets for British exports.[19]

Other historians have explained the 'new imperialism' as a diversion of attention away from severe social problems within Britain,[20] exacerbated by the Great Depression, changes in class configurations, the demands for Irish Home Rule, and the problems contingent on an almost unprecedented population growth (between the census of 1801 and the census of 1901 the recorded population of Great Britain had grown from 12 million to 42 million). The solution of the population problem for a number of the members of the Commission investigating the economic decline was colonial expansion, and emigration rather than birth control. Malthus had in 1798 drawn attention to the potentially fatal consequences of the population growth outrunning the means of subsistence. Mass unemployment caused by the Great Depression had seen the emergence of socialism within Britain and of organised labour movements. With the growth of capitalism and the modern professions, the middle classes were increasing in numbers and influence and The Reform Bills of 1867 and 1884 had produced a much larger electorate which led to enormous changes in party organisation and the realisation of the importance of propaganda.[21] Propaganda was to be supported and eased by the arrival of the 'popular press' (which was notoriously jingoistic), and the improvements in literacy brought about by mass elementary education. Expansionism provided a spurious appeal to class unity, a means to confirm Britain's position as a great power within the world, and an orientation of public attention away from internal problems towards international concerns as well as providing escapism:

One promise held out by imperial expansion was that of escape from the pressure of unwelcome social change at home, and the creation of 'traditional' English life overseas.[22]

Patrick Brantlinger has argued that this pattern (the deflection of public attention away from domestic problems) is to be found in the nineteenth-century novel: he shows how the themes of late nineteenth-century culture gradually shift from domestic class-conflict to an increasing concern with racial and international conflict. Before Brantlinger, Mackenzie had discovered in the changing forms of popular theatre in the nineteenth century a similar phenomenon – by the end of the century, he demonstrates, class antagonism has virtually disappeared from melodrama:

By then, imperial subjects offered a perfect opportunity to externalise the villain, who increasingly became the corrupt rajah, the ludicrous Chinese or Japanese nobleman, the barbarous 'fuzzy-wuzzy' or black, facing a cross-class brotherhood of heroism, British officer and ranker together.[23]

Brantlinger argues that imperialism functioned as a kind of ideological safety-valve, deflecting working-class radicalism and middle-class reformism into non-critical paths.[24] Noisy imperial propaganda was certainly to have this effect, but it is doubtful whether imperialist expansionism was solely influenced by an impulse to quieten unrest within Britain. Other historians have explained the rash of annexations as a response not to domestic problems, but to uprisings on the edges of the Empire.

## AN EXPANSIONISM OF FEAR?

In their study of the causes of late nineteenth-century expansionism in Africa, Robinson and Gallagher tend to play down internal problems as a stimulus for 'new imperialism' and argue instead that such expansionism became necessary as a response to a series of uprisings and rebellions in the last decades of the century:

> the so-called imperialism of the late Victorians began as little more than a defensive response to the Irish, the Egyptian and the Transvaal rebellions.[25]

They argue that being compelled to respond to such rebellions forcefully, the British manoeuvred themselves into more and more compromising positions, in which they found themselves annexing territories to crush rebellions. British experience of nationalistic rebellions had begun earlier in the century with the Indian Mutiny of 1857. A fear of revolt increasingly prevailed in British imperialist policy from the time of the Indian Mutiny (1857) onwards:

> The Indian Mutiny and the social upheavals which followed hard on the heels of European penetration throughout the Near and Far East left a lasting disenchantment in London and Calcutta about the possibility of westernising the Oriental . . . Victorian rulers had learned much more about the depths of reactions which too much meddling could stir up in Oriental societies.[26]

The later rebellions which broke on the edges of the empire, and reinforced the already deeply-entrenched fear of revolt, began in the Transvaal. The armed rebellion of the Boers in 1880 forced the British to a retrocession of the Transvaal, and the recently-annexed territory became a republic once more, although Britain retained a power of veto over the republic's relation with foreign powers and bordering tribes:

> Gladstone's government had not only hauled down a flag in the Transvaal, they had left a rebellion unpunished and a humiliating defeat unavenged. . . .
> The Imperial position in South Africa had been shored up for the time being; but the experience of the crisis of 1880–1 left deep marks upon the future.[27]

This period seems to have been marked by a series of nationalistic revolts breaking wave upon wave over a government unsure of its policies for dealing with 'native' uprisings. Soon after Gladstone's ministry had 'patched up' the Transvaal crisis and quietened the

Irish nationals, the Egyptian revolt broke open. Initially Gladstone's policy had been minimum interference in Egypt, but as negotiations failed, Gladstone authorised an expedition to Egypt which caused nationalistic feeling to flare up and resulted in Britain finding itself in occupation of Egypt:

> They had no long-term plan to occupy Egypt and saw no strategic need to do so. They had muddled and drifted with events. Each fateful step seemed to be dictated by circumstances rather than will.[28]

This muddle and confusion drew Britain into an occupation of Egypt (albeit reluctantly and, as they believed, temporarily) which changed the balance of power in Europe and became the starting-point for the extraordinary Scramble for Africa which characterised European imperial activity in the 1890s. British policy became adapted to and influenced by a series of revolts and uprisings which shocked the British public and forced the government into 'desperate expedients', annexing territory rapaciously in order, paradoxically, to defend itself and its routes to the East:

> For the Victorians at mid-century the excellence of moral suasion and free partnership had seemed self-evident. But now this belief was being shrunk by fears of subversion and disloyalty. Too often the old aspirations to liberate and improve the world had been ungratefully accepted or surlily refused. Orientals and Africans had been shown the way. They had not followed it . . . . Step by step, the easy British optimism modulated into an injured resentment and a harsher outlook . . . . Hence they were driven into abandoning creative policy and replacing it by cold administration and control. Prestige became all-important to them. So too did insurance. Policy grew more and more committed to the warding off of hypothetical dangers by the advancing of frontiers . . . . The frontiers of fear were on the move.[29]

## IMPERIAL PROPAGANDA: MILITANT MASCULINITY AND RACISM

In his discussion of the stages of 'new imperialism', James Sturgis notes that within the period of what he terms 'conscious imperialism' and dates as 1892–1902, the emergence of the popular press played a significant part in conducting public opinion: 'Newspapers no longer acted mainly as mere purveyors of official opinion but as conduits of public opinion.' During this period, he adds, 'late imperial ideology established a kind of hegemony over British cultural life' particularly by means of the popular press. Alfred Harmsworth, for instance, founded the *Daily Mail* in 1896; it gloried in the new imperialism and tapped a new market in his paper 'written by office boys for office boys' which was: 'a barometer of a gradual change which conformed to the almost monolithic imperialist stance of the metropolitan press in 1900'.[30]

John Mackenzie[31] catalogues the multiplication of 'vehicles of imperial propaganda' in this period. By the end of the century there had been a significant reduction in the cost of book production, which enabled an increased circulation of ideas and increased opportunities for imperial propaganda. Advertising, due to the technological advances in colour lithography, had become the purveyor of powerful visual manifestations of imperial ideology. Enamel advertising signs, often used as a means of advertising for imperial companies, increased rapidly from the 1880s onwards. Photography, bringing back images of the furthest corners of the empire, paved the route to European expansion in the late nineteenth century. Exhibitions of empire increased in number from the 1880s onwards and gained an increasingly propagandist flavour: a celebration of white man's successful transplantation to the farthest reaches of the globe. Imperial propaganda societies and leagues multiplied from the 1880s, such as The Primrose League and the British Empire Club, and many had their own journals. Imperialist propaganda was also to be found in societies which were not directly imperial in their concerns. Societies such as the Girls' Friendly Society and the Mothers' Union produced an ideal of motherhood and femininity which reflected imperial ideology. Imperialism was to pervade the eugenics and motherhood movements of the Edwardian era: mothers of the empire were to raise healthy sons to protect and expand the empire.[32]

Mackenzie also describes the rise of the public school ethos, characterised by athleticism and chauvinism, which disseminated itself to all classes through the emergence of juvenile literature. This literature, with its promotion of self-improvement and aggressive individualism, conformed to the pattern we have seen earlier: a deflection of attention to threats *outside*, rather than within, British society:

Whereas the dreadfuls had largely internalised crime and conflict in terms of domestic society, the new journals externalised them.

The world became a vast adventure playground in which Anglo-Saxon superiority could be repeatedly demonstrated *vis-à-vis* all other races, most of whom were depicted as treacherous and evil.[33]

As one might expect, these journals became increasingly xenophobic as the century progressed: the villains were always foreign, and the stories celebrated and ensured reward for the 'virtues' of self-reliance, individualism and athleticism. As with melodrama and imperial gothic the emphasis was placed on cross-class collaboration to defeat or suppress whatever was threateningly 'out there'.

Such literature was to pave the way for the rash of boys' associations in the 1890s. Such youth movements, Mackenzie observes, emerged out of a combination of the Volunteer movement and evangelical muscular Christianity. Alongside the scouting movement there were numerous other boys' associations of the same militant ethos, often organised by churches, such as the Anglican Church Lads' Brigade and the Catholic Boys' Brigade, and these were often initiated as a means to control and direct what was seen as the 'hooliganism' of working-class youth clubs. Baden-Powell's famous *Scouting for Boys*, a handbook for such proto-militaristic masculinity, appeared in 1899.

One could argue that in this age of conscious imperialism, when 'late imperial ideology established a kind of hegemony over British cultural life', that national identity seemed far from possessing a 'crisis-consciousness'. However, in the increasing compulsion in many areas of culture (in melodrama, and the genres of imperial gothic and juvenile literature, for example) to externalise the villain and in the rise of militarism and imperialist propaganda more generally, we can begin to see what historians of empire have identified as a growing siege mentality. Invasion fiction is also on the ascendency from the 1880s onwards (I shall return to this phenomenon later) and the pervasiveness of an assertive and muscle-flexing imperialist ideology is perhaps better seen as an expression of a national identity anxious to fortify itself against imaginary assailants.

## FEMINIST AGENCY

One of the most important areas of inquiry in tracking the social contexts of the rise of the *femme fatale* would seem to be feminist agency and agitation: is there any connection between the demands of the Women's Movement in this period and what might be described as the *femme fatale* reaction? The history of feminism has tended to ignore the 1890s, as Lucy Bland has observed recently. Bland has refuted the assumption that the period between the campaigns against the Contagious Diseases Acts of 1886 and the rise of militant suffragism in the early twentieth century was a period of feminist quiescence.[34] 1897 saw the amalgamation of different suffrage societies under the National Union of Women's Suffrage Societies and a suffrage bill looked close to victory in 1892 and again in 1897. She demonstrates that this period heard an 'increasingly voiced demand for a woman's right over her own body' and was characterised by the emergence of women's issues into the 'New Woman' novel, which came into its own in this period: 'the "new woman" novel was spot-lighting a host of horrors lurking behind the veneer of marital respectability'[35] (the double standard, venereal disease, incessant child-bearing and non-consensual sex). Sarah Grand is said to have invented the term 'New Woman' in an article of 1894 in reference to women who were entering higher education and new areas of employment. The word 'feminism' too, arrived in England from France in 1895. The main thrust of the Women's Movement in this period was a demand for changes in male sexual behaviour, the spectre of bestial male sexuality brought into public consciousness by the revelations of the White Slave Trade articles of 1885.

Patricia Stubbs, too, sees the emergence and development of New Woman fiction as a crucial part of feminist agency in the last years of the nineteenth century:

> The eighteen eighties and 'nineties saw the beginnings of a major revision in thinking about women and sex, a process in which literature played an important part.[36]

Novelists in particular, she argues, were beginning to change the received representations of women. Stubbs does not underestimate the achievements of the Womens' Movement from the 1870s and points out that by 1880 it had a firm organisational basis in suffrage committees. Agitation had resulted in the Married Women's Property Act of 1870 (with a second and more important Act in 1882) in which custody and maintenance rights had been extended. Women with necessary property qualifications won the local franchise in 1882 and by 1877 women were beginning to enter medical schools.

Although it is tempting to see the changing and more positive representations of women as coming out of the Women's Movement, Stubbs tends to question attributing such change to feminist agency. She links the changing representations of women amongst the writers of the New Fiction (and Stubbs cites Hardy, James, Meredith and Moore as examples) to a more general 'rejection of the moral imperatives which had accompanied the consolidation of the bourgeoisie in the middle years of the century':[37]

> By the end of the century morality had become for many writers a relative, not an absolute matter. The realist no longer believed in an absolute free will or, beyond a point, in individual moral responsibility, certainly not in individual moral autonomy.[38]

This alienation from social and political orthodoxy and the challenge to prescriptive moral and sexual ideology brought about major revisions in the portrayal of women. These changes in the novel coincided with advances in psychology (the pioneering work of Freud, Havelock Ellis and Edward Carpenter) and with advances in feminism, yet, Stubbs argues:

> there is no direct, causal link between developments in the novel and the emergence of either feminism or sexual psychology in the late nineteenth century. In the case of feminism there was, on the contrary, a definite breach between the novelists and parts of the movement, many women fearing anything which might associate their cause with 'loose morals'.[39]

Stubbs inclines to place these three movements – the emergence of feminism, changes in the novel and advances in psychology – as parts of a larger cultural development:

> They were all part of the disintegration of what had been a highly homogeneous culture, but which was now rapidly changing under new political and economic pressures.[40]

What may be of more use in the search for the contexts of the *femme fatale* phenomenon is what Stubbs describes as a conservative 'backlash' against such changes which occurs in the 1890s:

> The aims of the women's movement, modest though they were, taken together with the commitment of a number of important writers to a degree of sexual honesty in the novel, were greeted with alarm and dismay by a fundamentally conservative public

. . . . The character of the response – irrational, hysterical and dogmatic – can only be explained by the special nature of the challenge.[41]

This 'fundamentally conservative public' were also at this time to be challenged and discomposed by a series of widely-publicised trials, divorces, and general muck-raking, a chronicle of scandal-mongering which suggested a new mode of public discourse as Jeffrey Weeks, a social historian, suggests:

> a new mood is detectable from the 1880s and 1890s, and 1895 is a particularly symbolic year because the reaction to Wilde's downfall was indicative of the new mode in public discourse.[42]

Weeks catalogues a series of scandals which shook the British public in this period: all deeply challenging to moral purity and which incited renewed calls for moral purification. This period witnessed the campaigns against the Contagious Diseases Acts, scandal about police leniency to high-class 'madams', the White Slave Trade series of articles (1885), the divorce of Sir Charles Dilke (1886) and of Parnell (1890) and the scandals of the Cleveland Street homosexual brothel (involving the son of the Prince of Wales) and the Tanby Croft gambling scandal (involving the Prince of Wales).

The feminist movement, though at this stage it was concerned primarily with education and political rights for a select few, came to be seen as damaging to the basis of bourgeois organisation – the family, and to moral purity (premised on Woman as the Angel in the House). Those who denounced feminism took on an increasingly apocalyptic tone as the century progressed. In 1889 the *Westminster Review* predicted that the 'Ego' of woman:

> will yet roll over the world in fructifying waves, causing incalculable upheaval and destruction. The stirrings and rumblings now perceivable in the social and industrial worlds, the 'Bitter Cries' of the disinherited classes, the 'Social Wreckage' which is becoming able to make itself unpleasantly prominent, the 'Problems of Great Cities', the spread of Socialism and Nihilism, are all intimately connected with the ascent of [this] Ego.

An important strand in the backlash, or counterattack against feminism and the challenge to sexual and moral orthodoxy taking place in fiction, was to associate it with popular anxieties about a declining empire and a weakening moral fibre:

> It was widely believed at the time that moral and martial valour were closely linked, so when the whole character of English culture seemed in the 'eighties and 'nineties to be moving rapidly into a more permissive era (Ibsen, Wagner, Wilde, feminism, socialism), widespread anxieties about the supposedly declining 'moral fibre' of the nation combined with fears about Britain's ability to defend the Empire.[43]

In this moment of perceived crisis, writers and activists who challenged censorship or who insisted on greater sexual freedom in their lives and in their fiction or who called for women's rights were denounced as anarchists and revolutionaries who threatened the security of British culture, morality and empire. Individualism and the rights of women came under increasing attack in this backlash: all individual needs must be subsumed in the atmosphere of impending gloom, all must do their duty and uphold the threatened empire. Moral purity in this moment of crisis became paramount, as we can see in the rise of the moral purity organisations such as the National Vigilance Association (formed in 1885) and the National Social Purity Crusade (1901). Such associations, like the boys' associations, became increasingly more militaristic at the turn of the century. They saw themselves as the custodians of morality, besieged by the storm troops of the decadent and the impure.

## CULTURAL HEALTH AND ITS DIAGNOSIS

As the century progressed towards its close, debates about the state of Britain's culture and the 'moral fibre' of the nation became more urgent. In his article 'An Anatomy of Cultural Melancholy', J. E. Chamberlin describes the obsession with cultural health in the last decades of the century and the general influence of scientific and particularly medical speculation on cultural debate:

> cultural health in the last decades of the nineteenth century was most often measured by its evidence of disease. Quite naturally, this evidence was marshalled along lines supplied by the sciences, for science in general was beginning to take a particular

interest in abnormal or pathological states, from the perturbations of the planets to the palpitations of the heart.[44]

Chamberlin sees this growth of a particular interest in the abnormal as part of a larger concern with the state of culture: that the discussion of culture in the latter half of the nineteenth century 'increasingly turned upon some argument not as to what constituted but rather as to what afflicted culture'. Biology turned its interest towards the abnormal and the pathological as that which defied description or classification, or that which gave indications of being in a state of developmental decline.

By the end of the century the radical theories of Darwin and contemporary evolutionists had been translated into many different sub-sciences: those of craniology (the study of cranium sizes to measure the evolutionary development of certain races), criminology (the study of anatomical stigmata to measure 'inherited' criminal tendencies in 'deviant' individuals), and anthropology (the study of racial difference). The scientific study of racial difference had begun earlier in the century with the foundation of The Anthropological Society of London in 1863. This organisation aimed to be a free forum for the investigation of every aspect of human behaviour, but it was also to enable expansionism by contributing to a greater knowledge of (and hence power over) alien races. The Rev. Dunbar Heath, the Society's treasurer, declared in an address of 1868: 'the best legislator or politician is he who best understands the elements he governs; or, in other words, the best practical anthropologist'.[45]

One of the most pervasive late nineteenth-century assumptions, influenced by the development of anthropology, was that the white races of Europe were higher or more advanced in the evolutionary scheme than the primitive or savage races. In the evolutionary scale the white Aryan races were placed at the top of the hierarchy with the lesser races arranged in order of 'development' (and cranium size) beneath. Thus anthropology not only provided a means of power over native and colonised races (through 'knowledge' about such races) but also provided a model to justify and legitimise imperialism by arguing that lesser races needed the control and influence of superior races to safeguard and ensure their development. Evolutionary theory as it became translated into Social Darwinism (what some might call a 'misinterpretation of Darwin's ideas'):[46]

allowed an existing ethnocentrism to be wrapped in a covering of pseudo-scientific certainty. Ideas regarding the struggle for 'racial' survival were endemic among late-Victorians. Introducing a hardness into thinking about war and race, they could justify the imposition of rule over the 'child' races.[47]

Christine Bolt has shown that 'racial attitudes changed and hardened' during the late Victorian period.[48] This is partly due to the more widespread acceptance of biological determinism. The work of the anthropologists was important:

> because it gave the weight associated with ordered, empirical data to widely circulating ideas which seemed to conform to Victorian domestic realities and experience of the wider world. It appeared to confirm the inevitability of racial conflict, the validity of generalising about group characteristics, the desirability of racial purity, the need to control 'inferior' elements in any race, and the justice of imposing European civilisation on the hunting economies and cultural crudities of 'savagery'.[49]

Brantlinger has plotted the way in which an increase in racism can be seen as a direct response to the decline of faith in free trade and in the power of imperial might. Imperialism becomes self-conscious as it becomes problematic: 'imperialism as an element in British culture grew increasingly noisy, racist, and self-conscious as faith in free trade and liberal reformism declined'.[50] We can also argue that the more racist tendencies of late nineteenth-century imperialism, which functioned to reinscribe the superiority of the white Aryan races by means of categorising what was racially inferior, express an anxiety about the position of the superior races at the top of the evolutionary hierarchy.

Anthropological ranking had both enabled and legitimised imperialism earlier in the century, but it also provided a ready model for measuring developmental decline by the end of the century. Anthropology showed that while some of the backward races were still developing and could hope for a better and more advanced future, others were in a state of developmental *decline*, or atrophy. Science could not ensure, using this model, that the developmental superiority of the British race would increase or even remain stable.

## THE DIAGNOSIS: DEGENERATION

'Degeneration', defined by J. E. Chamberlin as 'the opposite of the theory of the progressive evolution of cultures',[51] became an anxious buzz-word of the late Victorians and provided a scientific terminology for expressed widespread concerns about imperial, racial and moral decline in Britain. Chamberlin proposes that degeneration 'is, in many ways, at the heart of the matter' of these debates and anxieties about the state of culture. This period produced a discourse of degeneration easily assimilated into biological, psychological and social theory.[52] While some saw the culture disintegrating as the empire declined, others insisted that cultural degeneration was the product of the degeneracy of its leading individuals.[53] E. Ray Lankester's *Degeneration*,[54] first delivered as a lecture, was published in 1880. Lankester, a distinguished disciple of Darwin, argued that some species represented not advanced versions of their earlier selves but atrophied forms of higher species, atrophy being defined as 'a gradual change in the structure, in which the organism becomes adapted to less complex and more varied conditions'.[55] Lankester proposed that degenerative evolution was not limited in its application to the field of zoology, but could be transposed into cultural debate and into social theory. His book posits the real possibility of degeneration with regard to the European races and articulates (scientifically) the widespread fear of 'cultural drift', a drift *backwards* down the evolutionary scale: 'possibly we are all drifting, tending to the condition of intellectual Barnacles or Asidians'.[56] Lankester argued that the 'unfit', the atrophied, were flourishing in a degraded environment in ever-increasing numbers, above all in the heart of London's underworld.

Max Nordau's *Degeneration*,[57] published in English translation in 1895, developed such degeneracy theories by taking as its focus decadent European literature. The decadents were to be the diagnosed scapegoats of Nordau's scheme rather than the supposedly 'degenerate' fecundity and overcrowding of the working classes. The book was widely read, in part because its publication in England coincided with Oscar Wilde's trial, which had drawn public attention to decadent art and homosexuality. The definition of the degenerate type was, of course, a means to classify abnormality or perverseness (the criminal, homosexual, prostitute, aesthete, or decadent artist) and inversely a means to articulate the imagined spread of degenerate characteristics threatening moral purity and cultural health. Fundamentally it became a means to enforce prescriptive normality and morality by a scientific demarcation of behavioural characteristics considered challenging to the *status quo* (the work of feminists and radicals of all kinds), as Boumelha argues:

> The spectre of 'degeneration' – a concept given particular promi-
> nence in and after Max Nordau's *Degeneration* (translated in 1895)
> – was an effective threat to hold over feminists who could not
> predict with 'scientific' certainty the effects of higher education or
> the vote upon the physiology of future generations . . . . This kind
> of sociobiology, with its direct and unmediated connection be-
> tween zoology and politics, dominated the sexual ideology of the
> last two decades of the nineteenth century.[58]

Christian morality gives way to the 'incontrovertible authority' of biological law. The law of biological determinism firstly enabled cultural disease as a concept to be assimilated and secondly enabled a kind of cultural scapegoating whereby those considered to have 'infected' the nation could be identified and registered degenerate.

For a country less sure about its power in the world, the possibil-ity of inverse progress (degeneration – either of individuals or of the entire race) both stimulated and provided a language for fears of cultural decline. If Britain's power in the world was slipping, could this be attributed to the degeneration of its leading members or of its working-class population residing in the London 'nether world'? Fear of decline or of degeneration was also fuelled by a sense of Britain's inability to defend itself should the need arise:

> As an imperial power under the twin pressures of economic com-
> petition and the possibility of nationalist risings in the colonies,
> Britain depended for its sense of security on a large and effective
> standing army. But it was widely supposed that the British work-
> ing class were in such poor physical shape that the army and the
> empire would collapse if it came to a large-scale war.[59]

## INVASION ANXIETIES

A number of literary historians have traced the development of the invasion scare story which begins to emerge in British fiction from the 1870s and which provides a key to changes in attitudes to Empire in the age of 'new imperialism'. Invasion scare stories are those in which 'the outward movement of imperialist adventure is reversed',[60]

just as degeneration anxieties are those in which the forward movement of evolutionary progress is inverted.

In *The Edwardian Turn of Mind*[61] Samuel Hynes observes that these
stories reach a peak in the years between 1906 and 1909 and decline
thereafter. Such stories include H. G. Wells's *The War of the Worlds*
(1897), *Dracula* (1897), Erskine Childer's *The Riddle of the Sands* (1903),
William Le Queux's *The War in the Air* (1908), Rider Haggard's *She*
(1887) and *Ayesha: The Return of She* (1904). The anxieties expressed
in these texts, writes Hynes, are of two kinds:

> a growing awareness of England's isolation from continental alli-
> ances and a conservative fear that radicals, by transferring power
> from the traditional ruling classes to the lower classes, would
> weaken England's will to defend itself.[62]

These stories illustrate how closely degeneration anxieties and invasion scares were linked. Both plot a narrative of decline and fall and
attempt to find a means to fend off imagined decline by identifying
the invader as either foreign or degenerate. The frontiers of Empire
and culture must be fortified to prevent barbarian invasion:

> Much imperialist fiction after about 1880 treats the Empire as a
> barricade against a new barbarian invasion; just as often as it
> treats the Empire as a 'dressing for dinner', a temporary means of
> preventing Britain itself from lapsing into barbarism.[63]

Hynes observes that the period in which invasion scare stories
reach a peak also sees a peak in degeneration anxieties exacerbated
by the the Boer War, which had undermined Britain's confidence in
her power and military strength. The Government formed an Inter-
Departmental Committee on Physical Deterioration in 1904 to look
into the causes of what was believed to be a deterioration in the
racial stock of Britain's working classes. Brantlinger associates the
rise of invasion stories with the development of spy stories, Wellsian
science fiction and imperial Gothic: all such fiction is on the ascendency from the 1880s onwards. 'Clearly,' Brantlinger writes, 'this was
not the fiction of a generation of writers confident about the future of
Britain or its Empire.'[64]

Heinz Gollwitzer, writing about imperialism from a wider, European perspective, sees the rise of invasion fiction as symptomatic of

the 'age of imperialism' and bound up with the rise of nationalism throughout Europe and an increase in 'great power' rivalry:

> the fear of being overreached, surpassed, crushed or encircled in one way or another, constituted a powerful factor in the imperialist's attitude towards life, particularly among statesmen and the military.[65]

The late nineteenth century witnessed the circulation throughout Europe of numerous 'danger slogans'. These were articulated as a series of 'perils': the black peril, the yellow peril, the American peril, even the 'white peril' (circulating in the Far Eastern countries). From the 1880s France and Central Europe feared the 'American peril': the danger of the United States economically outstripping Europe. Russia was feared too as a possible invader and as a economic competitor but the best-known source of the fear of invasion is what Gollwitzer terms the 'yellow peril' which projected a picture of the 'yellow', Oriental countries, numerically superior, rising up to clear the white man out of the Far East and becoming masters, perhaps, of the world.[66] Such widespread concern with conspiracies, spies, and invasion, Gollwitzer insists, must be seen as an effect of the advent of great power rivalry:

> Finally, it was only at a time when great politics had taken on world dimensions and people began to be concerned on a world scale with enemies, conspiracies, the creation of blocs and fronts, that the idea of a Zionist conspiracy to dominate the world could emerge and find credence.[67]

The increase in xenophobia in British fiction of this period, combined with widespread fears about the fitness of the British race and British culture, is both symptomatic of and conducive to a growing siege mentality in British imperialism. Paul Kennedy insists that the defensive expansionism of the late nineteenth century both affects and is affected by a 'growing climate of apprehensions and dissolving certainties' within late Victorian culture:

> The country became much more defensive, less willing to take chances, much more suspicious of foreign powers and much less tolerant of indigenous peoples; in consequence, much more in-

clined to take preemptive imperial actions, particularly since the government was under considerable pressure from domestic opinion to do so.[68]

Such historical and cultural research raises new questions about 'cause' and 'symptom': what 'causes' these changes in national identity so apparent from the 1870s onwards? Defensiveness and preservationism are to be found in many different areas: imperialism, invasion fiction, attitudes to race and evolutionary progress, attitudes towards the demands of the Women's Movement, fears about racial deterioration. It is too simplistic to prioritise changes in the security of empire as having a primary causal relationship to the development of a 'crisis-consciousness'. It would be just as easy to argue that developments in science 'caused' this new narrative of fear and defensiveness by positing the possibility of the obverse of progress: that great powers and great cultures can regress, can fall, can devolve. It is more useful to avoid compartmentalising these changes into 'cause' and 'symptom' and to maintain the plurality of change: that each of these changes are both causes *and* symptoms of a changing national identity. Invasion fiction, for instance, should not be seen as merely a symptom of changes in the security of empire, but as one of the vehicles which inscribe and confirm Britain's declining power and increasingly vulnerable position in the world. Imperialism likewise cannot be seen in isolation but must be observed in the context of changing notions of progress and evolution, and the influence of scientific developments. Xenophobia itself seems to have developed out of changing attitudes to the colonised, and fears about nationalist uprisings, but also out of developments in anthropology which were conducive to widespread fears in Britain about racial deterioration.

One way to avoid such division into cause and symptom is to use the word 'component' to indicate that these changes are part of a cultural system; components of a cultural system preoccupied increasingly with xenophobia, defensiveness and preservationism. The *femme fatale*, too, will be seen in the latter chapters as a component of a changing consciousness: she is one of the recurring motifs of the fiction of the late nineteenth century and takes her place amongst degeneration anxieties, the rise of invasion scares, anxieties about 'sexuality' and 'race', and concerns about cultural 'virility' and fitness. It is within the examination of the texts themselves that the importance of resisting the prioritisation of causes will be made evident: the individual texts produce discourses which circulate and interconnect with other discourses. It is the interweaving of such threads within the individual text, and the complex fabric of a culture to which that work is a contribution, that is to be the focus of this book.

## CLASSIFICATION PATHOLOGY

For a culture to diagnose itself as unhealthy or 'in decline', a medical or scientific model against which to measure itself becomes necessary. Science, as Chamberlin, has shown, had prepared such a model by the late nineteenth century. He has shown how the late Victorians had an 'instinct to turn to what was wrong in order to clarify, if not to define, what ought to be right'.[69] In attempting to define the weak spots in what was believed to be a culture in decline, scientific investigation increasingly centred upon defining abnormalities and searching out individuals or types who could be said to have 'infected' the nation:

> Whatever the scheme, some sort of causal relationship between the state of the culture and either its institutions or its individuals was generally accepted; and those who saw this state as degenerate reinforced this model by a psychological analogy that was of wide appeal, viz., that any cultural psychosis is at the very least preceded, if not caused, by an individual or collective neurosis.[70]

Incessant classification and naming became a feature of the late Victorian period: an instinct to define and measure culture by what it ought not to be. By the end of the century evolutionary theory had stimulated the establishment of new areas of science such as anthropology, criminology, craniology, all engaged in different ways with classifying and naming species, races, sexualities or deviant behaviour. Thus there is an increasing preoccupation in late Victorian culture with biological determinism: the fixing of gender, species, race and individual behaviour in terms of biology and inherited characteristics.

Many late Victorians, especially after the Wilde trial, felt that close attention had to be paid to identifying whatever was degenerate in society to ensure that degenerate characteristics were not acquired by the culture. Such investigations thus centred on what was considered alien or Other (not just alien races, but Woman, non-procreative sexuality, the insane or delinquent). In his study of Orientalism (the Western projection on to and will to govern the Orient) Edward Said once again sees the period from 1870 onwards as being distinct with a more 'manifest' Orientalism being constructed in this period:

> Along with all other peoples variously designated as backward, degenerate, uncivilised, and retarded, the Orientals were viewed in a framework constructed out of biological determinism and moral-political admonishment. The Oriental was linked thus to elements in Western society (delinquents, the insane, women, the poor) having in common an identity best described as lamentably alien.[71]

Classification is not limited to racial mapping in this period, but it does seem, as Said and Chamberlin have shown, to be generally limited to areas that resist classification or to groups considered alien, or to areas of human activity considered abnormal, pathological or degenerate. Women took up their place too in the anthropological hierarchical scheme. Measured by new 'modern' scientific methods (those of craniology, the measurement of cranium sizes; or by the methods of criminal anthropology, the study of inherited stigmata or bodily signs), Woman could be diagnosed and defined as a species inherently inferior in intelligence, as having innate criminal tendencies, and, where possessing an 'abnormally' powerful libido, atavistic.[72] The attribution of criminal and overtly sexual qualities to the black races was not new in the late nineteenth century, but science was to give racist and sexist generalisations scientific credibility. Woman became increasingly ranked with the black, the savage and with the animal: and given a low position on the evolutionary ladder by virtue of her cranium size.[73]

This period saw the 'founding of learned societies, journals, and academic institutions for medicine, anthropology, geography and linguistic studies' as Joanna de Groot[74] has shown, concentrating on the study of human characteristics, differences or cultures and bringing them firmly into the area of science, rationalism and professional expertise. The various sciences of Darwinism, craniology, criminology and anthropology were powerful and well-published in this period, fixing racial and gender characteristics, defining anybody deviating from their consigned place as abnormal and unnatural. The same, of course, was characteristic in medicine (with the entry of the sexual into the medical domain) for, as Michel Foucault has shown, the late nineteenth century saw a multiple 'implantation of perversions':[75] a clear and indisputable separation of the normal from the abnormal. It was a period, then, for all the reasons outlined above, that, in the areas of science and rationality, was obsessed with sexual and racial classification of all kinds, urgently seeking a hierarchical definition and inscription of superior/inferior races and, in medicine, the definition of normal and abnormal sexualities. In Foucauldian terms what we are witnessing is a process engaged not in stamping out the illicit and the anomalous but producing and regulating it.

## THE CLASSIFICATION AND FABRICATION OF SEXUALITY

As Michel Foucault and Stephen Heath would remind us, there is no such thing as a given sexuality, only an historical and cultural construction of 'sexuality'. It is this *fabrication* and classification of sexuality in the multiplying areas of the production of discourse in this period that can be witnessed in the late nineteenth century. The debates on sexuality and female sexuality (normal and abnormal, safe for men and threatening to men) were very much in circulation in the 1890s, a period haunted by fears of cultural degeneration, anxieties about the decline of empire and preoccupations with moral purity and its measurement.

'Sexuality', as Stephen Heath[76] has pointed out, is a nineteenth-century word. More importantly its first usage in a recognisably modern sense (meaning 'possession of sexual powers or capability of sexual feelings', *OED*) is dated 1889 and is found in a sentence from *Clinical Lectures on the Diseases of Women* by the physician James Matthews Duncan: 'in removing the ovaries you do not necessarily destroy sexuality in a woman'.[77] The word appears, then, in medical discourse and involves a (problematic) *female* sexuality, which substantiates the arguments against Foucault's lack of gender specificity in his analysis in *The History of Sexuality*, Volume 1. The date 'registers an historical moment and the context of a new awareness'.[78] It appears for the first time on the threshold of the 1890s.

Foucault, too, sees the last decades of the nineteenth century as playing a significant part in the construction of 'sexuality' (and it is unusual for Foucault to be historically specific). He states that in this period there was: 'a development of the judicial and medical control of perversions, for the sake of a general *protection* of society and race'[79] (emphasis mine). (Presumably Foucault is alluding to the

Wilde case here – 1895 – the medical and judicial systems combine to condemn Wilde's 'perversion': homosexuality.) Foucault adds more specifically that: 'It can be said that this was the moment when the deployment of "sexuality", elaborated in its more complex and intense forms, by and for the privileged classes, spread through the entire social body.[80] A 'multiple implantation of perversions', as I have mentioned earlier, takes place in this period and it was science that was to provide a new terminology for the sexually anomalous.

## MAPPING THE DARK CONTINENT OF THE OTHER

Historians have speculated about the 'causes' of this obsession with classification. Gillian Beer has written about the effect of the 'immense elongation of time' caused by the discoveries in geology and the emergence of a new study of prehistory. She speculates about the emergence of realism as a response to 'a dismayed recognition of the extensiveness of oblivion, the manifold and unremitting activities of forgetting'.[81] She argues that the Victorian fascination with history, with lineage, with the assemblage of record, even the rise of the detective story (with its emphasis on clues and the deciphering of traces) are all in some way bound up with 'deep anxieties about the extent of oblivion, the remoteness and unattainableness of origins', for after Darwin it was 'no longer possible to conceive of natural history as a tracking back to a recoverable origin'. The Victorian insistence on the 'real', she adds, can be seen as a response to the 'loss of a close-knit beginning and ending in the natural world'.

An alternative approach would be to suggest that what is happening is a response to a fear of the unknown and the unmapped, that the late Victorian crisis-consciousness responds to such fears by attempting to make the unknown world – the pathological, the alien, the abnormal – better-known. This response is itself a kind of colonising for, as the early anthropologists had pointed out, power over the colonised could only be maintained by an increase in knowledge about alien races. As Said has argued about Orientalism:

> the imaginative examination of things Oriental was based more or less exclusively upon a sovereign western consciousness out of whose unchallenged centrality an Oriental world emerged, first according to general ideas about who or what was an Oriental, then according to a general logic governed not simply by empirical reality but by a battery of desires, repressions, investments

and projections.[82] Orientalism is premised on exteriority, that is, on the fact that the Orientalist, poet or scholar, makes the Orient speak, describes the Orient, renders its mysteries plain for and to the West.[83]

I have already used the term 'mapping' to imply the imperialist and expansionist tendencies of a biological science preoccupied with classifying the abnormal, pathological and alien. This is an attempt to map the dark continent, and the dark continent should be understood as, not merely the geographical signified of that term – Africa – but as the domain of the Other, everything designated as *outside* late nineteenth-century British culture, moral systems, and normality. It is no coincidence that Freud refers to the unmapped region of the female mind and female sexuality as the 'dark continent'. The project of mapping the Unknown involves not a discovery of 'truth' but representation, a process which Said describes as conversion ('translation', 'transformation') of the strange and unfamiliar into the known. 'Knowing' the Orient (and in our context knowing and naming – classifying – the Other as the abnormal, the pathological) is also a process of reducing the imagined hostility of the unknown:

> efforts to bring the Orient closer to Europe, thereafter to absorb it entirely and – centrally important – to cancel, or at least subdue or reduce, its strangeness, and in the case of Islam, its hostility.[84]

What I have been trying to establish in this chapter is a parallel between what historians have seen as a defensive and fearful expansionism of late Victorian imperialist policy and the growth of classification which is, in itself, a kind of expansionism, pushing at the boundaries of what is known and mapping the Unknown. This too could be termed an expansionism of fear. Ronald Robinson and John Gallagher have described the complex development of the Scramble for Africa as not an annexation of this continent to *add* to the empire but as defensive preservationism of the old trade routes, an attempt to *protect* the existing empire. Similarly, biological interest in the unclassifiable (an expansionism into unknown lands) is not an annexation of these areas for their own sake but is stimulated by a need to preserve and protect the old standards upon which Britain's greatness was believed to have rested, the *status quo*:

> [British political expansion] of the late Victorians in the so-called 'Age of Imperialism' was by comparison negative, both in pur-

pose and achievement. It was largely concerned with defending the maturing inheritance of the mid-Victorian imperialism of free trade, not with opening fresh fields of substantial importance to the economy.[85]

It could be said that the old orthodoxies of morality, sexual roles, and prescriptive human behaviour were increasingly under attack, so in an effort to preserve and defend those orthodoxies new territories had to be annexed to ensure that preservationism was sustained.

Expansionism, it has been argued, masks a fear of invasion (annexations stimulated by a need to fend off the advances of other great powers or to prevent native uprisings and reflected in the rise of invasion fiction). Likewise, the obsession with racial 'mapping' and ranking (anxiously reinscribing the white male at the top of the evolutionary scheme of development) masks a fear of degeneration (again to be seen in the recurring fictional themes of regression, and in the genre of imperial gothic: the fear that the white man's place at the top of the evolutionary scheme is not so secure). All these preoccupations should be seen in the context of a pervasive preservationism in response to a crisis-consciousness: a desire to maintain the *status quo* and to maintain Britain's place in the world as an imperial power in a time of increasing challenge both internally (a challenge to the old orthodoxies) and externally (the challenge to the Empire). Historians have argued that Britain in the late nineteenth century saw itself as being in decline, experiencing 'cultural drift' – its national identity as a leading world power had been badly shaken and it sought to shore things up, to protect the frontiers of morality and empire. Classification and race-thinking became a means to postpone the crumbling of the frontiers, and a means to identify what were seen as the weak spots in the frontier as well as what was seen to be threateningly Other, outside the frontier.

SEXUALITY AND EMPIRE

Patrick Brantlinger who, like many historians of Empire or historians of imperialist fiction, dismisses (or assigns to footnotes) the work that has been done recently in the study of race and sexuality with regard to imperialist discourse, nevertheless uses an apt metaphor to describe the changing nature of British imperialism:

In British literature from about 1830 to the 1870s, white heroes rarely doubt their ability to tame various geopolitical mistresses – Africa, the sea, the world – and to bring civilised order out of the chaos of savage life.[86]

Brantlinger dismisses the importance of the gender of various invaders of the genre of imperial gothic – namely Ayesha and the female vampires of *Dracula*.[87] Yet in the terms of his metaphor used above the fact that these invaders are not just female, but sexually assertive and predatory women, is surely significant. By using such a metaphor – British inability to 'tame' mistresses – Brantlinger touches on the heart of the matter. What we are witnessing is a perceived decline in power and virility in the world (Britain is no longer able to compete successfully with the other great powers, nor is it able to 'tame' those it rules over) and inevitably sexual discourses were increasingly mobilised to speak about this decline in power. Edward Said has written about the increasingly sexual nature of imperialist discourse in the late nineteenth century:

> the space of weaker or underdeveloped regions like the Orient was viewed as something inviting . . . interest, penetration, insemination – in short colonisation . . . scholars, administrators, geographers, and commercial agents poured out their exuberant activity onto the fairly supine, feminine Orient.[88]

If the space to be colonised or penetrated is in itself a feminine and supine space then failure to carry out effective colonisation is imagined as a failure of virility. Cultural 'virility' (the ability to progress and evolve successfully – to propagate the race) was believed to be premised upon moral (and racial) purity. By extension cultural illhealth or lack of virility is understood as caused by a fall from moral purity upon which Progress and the Empire are built – a fall towards degenerative evolution. Lynda Nead has shown how anxieties about *decline* (of Empire and of sexual morality) are joined in the narrative of degeneration:

> It is surely significant that the language of moral and dynastic degeneration is the same: decline and fall; the terms plot both a moral and an imperial narrative and a fall from virtue can symbolise the end of an empire.[89]

How, one might ask of a book which claims to be about the fabrication of the *femme fatale*, does the sexually aggressive female fit into this scheme? The *femme fatale* is another of the components of this crisis-consciousness and she expresses a plethora of anxieties at once, or rather she is a sign, a figure who crosses discourse boundaries, who is to be found at the intersection of Western racial, sexual and imperial anxieties. The *femme fatale* emerges as a recurring figure in late nineteenth-century fiction alongside the emergence of degeneration discourses, invasion anxieties, and an increase in the classification of the abnormal and the pathological.

Christine Bolt, Joanna de Groot and Edward Said have all, in various ways, explained how race-thinking, and an obsession with the 'Other' becomes a means to define the self by assigning a place to what the self is not: '"race-thinking" in Britain was evidently cultivated as part of a general search for group certainty in a fast changing society'.[90] If we are to see this instinct for the classification and naming of the abnormal, the pathological and racially distinct (what we can call the Other) as a kind of defensive and paranoid expansionism into the Dark Continent of the Other, then we must be aware that this continent contains many Others and that Woman is one. The naming of the Other enables a preservation and defence of the not-Other (what is considered 'normal' and acceptable) by drawing fixed boundaries of definition and ensuring a reinscription of the moral superiority of the coloniser.

# 2
# Theoretical Perspectives

Somewhere every culture has an imaginary realm for what it excludes, and it is that zone we must try to remember *today*.[1]

The *femme fatale* is one of the inhabitants of an imaginary realm. As all images of Otherness, she is a stereotype, and the origin of the stereotype is in the manufacture of texts.[2] In this chapter I will be looking at other inhabitants of this imaginary realm and the ways in which cultures demarcate such zones in order to define themselves in terms of what they are not. In the previous chapter I examined the late nineteenth-century impulse to examine the abnormal and the pathological, the way in which late nineteenth-century culture sought to define what it was by diagnosing what afflicted it. This process is an act of mapping cultural zones, marking boundaries, and of creating and defining cultural Others.

## WOMAN AND THE BINARY OPPOSITION

The metaphorical space which the *femme fatale* occupies in late nineteenth-century culture is a space 'outside' normality, order, light, outside 'masculine' logic, reason, culture. Jacques Derrida has written about what he terms 'phallocentrism' which, he argues, is sustained by 'binary oppositions' deeply embedded in Western thought. Phallocentrism is summarised here by Ann Rosalind Jones:

> Derrida argues that the discourse of western metaphysics has been based on the construction of a fantasised sovereign subject, an idealised version of 'man'. From the beginning of philosophy, men have set themselves up as the central reference point of an epistemology built on a set of hierarchical oppositions in which 'man' (white, Graeco-Roman, ruling class) always occupies the privileged position: self/other, subject/object, presence/absence, law/chaos, man/woman.[3]

31

Binary oppositions in Western thought (as opposed to Oriental thought) are internalised as *hierarchical* oppositions: the element of each pair needing the dominance or subordination of the other for its meaning. The two terms are dependent upon each other, but the dependency is premised on imbalance and inequality between the terms.

Feminist criticism has written about the Otherness of Woman in a number of ways, both before and after the Derridean naming of this process as phallocentrism. Simone de Beauvoir's monumental and influential work, *The Second Sex*,[4] addressed this notion of Otherness in the representation of Woman, and in many ways initiated the analysis of female Otherness to be found in contemporary French feminist theory. For Beauvoir, Woman:

> is defined and differentiated with reference to man and not he with reference to her; she is the incidental, the inessential as opposed to the essential. He is the Subject, he is the Absolute – she is the Other.[5]

Beauvoir relates this definition and differentiation process to a primordial expression of a duality to be found in most primitive societies and mythologies: an expression of the duality of Self and Other. Others have always existed but were not always attached to the division of the sexes.[6]

We can see that Beauvoir's analysis corresponds to the Derridean binary opposition, although her focus is different from that of Derrida, taking as her subject the mythologising of woman in Western literature and thought. It is where she proposes the existence of plural Others in masculine thought, that she comes closest to the Derridean theory of phallocentrism. Woman, she argues, has not been the *only* Other, nor has she kept the same importance throughout history, but she *is* always defined as the Other:

> her ambiguity is just that of the concept of the Other; it is that of the human situation in so far as it is defined in its relation with the Other . . . . And here lies the reason why woman incarnates no stable concept.[7]

Woman is, of course, as Beauvoir reminds us, not the only incarnation of the Other. Woman occupies the imaginary realm beyond the demarcation '/' of the binary opposition but, as we can see, there are other occupants and cultural anomalies to be found in this zone:

White/Black
Good/Evil
Man/Woman
Self/Other
Subject/Object
Presence/Absence
Law/Chaos
Occidental/Oriental.

## THE CONSTRUCTION OF RACIAL OTHERNESS

Edward Said in his study of Orientalism (the way in which Western thought had systematically generalised the Oriental as Other) uses the term 'binomial opposition' to describe this same process. He writes of the complex historical and cultural circumstances out of which such a tendency to categorise evaluatively emerges in the nineteenth century:

> One of them is the culturally sanctioned habit of deploying large generalisations by which reality is divided into various collectives: languages, races, types, colors, mentalities, each category being not so much a neutral designation as an evaluative interpretation. Underlying these categories is the rigidly binomial opposition of 'ours' and 'theirs', with the former always encroaching on the latter (even to the point of making 'theirs' exclusively a function of 'ours'). This opposition was reinforced not only by anthropology, linguistics and history, but also, of course, by the Darwinian theses on survival and natural selection, and – no less decisively – by the rhetoric of high cultural humanism.[8]

Definitions of European culture, premised on the widespread belief in the superiority of the European races, necessitated a rigid demarcation of what was not 'our' culture, but 'theirs' in hierarchical contrast. To define 'us' (as superior) meant locating 'them' (as inferior) and banishing 'them':

> For every idea about 'our' art spoken for by Arnold, Ruskin, Mill, Newman, Carlyle, Renan, Gobineau, or Comte, another link in the

chain binding 'us' together was formed while another outsider was banished.[9]

The most important point about binary oppositions, or binomial oppositions (whatever one chooses to call this setting up of hierarchical difference in binary terms or pairs) is that those who reside in the imaginary realm are *placed* there by the cultural system (ideology). Frantz Fanon shows similarly how the 'Negro' has been constructed as an outsider in the Western imagination. The Negro has been made to be a symbol of sin, the archetype of the lowest set of values:

> In the remotest depth of the European unconscious an inordinately black hollow *has been made* in which the most immoral impulses, the most shameful desires lie dormant [emphasis mine].[10]

Patrick Brantlinger tells of the genealogy of the myth of the Dark Continent in the Western imagination and demonstrates its development throughout the nineteenth century. This is an extension of what Fanon and Said have described as the process whereby the non-Westerner or the non-white is made into a separate species. Africa, the Dark Continent, came increasingly to be seen as a centre of evil, possessed by a demonic darkness which it was the duty of the white man to 'illuminate' with Western values or to exorcise.[11] The Dark Continent became one of the imaginary realms of the late Victorians. The Negro did not just reside in the Dark Continent, but *was* (psychologically) that imaginary realm and, as such, was represented not merely as the absence of Western values, but the negation of those values:

> He is, let us dare to admit, the enemy of values, and in this sense he is the absolute evil. He is the corrosive element, destroying all that comes near him; he is the deforming element, disfiguring all that has to do with beauty or mortality; he is the depository of maleficent powers, the unconscious and irretrievable instrument of blind forces.[12]

## NON-WESTERN SEXUALITY

The sexual dimension of the human experience is one of those most commonly divided into the 'normal' and the 'deviant', the 'good' and the 'bad' . . . . For a secure definition of the self, sexuality and the loss of control associated with it must be projected onto the Other. Fantasies of impotency are projected onto the Other as frigidity, fantasies of potency as hypersexuality . . . . Sexual norms become modes of control.[13]

The non-Westerner fabricated by the Westerner as the epitome, or stereotype of the outsider, is (necessarily) imagined to have a sexuality considered abnormal, or threatening. This allocation of threatening sexuality to the Oriental or the Negro is a double process: firstly the non-Westerner is imagined to possess a sexuality which is Other to Western concepts of permissible or moral sexual practices, and secondly this allocation can be seen as a projection of European desires and fantasies on to the Other:

> For the majority of white men the Negro represents the sexual instinct (in its raw state). The Negro is the incarnation of a genital potency beyond all moralities and prohibitions.[14]

Said and Fanon, in their separate works, have shown how this fantasised and dangerous sexuality is attributed to both the Negro and the Oriental. Said has shown how the Orient came to be seen as a place of unlimited sexual license and experience unobtainable in Europe.[15] In time 'Oriental sex' came to describe a commodity of mass culture, available inside Europe.

Joanna de Groot has taken Said's observation one stage further by showing how the Orient as a place of projected fantasy and mystery, an imaginary realm of desire, was also seen as a realm essentially *feminine*, and therefore needing to be controlled, being susceptible to and in need of protection (restraint). She has shown, as Said does not, that 'women were presented as the *means* for finding out about the Orient'.[16] Their veils and harems become the symbol of Oriental mystery, a demarcation of (sexual) space prohibited to man. The Dark Continent, too, as an imaginary realm came to be seen as essentially feminine, Africa as a barbaric mistress to be tamed or explored and thus rendered less threatening. The Dark Continent likewise becomes a term to describe the mysteries of Woman, significantly employed by Freud to describe the mystery of female psychology. The imagined qualities of Woman, Africa (the Dark Continent), the Orient, and deviant sexuality, cross boundaries, so that the Negro is said to possess a deviant sexuality, so that the sexual female possesses negroid qualities, so that the Orient possesses female qualities and so on. The traffic of racial and gender stereotypes moves in many directions:

> while the Orient came to be explored and characterised through images of gender and sexuality, it is equally important that the 'oriental' became an image through which gender and sexuality could be defined within European culture.[17]

Since all the signs and qualities of Otherness derive from the same deep structure in cultural formation, various signs of difference will be linked. The inhabitants of the imaginary realm will share the same qualities and characteristics; they will be perceived as belonging to the same 'family'.

## THE COMMON IDEOLOGICAL GROUNDING OF SEX AND RACE

Joanna de Groot's groundbreaking study of the ideological parallels and interactions between 'sex' and 'race' argues that 'nineteenth-century representations and discourses of sexual identity and difference drew upon and contributed to comparable discourses and representations of ethnic, 'racial' and cultural identity and difference'.[18] The reason for this is, in the words of M. Maynard and A. Brittan, that 'racism and sexism belong to the same discursive universe'.[19] The growth of biological determinism in the sciences in the nineteenth century facilitated this merging of the discourses of 'sex' and 'race'; in other words concepts of sex and race in effect were created by the same anthropological sciences in the late nineteenth century. Biological determinism affects class, but class can always be subject to political reform and is less easily contained by the categories of biological essentialism. De Groot argues that there are structural connections between the treatment of women and non-Europeans in the language, experience and imaginations of Western men. It becomes increasingly difficult to disentangle the discourses of sex and race in nineteenth-century culture. Imperialists speak of penetrating the Dark Continent; Jung celebrates Freud's 'passions for knowledge which was to lay open a dark continent to his gaze';[20] criminologists studying the prostitute look for negroid or 'atavistic' features; the Oriental man is feminised.

The interaction of 'sex' and 'race' discourses in the nineteenth century arose from the observation of biological difference:

> Whereas the theories and practices related to 'class' distinctions and relationships were founded on the new 'sciences' of political economy and social investigation, theories and practices related to 'race' and 'sex' drew on biological, anthropological and medical scholarship, often grounding themselves in part on observable and 'inescapable' physical aspects of difference. The inequalities inherent in male–female relationships and western hegemony in the world in the nineteenth century involved elements of personal intimacy and cultural encounter very different from the experiences and perceptions which constructed the history of 'class' in that period.[21]

In other words, the ideological grounding of 'sex' and 'race' shared the same scientific scholarship at base, and a different grounding from that of 'class'. The common grounding of 'sex' and 'race' in such discourses is that of *difference*: scientific scholarship grounded on 'observable and inescapable physical aspects of difference'. This was due in part to elements of 'personal intimacy and cultural encounter': the problems of Otherness – racial, cultural and sexual.

## THE POSITIONALITY OF OTHERNESS

> Where is she, where is the woman in all the spaces he surveys, in all the scenes he stages within the literary enclosure? We know the answers and there are plenty: she is in the shadow. In the shadow he throws on her; the shadow she is. Night to his day – that has forever been the fantasy. Black to his white. Shut out of his system's space, she is the repressed that ensures the system's functioning.[22]

The *femme fatale* comes in many guises, but she is always Other. She is always outside, either literally (the female vampires in Stoker's *Dracula* beckon from outside the circle of the Holy Wafer, beckon to the pure woman protected inside the circle) or metaphorically, for as sexually fatal woman she represents chaos, darkness, death, all that lies beyond the safe, the known, and the normal. In effect, the major common feature of the *femme fatale* is that of *positionality*: she is a multiple sign singularised by her position of Otherness: outside, invading, abnormal, subnormal and so on. Furthermore, it is significant that in the texts I shall be examining, the outstretched and imploring arms of the predatory female are a recurring feature from Lucy's 'Come . . . my arms are *hungry* for you' (*Dracula*) to Ayesha's killing embrace of Leo (*She*), to the outstretched arms of the black mistress of Kurtz bringing down the twilight (chaos) on to the imperial explorers of the Congo (*Heart of Darkness*). If, then, she is a sign of multiple Otherness (chaos, darkness, atavism, twilight, other worlds, even death) then her outstretched arms desire, in the male imagination, to draw the male down into that Other world.

Toril Moi's *Sexual/Textual Politics* provides a crucial expression of this marginality, a summary of the works of Irigaray, Cixous and Kristeva:

> If, as Cixous and Irigaray have shown, femininity is defined as lack, negativity, absence of meaning, irrationality, chaos, darkness – in short, as non-Being – Kristeva's emphasis on marginality allows us to view this repression of the feminine in terms of positionality rather than of essences. What is perceived as marginal at any given time depends on the position one occupies. A brief example will illustrate this shift from essence to position: if patriarchy sees women as occupying a marginal position within the symbolic order, then it can construe them as the *limit* or borderline of that order. From a phallocentric point of view, women will then come to represent the necessary frontier between man and chaos; but because of their very marginality they will also seem to recede into and merge with the chaos of the outside. Women seen as the limit of the symbolic order will in other words share in the disconcerting qualities of all frontiers.[23]

Woman's position on the frontier is a *double* position depending on the type of woman. The idealised woman (the woman seen as representative of a higher and purer nature, as Virgin or Mother of God) is conceived as an inherent part of the *inside* of the frontier (protecting and shielding the symbolic order from chaos). The second type, the woman vilified as Lilith or the Whore of Babylon, is to be found on the *outside* edge of the frontier, part of the chaotic wilderness outside, representing that darkness and chaos.

We will see this division starkly illustrated by the Lucy/Mina dichotomy in *Dracula*. Firstly, Lucy, in her vampiric transformation, struggles with the wreaths of garlic flowers, pushing them from her or breaking the circle in her nocturnal and vampiric state and clasping them to her in her 'pure' state. As 'vampire', she persistently searches for a way *out* of the protective circles the men (the 'experts') place around her. More strikingly, perhaps, Mina, venerated as 'one of God's women', and functioning as protectress of the band of men, remains just *inside* the circle of the Holy Wafer, with the sexualised vampire sisters just *outside* the circle begging her to join them. It is the second woman, the woman conceived of as *outside* the circle, or beyond the frontier, that will be the subject of this book. She partakes of the qualities of all that is beyond the frontier (Other) in the male imagination.

More importantly, it is the proposition, outlined above by Moi, that Woman shares in the disconcerting qualities of all frontiers, that I would like to emphasise here, and the observation that 'What is perceived as marginal at any given time depends on the position one occupies.' This formulation of the nature and positionality of Otherness extends Beauvoir's reading of Woman as Other, but as not the only Other. It implies that Woman is in some senses the only Other, or rather the Other around whom the qualities of all Others collect in the male imagination. Hence the multiple signification.

In Moi's formulation the *femme-fatale*-as-sign (the woman just beyond the frontier, merging with chaos) signifies all that lies beyond the frontier or sign '/': the signifying frontier marking the distinction of the two elements of the binary opposition: the sign that marks the end of order and the beginning of Otherness. For many reasons, frontiers, margins and boundaries were important and expressive metaphors of the last decades of the nineteenth century. We have seen how the late nineteenth century saw a growth in classification of all kinds, a preoccupation with ranking ethnic groups (in the sciences of anthropology and craniology), with classifying the criminal as a particular and physically recognisable type (in the sciences of craniology and criminology) and with classifying sexuality and 'implanting' a multiplicity of sexual types including the homosexual, the nymphomaniac, the masturbator (the growth of the medical analysis of sexuality). We can see these strategies as a means of dealing with anxieties (not individual but *cultural*) about merging and the breaking down of boundaries. Biological determinism itself is a way of fixing 'Others', believed to be themselves safely fixed by inherited and biological features.

To dissolve the distinctions made by racial classification would result in the merging of species. To dissolve the classification of the criminal as a distinct physical type (recognisably Other) would be to admit the possibility of criminality in everyone. To dissolve the distinctions of gender roles would be to admit women into previously 'safe' male areas: the club, higher education, certain male-dominated areas of work, and more importantly, into the franchise. Merging or dissolution of such boundaries would, moreover, bring on the spectre of degeneration of all kinds and herald the end of Empire. Nordau's diagnosis of creeping degeneration in Europe specifies the *loss of form* or *outline* (the lack of clear distinctions) to be a symptom of such degeneracy. He writes:

> Over the earth the shadows creep with deepening gloom, wrapping all objects in a mysterious dimness, in which all certainty is destroyed and any guess seems plausible. Forms lose their outline and are dissolved in floating mist.[24]

This is the twilight world, or dusk, of the *fin-de-siècle*, the gloom and mist, the shapelessness out of which the *femme fatale* so persistently looms in her fictional worlds. The 'imaginary realm', the 'literary enclosure' of the *femme fatale* is a twilight one and her form is often dissolved in floating mist.


## FANTASY

Rosemary Jackson sees Stoker's *Dracula*, like other fantastic texts, as 're-enforcing a bourgeois ideology':

> The shadow on the edge of bourgeois culture is variously identified as black, mad, primitive, criminal, socially deprived, crippled or (when sexually assertive) female. Difficult or impalatable social realities are distorted to emerge as melodramatic shapes – monsters, snakes, bats, vampires . . . femmes fatales. Through this identification, bad social elements can be destroyed in the name of exorcizing the demonic.[25]

Thus fantasy (and specifically Stoker's *Dracula*) has a normalising activity, identifying such a normality as middle-class, monogamous and male-defined, and seeking to destroy or exorcise that which it has named abnormal.

In summarising the work of Bessiere and the *limits* of fantasy, Jackson writes:

Presenting what cannot be, but is, fantasy exposes a culture's definitions of that which can be: it traces the limits of its epistemological and ontological frame.[26]

Dracula, then, in such a definition, as existing 'outside', points to the edges of the real; *Dracula*, as the text, 'traces the limits of (culture's) epistemological frame'. By representing what *cannot be*, the absent, it also frames what *can be*, what is allowed to exist inside the circle. This is also true of the *femme fatale*. She presents what cannot be, what is Other to late nineteenth-century culture's designated normality. Enduringly abnormal, she points to the limits of female normality.

Jackson and Bessiere correspond with Jameson's arguments in 'Magical Narratives: Romance as a Genre'.[27] Here Jameson insists that the concepts of good and evil are not metaphysical categories, but are as 'little natural, as historical and humanly "constructed", as say, the totemic systems of certain primitive tribes':

It is becoming increasingly clear that the concept of evil is at one with the category of Otherness itself: evil characterises whatever is radically different from me, whatever by virtue of precisely that difference seems to constitute a real and urgent threat to my existence . . . . The point, however, is not that in such figures the Other is feared because he is evil; rather he is evil because he is Other, alien, different, strange, unclean and unfamiliar.[28]

Evil, then, is always relative to each culture, or stage of culture. It is constructed as Other. It is all that is outside, taboo, and marks the limits, the frontiers, of what is socially and culturally acceptable: that which lies within the circle.

As I stated earlier, the Other is *made* Other – there is no natural Otherness. We must also look to positionality (cultural zoning into inside and outside realms) rather than essences. Fanon has written of the ways in which, throughout Western history the Negro has been constructed as outsider, the negation of Western values, the depository of all that is considered to be alien to Western culture. This he calls a 'mechanism of cultural projection': 'In Europe the Negro has one function: that of symbolizing the lower emotions, the baser inclinations, the dark side of the soul'.[29] Fanon challenges Jung's concept of the collective unconscious as located in the inherited cerebral matter of man and insists that the collective unconscious is constructed, that is to say, acquired:

the collective unconscious, without our having to fall back on the genes, is purely and simply the sum of prejudices, myths, collective attitudes of a given group . . . in fact the collective unconscious is cultural, which means acquired.[30]

Mechanisms of cultural projection are the means by which the collective unconscious is culturally fabricated. In this Fanon, like Jameson, insists that archetypes of Otherness, too, are culturally constructed and acquired. There is no natural Otherness, but only that which is made – fabricated.

Fanon argues that the white man projects his repressed on to the Negro, and this repressed includes sexual potential: an irrational longing for sexual license. With Woman the mechanism of cultural projection is more complex: within the hierarchies of Otherness, the black woman is yet more strange and more alien to the white man than the Negro male. Within the representation of the *femme fatale* there is a whole series of cultural projections taking place: where the *femme fatale* is black there is a simple projection of Western repressed on to the black woman. Where the *femme fatale* is white she bears the qualities of 'blackness': in other words, this mechanism of projection of the male Western repressed on to the white *femme fatale* has passed through the first stage of projection, so that the image of the black female (bearing a black, 'predatory' sexuality) is superimposed upon the white woman.

### SELF AND OTHER

Edward Said reminds the reader that it is:

perfectly natural for the human mind to resist the assault upon it of untreated strangeness; therefore cultures have always been inclined to impose complete transformations on other cultures, receiving these other cultures not as they are but as, for the benefit of the receiver, they ought to be.[31]

Of course, the articulation of anxieties about merging, about the dissolution of gender distinctions and national boundaries, cannot wholly be attributed to these very real ideological and political causes which I outlined in the previous chapter, but are equally bound up with the definition of *self* and Others: the importance of boundaries of the cultural body which define a unified self. As Joanna de Groot has observed in her study of 'sex' and 'race' in the nineteenth century:

> first in examining concepts of 'sex' and 'race' we are dealing with the terrain of male power; second such power should be understood not just as a practical function but also as a process of defining the self and others.[32]

In this she concurs with Foucault in not perceiving the strategies and discourses of the concept of Otherness as a deliberate, centralised strategy emanating from an ideological power base, but rather that these discourses come from and are produced everywhere, in all interactions with 'difference':

> The images of Otherness and subordination need to be understood as ways for men to explore and deal with their own identity and place in the world as sexual beings, as artists, as intellectuals, as imperial rulers, and as wielders of knowledge, skill and power.[33]

Similarly, Jameson's account of the means by which the categories of good and evil are defined indicates the same anxieties about the threatened unity of *self*:

> the concept of good and evil is a positional one that coincides with categories of Otherness . . . So from the earliest times, the stranger from another tribe, the 'barbarian' who speaks an incomprehensible language and follows outlandish customs, but also the woman, whose biological difference stimulates fantasies of castration and devoration, or in our own time, the avenger of accumulated resentments from some oppressed class or race, or else that alien being, Jew or Communist, behind whose apparently human features a malignant and preternatural intelligence is thought to lurk: these are some of the archetypal figures of the Other . . . .[34]

It is this process – the response to the sexual woman as evil and threatening because she is alien and Other, because her sexual Otherness 'stimulates fantasies of castration and devoration' – that we can see at work in certain of the texts and discourses studied. It is in the translation of such fears into ideological systems, systems corroborated by seemingly empirical sciences, into a construction of 'ethics', that we see the rationalising of primitive fears. Jameson argues that moving from Derrida to Nietzsche:

> is to glimpse the rather different interpretation of the binary op-
> position, according to which its positive and negative terms are
> ultimately assimilated by the mind as a distinction between good
> and evil. Not metaphysics but ethics is the informing ideology of
> the binary opposition . . . and it is ethics itself which is the
> ideological vehicle and the legitimation of concrete structures of
> power and domination.[35]

Not metaphysics but *ethics*: the reading of the predatory woman as evil (unacceptable) because she is Other. The establishment of Woman as the Other of the binary opposition informed by the ideology of *ethics* is a feature of the Victorian novel as Stephen Heath has argued:

> what is generally constant in the Victorian novel is a fascination
> with the image, the figure of 'the woman' – depicted, defined,
> displayed, diagnosed in a kind of ceaseless concern (the concern
> for identity, for who I, male, am, if, she, female, is elsewhere to *my*
> difference, 'the man'/'the woman', the one *from* the other, like
> Eve and Adam, the difference secured); and this simultaneously
> with her emergence as a medical problem for society and with her
> increasing reality as disturbance, engaged even in struggle against
> her position as 'the woman' and hence against his as 'the man'.[36]

I would like to propose at this point that while Woman-as-Other is a fixed concept inscribed in Western binary oppositions (either metaphysics – Derrida, or ethics – Jameson and Nietzsche) the construction of the sign of Woman located in specific discourses is a *historically shifting* construct. In other words, this is to propose that the constitution of the *femme-fatale*-as-sign depends upon *what else* (besides Woman) is considered to be culturally invasive or culturally and politically Other at any historical point.

## OTHERWORLDS AND UNDERWORLDS

Of the imagined zones of cultural or evolutionary darkness for the late Victorians, there are two of peculiar potency. The first is imagined as a geographical zone *within* civilisation: a dark Underworld located beneath the cities of progress, a zone characterised by poverty, sexual excess, degeneration, disease and corruption. The second is a place imagined as the depository of Otherness located *outside* civilisation: the Dark Continent itself – Africa – a place of disease, depravity and corruption. Both worlds, both imaginary realms, are characterised by darkness which even the light of progress and civilisation cannot penetrate. To encounter such zones is to risk contamination and corruption of the cultural self. J. S. Moffat, for instance, warned the missionary that in Africa he had to be:

> deeply embued with God's spirit in order to have strength to stand against the deadening and corrupting influence around him . . . . I am like a man looking forward to getting back to the sweet air after being in a coal-mine.[37]

Both myths express the fear of falling out of the light and into the dark, a fear of losing whiteness (regressing – degeneration), a fear of losing moral superiority, identity, status and class, and a fear of not being able to return to the privileged position once defiled by the Other realm:

> just as the social class fantasies of the Victorians . . . often express the fear of falling into the abyss of poverty, so the myth of the Dark Continent contains the submerged fear of falling out of the light into the abyss of social and moral regression. In both cases the fear has a powerful sexual dimension.[38]

Writing in a period haunted by decline and fall many writers of the late nineteenth century describe imaginary realms to which such a fall may take the White Man: the imaginary realms of darkness, disease and regression, whether the African Otherworld or the London Underworld within or beneath civilisation. H. G. Wells's *The Time Machine* creates an imaginary and divided realm: the dark subterranean world of the Morlocks and the surface world of the overcivilised and effete Eloi. The harmonious surface of the Eloi world is punctured by shafts or 'wells' through which the apelike Morlocks crawl at night to hunt their human prey. George Gissing entitled his novel about the London underworld: *The Nether World*, and Jack London described his vision of London in *The People of the Abyss*. General William Booth of the Salvation Army, echoing the title of Stanley's *In Darkest Africa* published only months before, entitled his study of poverty and disease in London, *In Darkest*

*London and the Way Out.*[39] Booth had read Stanley's descriptions of African gloom and darkness and had seen London. His paupers are described apocalyptically as the 'sinking classes', 'the submerged tenth', 'the multitudes who struggle and sink in the open-mouthed abyss' of a London comparable only to Dante's purgatory or to a Bosch painting: 'the borders of this great lost land are not sharply defined. They are continually expanding and contracting'.[40]

In his opening chapter Booth justifies his borrowing of Stanley's title by arguing that:

> while brooding over the awful presentation of life as it exists in the vast African forest, it seemed to me only too vivid a picture of many parts of our own land. As there is a darkest Africa is there not also a darkest England? Civilisation, which can breed its own barbarians, does it not also breed its own pygmies? May we not find a parallel at our own doors, and discover within a stone's throw of our own cathedrals and palaces similar horrors to those which Stanley has found existing in the great Equatorial forest?[41]

Just as imperial, racial and sexual discourses are interwoven in Western ideological systems (arising as they do from the same discursive universe), the two imaginary realms (the Underworld and the Otherworld) are superimposed upon each other in the cultural imaginings of the late nineteenth century; they share similar topographical features, in General Booth's words: 'the closer the mind dwells upon the subject, the closer the analogy appears'.

The late nineteenth century is noted for an attempt to quantify the numbers of prostitutes (especially those in London), and to regulate prostitution (rather than stamp it out) *via* the Contagious Diseases Acts of 1864, 1866 and 1869. These Acts attempted to control the spread of sexually transmitted diseases by enforced examination and/or compulsory hospitalisation of prostitutes. Lynda Nead concludes:

> The fear of prostitution and deviant sexual behaviour was organised in relation to much wider anxieties concerning political and economic crisis. Prostitution was moral *and* seditious; it was seen as a subversive system which could destroy the very roots of bourgeois society.[42]

The fallen woman would have fallen metaphorically out of this secure family-centred normality and into the subterranean depths of

London, a figure of contagion, disease and death as described in characteristically apocalyptic terms by General William Booth:

> Her word becomes unbelievable, her life an ignominy, and she is swept downward, ever downward, into the bottomless perdition of prostitution.[43]

'The prostitute', writes Lynda Nead, 'stood as the symbol of the dangerous forces which could bring about anarchy and social disintegration.'[44] Her association with contagion is figured in some of the visual representations of the prostitute by the symbol of the rat. Carrying contagion, infecting a city, the rat lives *under* urban streets in the sewers and darkness. It undermines society and can come up through any 'manhole' or drain like the Morlocks. Infestation of this kind, like the prostitute, can never be regulated, although the Contagious Diseases Acts attempted to control this infectious invasion by regulating and quantifying prostitution. Thus while the suffragette could be invading the franchise from *outside* (literally invading from her marginalised position) the prostitute was perceived as invading and undermining society from *beneath*, carrying contagious disease. The threat of the prostitute (residing in the London Underworld, destroying the roots of bourgeois society, invading *via* infection) could be conflated in the cultural imagination with other malignancies of all kinds as Lynda Nead points out:

> Socialism and communism were regarded as malignancies which could spread like a disease from the continent into England, and it was this network of fears which fed into and defined attitudes towards prostitution.[45]

## THE HISTORICAL SPECIFICITY OF OTHERNESS

> Women seen as the limit of the symbolic order will in other words share in the disconcerting qualities of all frontiers.[46]

It is to the historical specificity of the conception of Woman implied by Moi's proposition, that this book is addressed: that an investigation of the discourses mobilised by the *femme-fatale*-as-sign can be a means to investigate the frontiers of self and of cultural order and normality in a specific historical moment. In this period the multiple implantation of Others is to some extent due to what Foucault describes as an increase in power centres producing and inciting discourses: the discursive practices of the period. For Darwinism the Other is imagined as the spectre of degeneration signalled by the ape. For criminology the Other is the criminal, the evolutionary throwback in our midst (the 'beast' visibly present in society). For defensive/nationalist discourses the Other is out there waiting to invade. The *plural Other* is felt to be besieging: the self besieged by the non-self. It is the *conflation* of Otherness that is characteristic here; the conflation of anomalies in the literary imagination and in individual texts; the conflation of the sexual, colonial and linguistic encounter in Conrad, for instance, and Ayesha as *African* New Woman (though white), evolutionarily superior (though of Oriental origin), threatening sexual, political and female invasion:

> The representation of woman can never be contained within an investigation of gender; to examine gender is to embark on an historical analysis of power which included the formation of class and nation.[47]

To accept this proposition is to challenge Foucault[48] on the possibility of speaking about 'sexual discourses' at all, in that in this analysis the discourses of female sexuality are always attached to something else – they are formed from a plurality of Others. I do not challenge Foucault on the notion of there being multiple discourses of sexuality (corresponding to the multiple mechanisms from which they are produced and incited), but only on the point that such discourses cannot be separated and must not be separated from the cluster of Other discourses in which they are embedded: the evidence that female sexuality as Other is attached to simultaneous cultural anomalies through metaphors of anxiety.

What can also be seen alongside this phenomenon is a complex strategical situation (Foucault's phrase); an attempt to respond to the plural Otherness of the *femme-fatale*-as-sign by bringing her inside the realm of the known. If the function of a frontier in an imperialist moment (such as the *fin-de-siècle*) is both to be defended from invasion and to be extended outwards (to incorporate new territories and to extend the Empire) then we can read the various (medical, scientific) attempts to define a woman acting outside established norms for female behaviour as an attempt to incorporate the threat into the 'empire' of knowledge. The naming of this Other is an attempt to triumph over her Otherness. To name the deviant woman as *femme fatale*, prostitute, suffragette, New Woman, virago, degenerate, Wild Woman, Free Woman, is both to deny her difference and to regulate it.

Such a process – that of attending to the abnormal and the pathological in culture – has three motives or drives. The first is an attempt to *know* the alien in order to define the self. The second is to *know* the alien in order to disempower the chaos and perceived threat or violence of the Other. The third, and more sinister, drive is to know the Other in order to exorcise or expel or destroy the Other. This last process taken to its limit moves towards genocide. The Holocaust of the twentieth century is often seen as the result of extreme race-thinking in Europe around the turn-of-the-century. Catherine Clément has written of this last process of expulsion of the Other (in this case the deviant woman – the hysteric and the witch) in 'The Guilty One'. Drawing on the techniques used to treat hysteria by Freud and Breuer (significantly developed in the 1890s) she discovers a process which she terms 'cathartic expulsion' whereby a 'foreign body, real or metaphorical, must leave the body'.[49] She links this technique of expulsion to the exorcisms of the witch trials earlier in history, by showing that here, too, the foreign body must be expelled (if not destroyed) thus rendering the disorder inactive:

> And the definitive cure of the witch was to turn her over to the secular arm, which alone could reduce the disorder: reduce it . . . to ashes.[50]

We will see that cathartic expulsion is one of the methods used by the hunters of the *femme fatale*. In *Dracula* the vampire-hunters gather around the Undead body of the transformed vampire Lucy, in her tomb and perform a ceremony on her which is a fusion of medical operation (cliterodectomy?), rape and cathartic expulsion. In *She* the beautiful but terrifyingly powerful Ayesha is reduced to ashes in a bizarre devolution scene by the powers of Nature (manifested in the Flame of Life). Africa itself, the epitome of the mysterious Dark Continent and itself, as I shall show, a powerful and threatening woman's body, must be conquered and destroyed, or rendered powerless. Africa was seen by the late Victorians, as Brantlinger has shown, as a place of demonism, a land which needed to be exorcised:

> The British tended to see Africa as a center of evil, a part of the world possessed by a demonic darkness or barbarism, repre-

sented above all by slavery, human sacrifice, and cannibalism, which it was their duty to exorcise.[51]

What I have been tracking in this chapter is the ways in which, in Clément's words, late nineteenth-century culture creates an imaginary realm for what it excludes, that this imaginary realm is a kind of Dark Continent of Otherness, that the femme fatale is placed there along with other deviants and anomalies of late nineteenth-century culture. These deviants and anomalies interact with each other and partake of each other's qualities: the black woman is 'necessarily' sexually predatory and the sexual woman is 'necessarily' atavistic. The processes of phallocentrism and ethnocentrism (informed by the discourses of sex and race) are part of the same discursive universe. They do not merely connect but are symbiotic, parasitically feeding off each other, both occupied in locating and ultimately even expelling the Other, the non-self.

## THE DISRUPTION OF PHALLOCENTRISM

There were opponents to the dominant ideologies of the late nineteenth century which I have been describing here, of course. Literature did not merely encode, create or reinforce such ideologies. There were writers who consciously challenged the rigidly and prescriptively normative tendencies of the turn-of-the-century, and there were others who, perhaps unconsciously, disrupted the ethnocentrism and phallocentrism of imperialist ideology and of patriarchal systems.

Stephen Heath's *The Sexual Fix* proposes the possibility of the disruption of phallocentrism (the inscription of male positions):

> there are . . . very definitely, *uses* of language, discourses, inscribing male positions (spoken or written in and from the representations of the man in the particular – phallocentric – system of 'sexuality' we have been describing here); as also there are uses of language attempting to break the dominance of the inscription of those male positions . . . .[52]

In my reading of Hardy's *Tess of the d'Urbervilles* I have tried to draw out what I believe to be an attempt to break the dominance of the male reading of Woman, a disruptive and entropic use of representation, occasioned perhaps by Hardy's experience of moral alienation in the public reception of his novels. I will argue that Hardy, in formulating the 'something more to be said in fiction than has been said', is engaged in a process of pushing back or dissolving the boundaries of what can be said, a confrontation with the language of normalisation. I will argue too that Conrad's fabrication of various *femmes fatales* involves a mimicry of phallocentric stereotypes and discourses, a mimicry which suffers upon such stereotypes a form of implosion by overproduction. Both Conrad and Hardy, I will argue, seem in their different ways to be searching for another language, to be transgressing the rules of phallocentric stereotypes. These writers do not break with the stereotype of the *femme fatale* nor with the phallocentric discourses mobilised to describe her, yet they push these to their limit, eroding *via* overproduction.

I will argue that in the writing of Conrad and Hardy there is a textual self-reflectiveness, an awareness of language itself as a limiting process and, secondly, that there is in these texts an implicit questioning of unified self and a recognition of the impossibility of 'character' representation of any kind (seen in these texts as a discursive overdetermination of 'character' pushed to the point of rupture). This disruption of language and character representation and, more importantly, the disruption of previously unquestioned moral and ethical systems, can be seen to prefigure Modernism. The fragmentation of self and of character representation (the disruption of a realistic signifying practice which represents the ego as an indivisible unit), the impossibility of fixed knowledge, the relativity of ethics, of science and of ideology: all of these are recurring themes and preoccupations of Modernism.

# 3

# *Dracula*: A Social Purity Crusade

*Dracula*, as Geoff Wall has put it, is 'a persistently anxious text'.[1] Its central action dramatises the prevention of a foreign invasion by a reinforcement of frontiers and an attempt to identify and eliminate the weak spots in the barricades erected to repel the invader. As such it forms an early part of a particular genre categorised by Samuel Hynes in *The Edwardian Turn of Mind* as 'invasion literature'.[2] H. G. Wells's *The War of the Worlds*, published only a few months after *Dracula*, in 1897,[3] forms another early example of invasion literature. Wells describes the invasion of England by a 'superior' race from Mars. The Martians' world is cooling and they must find new territories for survival, using their superior intellect (they have an anatomy which is almost all brain) and strength to defeat and 'consume' the inhabitants. *The War of the Worlds* articulates the 'sense of dethronement' of man, as Wells calls it, or of declining imperial power.

Both texts employ the motif of a spreading circle (rather like the action of ink on blotting paper) as a signal of the insidious nature of the invader. The invader, once inside, moves by degrees, stealthily and steadily gaining new ground, inch by inch, like a disease. Wells describes the impact of the Martian weapon, the black terror:

> From a balloon it would have seemed as if some monstrous pen had flung ink upon the chart. Steadily, incessantly each black splash grew and spread, shooting out its ramifications this way and that, now banking itself against rising ground, now pouring swiftly over a crest into a new found valley, exactly as a gout of ink would spread itself upon a blotting paper.[4]

Harker too discovers Dracula's campaign map (like Wells's chart seen from above) and finds there three small circles around Dracula's points of entry: Exeter, Whitby and London. Later Van Helsing is to warn that Dracula's invasion is spreading: 'The circle goes on ever widening, like as the ripples from a stone thrown in the water'.[5]

52

As the invaders acquire new territory, the series of small circles is finally assimilated into one mass, much as the imperial maps marked in coloured ink described by Marlow in *Heart of Darkness*.[6] The lives of both the Martians and Dracula are supported by the assimilation of the blood of their victims: the Martians pipe fresh blood straight into their veins and Dracula drinks his. Such efficient carnal appropriation, dispensing with the unnecessary paraphernalia of digestion, confirms these invaders as superior beings. This is a vampiric version of the evolutionary maxim: the survival of the fittest – the victim of the struggle will be *consumed* by the evolutionarily superior victor to increase its size and strength.

In an article on imagination written by the Earl of Dunraven in 1892 and published in *The Nineteenth Century*, the discourses of invasion and degeneration are fused by the deployment of a metaphor of consumption.[7] Here the Earl of Dunraven warns that immigration is detrimental to the British nation, causing a 'paralysing, demoralising, body-and-soul destroying effect upon our people'. He argues that immigration can only be permitted if the quality of the material is 'digestible' and if industry is in a position to 'absorb' it:

> Whether immigration be good or bad for us depends upon the quality of the material arriving on our shores, upon the condition of these industries which have to absorb it, and upon the general tone of the national digestion. The material is, in my opinion, intrinsically bad. But even if it were good, it could not benefit us unless our population were in a position to assimilate it properly and convert it to their own use.[8]

Buried in the sub-text of this article is a struggle for survival couched in metaphors of digestion: who is eating whom? If such immigrants are allowed to enter they must be assimilated (consumed) and 'converted' to the use of British industry: a form of amoebic ingestion.[9] Similarly the Martians of Wells's novel and Dracula himself are immigrants. They are invaders of a particular kind; they must assimilate blood and territory in order to sustain life and grow strong. In the struggle for evolutionary superiority which both texts play out, these invaders must be themselves assimilated and 'converted'.

*Dracula* is a text which places emphasis on territory: what is inside and threatened and what is outside and threatening. The aim of the alliance of men (inside) is to form perfect protective circles of discourse (so that there are no gaps in knowledge); to form perfect sealed circles around their women (to 'protect' them); and finally to surround and assimilate Dracula himself. Dracula is always outside trying to get in: planning his invasion of England in Transylvania, beating on the window as a bat, working on the weaknesses of others to allow him entry. The alliance is always on the inside, strengthening the fortifications, anxiously sealing gaps. Such frontiers are not merely geographical frontiers, but frontiers as protection and restraint of female sexuality, frontiers which ensure the censorship of fiction and frontiers as definition of the self and of the social body.

The opening chapters of *Dracula* tell of Jonathan Harker's journey into the unmapped and Other country of Transylvania. It records, through Jonathan's journal, the gradual breakdown of his reason and his sense of self as he travels from the West to the East. The superstitions, customs and lack of Western punctuality trouble Harker, and his journal becomes the tool whereby he protects his reason, his self:

> Let me be prosaic as far as facts can be; it will help me to bear up, and imagination must not run riot with me. If it does I am lost. (*Dracula*, Harker's journal, p. 25)

Harker's fear is of losing his reason to imagination, losing his *self* to this unmapped, untimetabled country and of being *absorbed* into it. In response to his fear he colonises the Unknown, assimilates the Unknown into written form. Having entered this new territory, Harker feels it might *absorb* him:

> Soon we were hemmed in by trees, which in places arched right over the roadway till we passed as though through a tunnel, and again frowning rocks guarded us boldly on either side. (*Dracula*, Harker's journal, p. 12)

*En route* to Dracula's castle, the metaphors of threatening enclosure which Harker uses to describe his experience of geographical Otherness, multiply. Wolves close around them like a 'moving circle' whilst Harker experiences 'a paralysis of fear'. Only Dracula, disguised as the 'strange driver' can dissolve the circle of the Unknown: for him this 'living ring of terror' (the circle of wolves) is some 'impalpable obstacle'.

Harker's experience of enclosure by the trees and then by the wolves is soon to be repeated by the attack of three female vampires within the castle who threaten to assimilate him, transubstantiate him into the Undead. (Wolves in this text are consistently interchangeable with vampiric females – later, a zoo-keeper asserts 'you can't trust wolves no more than women'.) Throughout such attacks on his reason the quasi-legal language of Harker's diary traces his attempts to keep a grip on the Known.[10] Trapped in the castle, Harker's investigations take him nowhere; all his energies in this last section of the novel are used in trying to find gaps in Dracula's fortifications, to escape from the inside. He does escape but is finally 'lost', suffering (as we find out later) from physical and mental breakdown. He is finally consumed in the 'imaginative whirlpool' of Transylvania, that Otherworld, and there he loses his reason, his recording voice, himself.

As investigative readers, replacing Harker as detective, we become aware in the next section of this novel, that Dracula is invading England. In the gaps between the fragmented accounts which characterise this section,[11] in the darkness, offstage, Dracula is invading England, *via* Whitby. Dracula, as Unknown, leaps from the wrecked boat in the form of a wolf and disappears into the darkness, 'which seemed intensified just beyond the focus of the spotlight' (*Dracula*, p. 79). The searchlight, like the discourse, cannot illuminate or reach him; he is beyond rational inquiry. Although we are firmly placed in the modern, technological world of transmitted information (the telegram, shorthand, the typewriter, the phonograph, the newspaper), all these devices are impotent, for they cannot illuminate the Unknown. Each person's knowledge of events is, as yet, partial and Dracula is able to invade Whitby because there are such gaps in the fortification of knowledge. The searchlight must extend its range, the investigations must come together and extend their range of inquiry and knowledge.

Van Helsing enters the text, combining the roles of psychic investigator, detective, psychiatrist, philosopher and scientist. As David Seed[12] has shown, he counteracts the fragmentation of knowledge by accelerating the process of collaboration. The journals begin to be exchanged and the surface of the text changes, with one account often finishing where another takes over. As the gaps close, Dracula becomes better-known. Such group strength depends, as Van Helsing insists, on the constant production of discourse. Mina and Jonathan

Harker transcribe all of the individual discourses into one uniform whole: 'Mrs Harker says they are knitting together into chronological order every scrap of evidence they have . . . by dinnertime they will have a whole connected narrative' (*Dracula*, Seward's diary, p. 225). The connection of narrative is crucial for it is such connection that forms the barricade against Dracula. Every now and again someone fails in their duty of constant group confession and when such concealments occur a gap is opened in the 'knitting' of collaborative discourse, through which Dracula can enter. Mina is excluded from the alliance by virtue of her 'weakness' as a woman.[13] She is kept 'in the dark' and it is in this darkness that she is seduced by Dracula, seemingly in a dream. She falls silent, deciding not to share her nocturnal experience with her husband, fearing to worry him further, yet by the time this 'seduction' is discovered it is too late, for she is already contagious.

Mina moves, then, from being one of the strongest parts of the alliance, the frontier, to being one of its weak spots. Earlier, Lucy had been one of the weak spots, being Dracula's first victim after his entry into England. There is, in the text, a latent accusation of complicity: Lucy seems destined to be Dracula's victim. Even before his invasion she is prone to sleepwalking, is weak, flirtatious, even articulates a desire to be polygamous and does not take easily to confession: 'I cannot tell you how I loathe talking about myself', she confides to Dr Seward, who is examining her. Mina, too, falls silent at a crucial point in the battle against Dracula. In describing her experience, she confesses: 'strangely enough I did not want to hinder him' (p. 287). The other main human weak spot in the fortifications against Dracula is Renfield, the pet lunatic of Seward's lunatic asylum who is tricked by Dracula into allowing him entrance. Those who are weakest at the frontier, those who are most likely to be offenders, are women and lunatics.

By the end of the novel the alliance have extended their empire of knowledge about Dracula into the Otherworld itself – Transylvania. Such collaboration, based on constant confession and informed by science, has pushed the monster back into his own territory where the hunters can surround and assimilate him. Earlier Harker was 'encompassed . . . hemmed in on every side' yet, by the end of the novel, the alliance close in like wolves upon the fleeing cart carrying Dracula and, surrounding it, force it to stop.[14] The staked Dracula crumples into dust, seemingly destroyed but actually contained and absorbed by the opposing alliance. Dracula disappears, but a boy is born on the anniversary of his death, carrying the names of 'all our little band of men together' – representative of the new empire, born out of the absorption of the Unknown. Dracula is squeezed out of the gaps in knowledge as they close and, once produced, he is consumed and converted by the discursive alliance.

## PATROLLING WOMEN

The professor and I took it in turns to watch, and we never left her for a moment unattended. Quincey Morris said nothing about his intention, but I knew that all night long he patrolled round and round the house. (*Dracula*, Seward's diary, p. 152)

Vampires in this novel are predominantly female: four out of the five women in the novel are vampires and there is only one male vampire – Dracula himself. Women are at risk for Dracula is 'heterosexual', attacking only women. These women once 'converted', become openly sexual – assertive, voluptuous and seductive: 'Come to me, Arthur.' [Lucy entreats] 'Leave the others and come to me. My arms are *hungry* for you'. (*Dracula*, Seward's diary, p. 211; emphasis mine)

To protect their women from such unrestrained sexuality (and to protect themselves from these hungry women), the men must maintain closed circles around their women, for Dracula will invade through any gaps. The men use a variety of protective measures to seal these women: wreaths of garlic flowers, crucifixes on gold chains, putty containing Holy Wafer to seal a tomb and Holy Wafer sprinkled in a circle on the ground to ensure that the vulnerable woman is not enticed outside by the vampire 'sisters'. Once the process of corruption begins, such women will be pushing at their constraints, insistently searching for a way out, as Mina observes of Lucy:

Twice during the night I was awakened by Lucy trying to get out. She seemed, even in her sleep, to be a little impatient at finding the door shut, and went back to bed under a sort of protest. (*Dracula*, Mina Harker's journal, p. 93)

If gaps are made in such male fortifications they are primarily made by women. Lucy's mother twice removes the garlic flowers from around her neck. A maid removes the gold crucifix again protecting Lucy, and three maids lie in drugged sleep whilst Lucy is being attacked. It is the three vampire women who try to draw Mina through her male fortifications into the sisterhood of unrestrained female sexuality with their cry: 'Come, sister. Come to us. Come! Come! Come!' (*Dracula*, Memorandum by Van Helsing, p. 367) Women cannot be entrusted with the sexual protection of their own kind. They are weak, naturally immoral, untrustworthy.[15] Such women, once sexualised, can only be 'corrected' by quasi-medical rituals to restore purity. The alliance gather with elaborate ritual in a circle around the Undead Lucy to drive a stake through her. Christopher Craft has observed, moreover, that the elaborate rituals of correction (what he terms the 'pacification program') are reserved for the *female* vampires; they are neglected in the staking of Dracula himself.[16] Like Dracula, Lucy is surrounded and absorbed, through death. She cannot be allowed to remain 'outside', Unknown, 'sexualised' and Other, but must be reabsorbed into the Known even if this process demands her 'death'.

## PATROLLING FICTION

Stoker's article 'The Censorship of Fiction',[17] published in *The Nineteenth Century* in September 1908, draws on metaphors of collaboration and frontier-building in his description of the invasion of immoral fiction. The year was crucial in the censorship debate, which had become a public issue in the last decades of the nineteenth century. In 1908 a group of well-known writers, poets and playwrights gathered together to sign a petition objecting to the official censorship of plays. In 1907 two so-called 'problem' plays had been suppressed by the Examiner of Plays and refused a licence.[18] This petition was to draw attention yet again to the problems of official censorship and state control of moral issues. The series of state morality and censorship trials in the last decades of the nineteenth century (Wilde, Vizetelly, Bradlaugh-Besant and Havelock Ellis) and the pervasive sense of moral decline of the nation and the empire had brought conservative, quasi-military organisations to the fore, campaigning for greater state control of the arts. The National Social Purity Crusade had formed in 1901, sponsored by the National Vigilance Association. In 1908 the National Social Purity Crusade reformed as the Forward Movement (one can see the development of progressively military metaphors in the naming of such groups). These were the troops marshalled against the decadent and degenerate artists clamouring for freedom from censorship, and Stoker was to find his allegiance with these vigilantes of morality. On 4 April 1908, an announcement appeared in *The Times* announcing the formation of yet another social purity organisation:

> Not only in London, but in all great cities and towns, there is an inevitable demoralisation that can only be arrested and replaced by a higher tone through *combined action*. For this object the forward movement of the National Social Purity Crusade has been inaugurated . . . . [emphasis mine]

Stoker's article makes similar reference to combined, 'military' action, drawing on the militarism prevalent in the Christian social purity associations of the turn-of-the-century.

Stoker addresses his article to the signatories of the petition and to the numerous authors of declamatory demands for freedom from censorship to be found in the newspapers and periodicals in 1907–8. As ex-manager of the Lyceum which had prided itself in its production of 'safe', family plays and had been opposed to the staging of so-called 'problem-plays' inspired by the work of Ibsen, Stoker's allegiance with a social purity associations is not surprising. What is significant, however, is the language used in this article, in which 'fiction' is seen to be interchangeable with Stoker's emphasis on the patrolling of women in *Dracula*. Stoker argues that censorship must be enforced in an age such as his own, in which there is evolving 'a class of literature so vile that it is actually corrupting the nation' (p. 483). Such writers 'have found art wholesome and made it morbid; they found it pure and left it sullied' (p. 485). Such a description parallels Dracula's insidious invasion of territory and women and his effects there. His 'converted' women become 'morbid' and 'sullied', sexualised and impure, just as the writers of this class of literature corrupt their readers and sully art. The spread of such literature, like Dracula himself, corrupts by contagion, brings pollution and disease. Mina, after her 'corruption' by Dracula, repeats the word 'unclean, unclean', and 'rubs her lips as if to cleanse them from pollution' (*Dracula,* p. 288). In this article Stoker implies that such moral depravity is contagious both to fiction and to women,[19] like venereal disease: 'If the plague-spot continues to enlarge, a censorship there must be' ('The Censorship of Fiction', p. 486).

Stoker's article reveals a tendency to conflate ethics and aesthetics: fiction must be kept clean just as the Empire must be kept clean. Social and moral purity of the nation depends upon what it consumes. Stoker draws on disease metaphors in his analysis of the state of art and of culture. He insists on collaboration, restraint, and constant vigilance in the work of maintaining social, cultural and moral purity. If moral depravity is an illness and a plague of British culture, it must be dealt with 'medically' and even 'surgically' (Stoker insists that immoral fiction should 'come under the knife of the censor'). The censor is perceived as surgeon/mutilator and the censored as the operated on or the mutilated. Such language parallels the discovery by Mina of the two enlarging spots on Lucy's neck:

> I looked at her throat just now as she lay asleep and the tiny wounds seem not to have healed. They are still open, and if anything larger than before . . . they are like little white spots with red centres. Unless they heal within a day or two, I shall insist on the doctor seeing about them. (*Dracula*, Mina Harker's journal, p. 95)

The 'knife of the censor', too, parallels the staking of Lucy (the purification/'pacification program'), now thoroughly corrupt, in order to restore her to the state of purity. Both literature and women must be pacified and purified by the authority of the morality associations.

As shown earlier, *Dracula* implies a complicity on behalf of the human weak spots, especially Lucy, but also Mina and Renfield. These weak spots, lacking sufficient strength or self-restraint, must be protected or they will become corrupt. Censorship, too, Stoker insists, exists to protect the weak:

> censorship . . . is based on the necessity of perpetually combatting human weakness . . . the weakness of the great mass of people who form audiences, and of those who are content to do base things in the way of catering for those base appetites . . . . The vice of the many of the audience is in the yielding to the pleasant sins or weaknesses of the flesh, as against the restraining laws made for the protection of higher effort. (Stoker, 'The Censorship of Fiction', p. 481)

Censorship, in Stoker's terms, is to be a kind of battle against evil and a collaborative enterprise:

If progress is to be good and is to be aimed at the organization of natural forces, the powers of evil, natural as well as arbitrary, must be combatted all along the line. It is not enough to make a stand, however great, here and there, the whole frontier must be protected. ('The Censorship of Fiction', pp. 481–2)

Similarly *Dracula* shows that 'progress' can only be maintained by vigilant collaboration in protecting the whole frontier: the narrative moves from fragmentation to collaboration and the alliance learns through its mistakes the importance of patrolling women and of compelling them to speak: 'Good women tell all their lives.' Property of all kinds must be protected in this high-capitalist world; both empires and women must be protected by such sealed circles.[20] As in *Dracula*, Stoker is clear about what is 'inside' and what is 'outside':

as the object of an external power is to prevent a thing of possible good from straying into the region of evil, the mandate should be to prevent excursion beyond the outmost point of good. ('The Censorship of Fiction', p. 480).

He also specifies the type of evil to be resisted as 'that arising from the sex impulses' (p. 483). Organised morality he imagines as a great dam established against the 'natural' forces of sexuality and depravity, which will be thundering against it at all times.[21] It is the 'sex impulses' which constitute the flaw in the mason-work of such a dam. In the context of *Dracula* the flaw is Woman, for it is women who allow Dracula entry. 'Indeed,' Stoker exclaims, 'women are the worst offenders in this breach of moral law' ('The Censorship of Fiction', p. 485).[22] If the criminality and amorality of Woman cannot be restrained voluntarily, it must be enforced. 'Restraint' is the key word for Stoker, a word he uses repeatedly in this article, for, he states, 'freedom contains in its very structure the germs of restraint' ('The Censorship of Fiction', p. 479).

This article, then, re-enforces, and in some sense decodes, motifs and preoccupations also present in *Dracula*, yet published ten years later. Indeed Dracula himself is called an 'author' by Van Helsing: 'But there remains a greater task: to find out the author of all this our sorrow and to stamp him out' (*Dracula*, Seward's diary, p. 217). Whilst it seems contradictory to place this article alongside some of the explicitly erotic passages in *Dracula* (and in later novels), what seems to be happening is that the novel enacts its own censorship. It shows the 'operation' of censorship at work, simultaneously producing sexuality and appearing to restrain it. It produces desire and sexuality, offering vicarious fulfilment, whilst attempting to expel itself of such desire. In Van Helsing's words, Dracula is 'creating a new and ever widening circle of semi-demons'. This image is used geographically, too, to demonstrate Dracula's invasion marked on his map: circles around Whitby, Exeter and London, which will presumably enlarge. To combat this widening circle, Van Helsing and his men, as censors, must form a circle of restraint, made up from the continuous production of discourse, knitted together. This will enlarge and push back Dracula from the frontiers and ultimately enable him to be assimilated.

Dracula's principal function is to invade, to break down the fragile boundaries put up by the alliance. In the *Literature of Terror*,[23] David Punter sees Dracula as blurring the lines (taboos) which 'enable society to function without disruption'. He sees Dracula as blurring the line between man and beast, blurring the line between man and God ('by daring to partake of immortal life'); blurring the line between man and woman ('by demonstrating the existence of female passion'). 'He is a shape changer, a merger of species, the harbinger of social collapse.'[24] In this sense Dracula represents a fantasy of 'no limits', of the violation of cultural taboos, of unlimited desire. Van Helsing and the alliance, in opposing such dissolution, must preserve the status quo, must prevent such merging of species, such blurring of the boundaries of morality. They must maintain taboos, distinctions, sexual segregation and social order. They must above all be vigilant.

## STRATEGIES OF SOCIAL AND SEXUAL VIGILANCE

### Policing the drawing-room

Stoker's investigators, his teams of inquisitors, stress vigilance in the search for and treatment of what are seen as the evil and destructive (sexual) energies in human interaction. In Stoker's *The Lair of the White Worm*,[25] of 1911, the forces of good struggle with evil in the person of Lady Arabella March, a local widowed landowner whose husband had died under mysterious circumstances, and with the sultry Mr Caswall, the local squire. The protagonists, united in their common pursuit of and determination to stamp out such predatory sexuality, and in their belief that Lady Arabella is the human manifestation of an antediluvian white worm which feeds on children and that Caswall is her dastardly partner in crime, persistently employ the language of warfare and struggle; they insist on collaborative investigations. All such investigations are coordinated by Sir Nathaniel de Salis and the text reads as a report of the proceedings of the investigators in their vigilance campaign for social and sexual purity:

> At half-past three the next day, Edgar Caswall called at Diana's Grove. Lady Arabella met him on the roadway and walked beside him towards Mercy Farm . . . . They found Lilla and Mimi at home and seemingly glad to see them . . . . The proceedings were a repetition of the battle of souls of the former visit . . . . This time the struggle for supremacy of will was longer and more determined . . . . (*The Lair of the White Worm*, p. 77)

All such social encounters between any combination of the protagonists and the evil forces follow a similar pattern: psychic battles of will between the 'pure' and the depraved. Stoker's text records the raw psychic energies beneath discourse – the sexual power that the vampiric Caswall tries to exert over the innocent cousins, Lilla and Mimi, and their attempt to overpower him with the strength of their purity. In such scenes Mimi is usually victorious, driving Caswall out through the door using only the power of her gaze. Like *Dracula*, the text incorporates its own scepticism:

> Just fancy how any stranger – say a doctor – would regard her, if she were to tell him that she had been to a tea-party with an antediluvian monster, and that they had been waited on by up-to-date menservants. (*The Lair of the White Worm*, p. 124)

While aware that such 'knowledge' is unlikely to be believed, Stoker's text, and his protagonists, uncover the silent energies of power and sexuality beneath seemingly innocent situations and insist that we find such energies everywhere, especially in the drawing-room. Dracula, too, soft-voiced, dignified, well-read, disguises his 'disease', his depravity all too well. His victims are never sure in their dream-state whether their nocturnal visitations are fantasies or real experiences. We must readjust our sight, the investigators warn, for no situation is innocent. We must be vigilant at all times, especially when such predatory sexual monsters as these stalk the drawing-rooms of the middle classes.

Stoker describes these silent sexual energies as part of a struggle for power or as a vampiric exchange of power which leaves the victor stronger and the victim weaker[26] – a form of predatory transubstantiation. Caswall seeks domination over the two women, Lilla and Mimi, and to achieve this, drains their energy: 'The weaker Lilla seemed, the stronger he became, just as if he were feeding on her strength.' (*The Lair of the White Worm*, p. 42) Sir Nathaniel, like Van Helsing, is astute enough to see the sexual element and insists that the group must play the masculine against the feminine – the investigators must maintain a constant surveillance of the 'feminine' and of female wiles:

> It strikes me that, as we have to protect ourselves and others against this feminine nature, our strong game will be to play our masculine against her feminine. (*The Lair of the White Worm*, p. 111)

Similarly, *Dracula* deploys board-game analogies to support Van Helsing's insistence on careful planning in the campaign against Dracula. Van Helsing and his men seek out Dracula's last pieces left on the board – here, coffins of Transylvanian earth which have been deposited at various locations throughout England. Once they have ascertained how many boxes are missing by exploring the house at Carfax, Van Helsing adds: 'It has given us opportunity to cry "check" in some way in this chess game, which we play for the stake of human souls.' (*Dracula*, Harker's journal, p. 253) The loss of the weak to the strong (Lilla to Caswall) is almost incidental, as are the multiple deaths of parents in *Dracula*: pawns are easily dispensed with when there are larger pieces to capture: there is more 'at stake'. In such a serious game, where the inquisitors risk human lives or, worse still, human souls, strategies must be constructed and continuously revised as information about the movements of the opponent become better-known. All players must be prepared in advance and must be able to conceptualise several moves in advance or there will be casualties. The texts deploy various strategies in their vigilance campaigns. As each strategy is tested and fails, new and more radical (and often violent) means must be found to ensure social and sexual purity.

### A secret life should have no omissions: strategies of interrogation

> all the records chosen are exactly contemporary, given from the
> standpoints and within the range of knowledge of those who
> made them. (*Dracula*, Prefacing Note, p. 1)

Stoker's textual note makes explicit the radical structure of this narrative which, dispensing with an omniscient narrator, puts in its
place a series of contemporary records given from the 'standpoints'
of those who have experienced the 'history' of Dracula. Yet, the
papers produced have 'been *placed* in sequence'; 'all *needless* matters
have been *eliminated*' and all records have been '*chosen*' (emphases
mine). There is, then, a controlling, ordering, censoring presence in
the text and a continuous incitement to discourse in order to produce
the text, the record of Dracula.

*Dracula* depends upon diverse contemporary records (written and
spoken) to fill out its bulk as a text and to discover the truth about
Dracula – to gain knowledge. The final text (although merely a 'mass
of typewriting') is the sum of all that is to be discovered about
Dracula's intentions, history, movements, attacks and habits. The
'records' are made up from almost any form of written material:
ship's logs translated from Russian, cuttings from newspapers, memo-
randa, telegraphs, undelivered notes, doctor's reports, as well as
letters, journals and diaries. The analogy of a collage would not be
inappropriate for the text in the first stages of its production – a
visual and aural collage: different handwritings and dialects, scraps
of newspaper cuttings pasted into journals, and printed telegrams. It
would even have included non-written material: Seward's phonograph. As the production team progresses, this fragmented record is
transcribed into a uniform typewritten script. There is enormous
relief evident in the production team as the processes of exchange
and collation begin. As the text moves from fragmentation to uni-
formity, from the oral to the written, the group gains strength and
knowledge, through group validation.

Stoker's *Dracula* is a confessional novel. It will take information
from anybody and everybody, anywhere and everywhere. It consumes voraciously and then submits its discourses to an ordering,
censoring process. The text, then, depends on its contributors trans-
forming their private experiences into communicated discourse. It
will produce the truth about Dracula – the text itself – only by these
means. Inciting discourse, by any means, then, becomes an absolute
necessity for the production of 'truth' and the production of 'text'.

For this reason, devices for recording, transcribing, ordering and storing of such personal discourses are essential to the text. Such discourses must be stored appropriately: all the explicitly 'erotic' passages of the text are confined to confidential, private modes of writing (journals and diaries). Stoker's emphasis on the modern means of recording and transmitting information is not, then, merely to emphasise the modern moment in which such mystery occurs, but is also the means that the text deploys for drawing attention to the means of its own production. A whole series of such devices are mentioned in *Dracula*: shorthand, travelling typewriters, phonographs for recording, and telegrams, letters, ship's logs, and press articles for transmitting information.

Foucault's *The History of Sexuality*, Volume 1, traces the history of the 'discursive explosion' of sexuality in the late eighteenth and nineteenth centuries:

> Incitements to speak were orchestrated from all quarters, apparatuses everywhere for listening and recording, procedures everywhere for observing, questioning and formulating.[27]

It is Foucault's thesis that sexuality, far from being repressed in the nineteenth century, was forced into manifold discourses. In the areas of economy, pedagogy, medicine, and justice, sexual discourse was to be incited, extracted, distributed and institutionalised.[28] Stoker's text, as we have seen, demands such verbosity for its very existence. What is the excuse for such verbosity? To incite, extract, distribute, and institutionalise Dracula. Because of the structure of the narrative, Dracula is never able to appear or speak for himself. He surfaces through the accounts of the contributors, and is always the product or content of another's discourse. Discourse alone produces him and to produce him, as the excuse for the text's existence (and its secret), such discourses must be incited. The final text resembles a 'confessional dossier' based on interrogations, consultations, autobiographical narratives and letters.[29]

Dracula, the vampire, is the secret to be discovered in the text. In this sense he corresponds to Foucault's secret-to-be-discovered: sexuality. In no other vampire novel, except perhaps Le Fanu's *Carmilla*,[30] is the act of vampirism made so explicitly erotic. Dracula attacks only women; his methods are seductive and hypnotic. Vampirism is contagious: it sexualises its victims. Dracula represents a threat to the bourgeois family, monogamy, sexual restraint. He must be 'sterilised', either in the sense of being made sterile as a degenerate throwback whose 'progeny' will carry the degenerate strain of the species (eugenics), or 'sterilised' as if he carried an hereditary sexual disease.

Dracula and the female vampires are the hunted. Who then are the hunters in this text, or in Foucault's term 'the local power centres' who compel the hunted into discourse? James Twitchell, in *The Living Dead*,[31] shows how in earlier versions of the vampire myth there was primarily a single vampire-hunter, usually a priest or a 'dhampire' (a son of the vampire who intuitively understands how the parent will act). In Stoker's *Dracula*, we have not one, but several vampire-hunters corresponding to the Foucauldian theory of the proliferation of power centres producing and inciting sexual discourse in the nineteenth century. Such 'manifold mechanisms' in this text, the producers of information, are primarily medical men and lawyers backed up by the financial resources of an aristocrat and a rich American.

The most powerful of the vampire-hunters is Van Helsing, described here by his student, Dr Seward:

> [he] knows as much about obscure diseases as anyone in the world . . . He is a seemingly arbitrary man, but that is because he knows what he is talking about better than anyone else. He is a philosopher and a metaphysician and one of the most advanced scientists of his day. (*Dracula*, pp. 111–12)

Van Helsing remains largely silent in the text; that is, he produces few written accounts by his own hand. His speech, like Dracula's, is reported by others. He functions as a still centre, organising and controlling the other hunters to go out and find information and to bring it back. He is one of many such characters in Stoker's work.[32]

## Good women tell all their lives

For these characters to have an ordering, organising function in these texts, they must encourage the other members of the respective 'alliances' to produce material; to be able to order and organise, they must have material to work on. Their relationship to the members of the alliance is similar to that between analyst and patient. Van Helsing functions similarly as confessor both in the religious and the psychoanalytic senses – he is Catholic and a medical man specialising in psychic phenomena.[33] In Foucault's terms, confession produces sexual discourse while appearing to repress sexuality. Van Helsing, as confessor, produces Dracula while appearing to try to stamp him out.

Mina Harker, too, is an integral part of the production process. While Van Helsing incites discourse, Mina processes the results, placing the material in sequence. Van Helsing is one part of a strategy of production, articulating an insatiable need for more and more discourse. Group strength, he insists, depends on constant recording, constant confession:

'Good women tell all their lives . . .'. (*Dracula*, p. 184)

'Nothing is too small, I counsel you, put down in record even your doubts and surmises.' (*Dracula*, p. 118)

'Go on, friend Arthur, we want no more concealment. Our hope now is in knowing all. Tell freely.' (*Dracula*, p. 285)

Foucault traces a line between the Catholic injunction to confess through the examination of conscience:

Tell everything, not just consummated acts, but all sensual touchings, all impure looks, all obscene remarks, all consenting thoughts[34]

to the scandalous literature of later centuries: Sade's injunction to confess in *The One Hundred and Twenty Days of Sodom*: 'to recount the most numerous and searching details'. Such confessional novels include the anonymous pornographic volumes of *My Secret Life* of the latter half of the nineteenth century. Here the narrator announces his intentions:

to write my private life freely as to fact and in the spirit of the lustful acts done by me or witnessed; it is written, therefore, with absolute truth.[35]

Later, he writes, strangely echoing Van Helsing: 'a secret life should have no omissions'.[36] Furthermore, he believes his writing constitutes a 'secret history' as a contribution to science, and more specifically psychology. Stoker's prefacing note, too, makes a similar claim: that such detailed personal accounts constitute a 'simple history'.

Many of the numerous articles on Stoker's *Dracula* reveal the similarity between the good (the alliance of men) and evil (Dracula and the female vampires) in the text.[37] Indeed any detailed study of the novel reveals that almost all the on-stage killing is executed by the 'good men', who may also be considered responsible for the death of Lucy through risky blood transfusions. They are certainly responsible for the 'deaths' of Dracula and the female vampires. They also initiate the sadistic, overtly sexual staking of Lucy. Lastly whilst Dracula is scrupulous about staying within the law, the 'good men' frequently transgress it, breaking into tombs and private houses, forging death-certificates, and resorting to bribery.

Van Helsing not only incites discourse, but he also initiates action and makes sure that it is 'correctly' carried out. Furthermore, he is almost the only character who is not stricken with doubts about his own sanity. The novel is sceptical about the reliability of its own narrators, who cannot be sure even of their own sanity.[38] Van Helsing, I repeat, is the only character free from such doubts. But Van Helsing is also the figure most like Dracula. As Christopher Craft has observed about Van Helsing's insistence on blood transfusions: 'A perverse mirroring occurs, as puncture for puncture the Doctor equals the Count.'[39] He is Dracula's opposite number in the structure of the text, but is also, in many ways, his mirror-image. Like Dracula his origins are obscure. Like Dracula he is 'foreign' and has problems with the English language. Like Dracula he is a father-figure. Like Dracula he can hypnotise, and uses his power to gain control over Mina.

If, then, we have good reason to doubt the testimonies of the main narrators, we also have good reason to doubt the motives of Van Helsing, who initiates so many sadistic rituals. His entry into the novel works as a catalyst to the production of Dracula, forcing him out of hiding and into discourse. If Dracula is vampiric, needing new blood to sustain his 'life', then Van Helsing is similarly vampiric as confessor, needing new discourse to maintain his creation: the text. I use Van Helsing here to include the other members of the alliance, or production-team, with Van Helsing as the principal force behind it. It is Van Helsing who articulates the text's thirst for discourse with his insistent injunctions to confess. Like the other similar characters in Stoker's texts (most particularly Sir Nathaniel from *The Lair of the White Worm*), Van Helsing is a kind of still centre, constantly available for consultation and interpretation. He is an analyst (particularly so when one remembers that he is Catholic, a hypnotist and a medical man) and, as we have seen in Foucault's work, psychoanalysis plays an important part as one of the 'manifold mechanisms' for producing sexual discourse or the 'truth about sex'.

In psychoanalysis the production of words is from the patient to the largely silent analyst. In Stoker's *Dracula* the flow of words is from below, through Van Helsing and into the text. Van Helsing insists on discourse, while contributing few of his own words directly. While Dracula is the vampire of blood, Van Helsing is the new vampire of discourse. The confession or (neurotic) discourse is the blood of the text and Van Helsing draws it out to render it into knowledge, to transubstantiate it into text (*via* Mina as transcriber and recorder), into the final interpretation. Such is the medical power over the body, insisting on more discourse in order to render its own theories strong. Neurotic discourse is the blood which will feed the new monster, the science of sexology and its demand is primarily for records of the secret lives of *women*: 'Good women tell all their lives.' Lucy is vulnerable and dangerous precisely because she does not take easily to confession. Likewise psychoanalytic theory is supported by numerous case-studies carefully transcribed by Freud, records of the secret lives of Freud's patients – the secret lives of numerous women: Anna O, Dora, and others. Power over the body is maintained by the blood of confession and such incitement is powerful because it takes such blood for its own, to convert it into new forms. Confession, or discourse, in *Dracula* comes from unlimited sources (ship's captains and zoo-keepers as well as the band of vampire-hunters) so that there is a large-scale blood or confession transfusion, transfused into the 'body' of the text.

> At issue is not a movement bent on pushing rude sex back into some obscure and inaccessible region, but on the contrary, a process that spreads it over the surface of things and bodies, arouses it, draws it out and bids it speak, implants it in reality and enjoins it to tell the truth: an entire glittering, sexual array, reflected in a myriad of discourses, the obstination of powers and the interplay of knowledge and pleasure.[40]

Similarly the movement of the text is not to silence Dracula, but to arouse him, draw him out and bid him speak. The vampire-hunters become the vampire-producers, drawing out the blood of discourse to render the text strong: the manifold mechanisms of the incitement to discourse. Strategies of interrogation and the means to record and transcribe the material produced under interrogation – the secret sexual life – are of paramount importance in the campaign against Dracula.

## DIAGNOSIS

### Case histories: reading the *femme fatale*

Just as scientific knowledge is the means by which Dracula is identified, known and finally expelled, such knowledge is invaluable in the search for readable signs by which to diagnose Lucy's contagious disease. Van Helsing draws upon unfashionable and occult knowledge – garlic, Holy Wafer, crucifix – but his investigation is also informed by modern science: criminology, craniology, evolutionary theory, hypnotism as it is used in psychoanalysis and confession, 'the talking cure'. Science is to provide the empirical data to inform the vigilance that the text demands. The 'records' of investigative procedure upon which Stoker's text is founded, coordinated by a quasi-scientist and collated to form empirical data – are in many ways a case-study of Lucy Westenra, her diagnosis and treatment, and a means to draw attention to ways of identifying the *femme fatale*, the degenerate female. The inquisition must know what signs to look for.

Late nineteenth-century 'sexology' tended to classify in terms of race and class: sexually-voracious women were more likely to be found amongst the working-classes or in 'primitive' cultures, and pornography reflects such assumptions.[41] Sexual insatiability, or nymphomania, when identified in prostitutes, working-class or primitive women could be read as 'proof' of atavism or degeneration.[42] When diagnosed amongst those of the middle classes it was more likely to be read, as above, as insanity or hysteria.[43] To become sexual to this degree was to fall, to fall from middle-class womanhood and hence out of the circle, into that Other world. 'Nymphomania' as a condition – itself part of the multiple implantation of perversions which Foucault identifies as a strategy of late nineteenth-century culture – had to be fed with convenient case-histories, all of which were readily supplied by the scientists: Havelock Ellis, Krafft-Ebbing, and others. Krafft-Ebbing, in *Psychopathia Sexualis*, reports the case-history of a girl who

> suddenly became a nymphomaniac when forsaken by her betrothed; she revelled in cynical songs and expressions and lascivi-

ous attitudes and gestures. She refused to put on her garments, had to be held down in her bed by muscular men and furiously demanded coitus. Insomnia, congestion of the facial nerves, a dry tongue and a rapid pulse. Within a few days lethal collapse.[44]

Lucy, of course, sexualised, exhibits all the symptoms of nymphomania: from the pure woman she becomes the fallen and insatiable woman, who must also be held down. She is lustful, voluptuous, demands that Arthur come to her and finally absorbs the 'blood' of four men.

Cesare Lombroso and William Ferrero, interestingly drawing on mythical archetypes, report that 'Nymphomania transforms the most timid girl into a shameless bacchante'.[45] Once again this is precisely Lucy's condition. Before Dracula's attack she laments: 'Why can't they let a girl marry three men, or as many as want her, and save all this trouble? But this is heresy and I must not say it.' (*Dracula*, Letter from Lucy to Mina, p. 59) The symptoms, here voiced in a private letter to her friend Mina, are already in place but they will not be identified until the individual records are brought together. During her transformation, the duality of Lucy's sexuality develops. Whilst awake she clutches the circle of garlic flowers to her, whilst asleep she pushes them away. At night she is forever looking for a means of escape. Seward, the doctor of the insane, well-used to formulating closely-observed case-studies, notes and records this duality:

> I noticed the difference in her between sleeping and waking. Whilst asleep she looked stronger, although more haggard and her breathing was softer, [when awake] she looked her old self, although a dying one. (*Dracula*, Seward's diary, p. 153)

Once vampirised, Lucy becomes that 'shameless bacchante' seen from afar through the trees of Highgate Cemetery. Seward, continuing to observe his case-study, describes her as a 'nightmare' of Lucy with bloodstained mouth, voluptuous and carnal. Seward is both repelled and attracted to this nightmare/fantasy of the sexually-released woman. Behind such fantasies lies the spectre of the New Woman, demanding the recognition of autonomous female sexuality: the New Woman who will some day 'do the proposing herself' (*Dracula*, p. 89). The New Woman was, moreover, widely believed to be sexually and morally degenerate.[46] Mrs Lynn Linton, for instance, terms the New Woman the 'Wild Woman' in a series of articles in *The Nineteenth Century* in 1891 and implies that her degeneracy is *contagious*:

> Creatures impatient of restraint, bound by no law, insurgent to their finger-tips, and desirous of making all other women as restless and discontented as themselves . . . they would incite the women to revolt against the rule of seclusion.[47]

It is perhaps no coincidence that 1897, the year of the publication of *Dracula*, saw the amalgamation of the different suffrage societies into the National Union of Women's Suffrage Societies.[48]

## Sexuality and regression

Stoker's insistence on sexual inquisitions and investigations, coupled with the prevalence of the quasi-militaristic moral purity associations of the turn-of-the-country (whose discourses Stoker draws upon) indicate cultural anxieties of a particular historical moment. The cultural and political implications of Darwinism and evolutionary theory were still being worked through at the turn of the century.[49] Evolutionary theory raised so many anxious questions about sexuality, about the beast within, about the primal slime from which man was supposed to have crawled. If man had evolved from such primal slime, had grown in stature from his appalling ancestor, the ape, if he were moving forward, progressing, then could not the reverse be possible – degeneration?[50] Was the terrible beast, the sexual beast, fully exorcised, or was he (or more importantly *she*?) still lurking beneath the facade of civilisation – in disguise?

Stoker's texts are not alone in expressing this anxiety. In *The Literature of Terror*, David Punter, argues that the whole genre of what he terms 'decadent Gothic' enacts such fears of regression and degeneration. All are concerned in some ways with 'the problem of the liberation of repressed desires'.[51] In this genre he places 'four of the most potent of literary myths': Stevenson's *Dr Jekyll and Mr Hyde* (1886), Wells's *The Island of Doctor Moreau* (1896), Wilde's *The Picture of Dorian Gray* (1891), and Stoker's *Dracula* (1897). Stevenson, for instance, exploits anxieties about scientific progress and the direction of such 'progress', if undertaken without moral guidance. Hyde, the monster, is part of the social, civilised being of Jekyll and is unleashed: 'My devil had long been caged, he came out roaring'. Often the awakening of such monsters is caused by misplaced scientific experiment, like the sadistic experiments of Doctor Moreau. Such texts play out a particular anxiety: the issue of relations between the human and the bestial caused by the theories of evolutionary progress.

As such, then, a cursory glance at the impact of these 'new' scientific concepts on *Dracula* will show us that, like other texts of the period, *Dracula* articulates fears about degeneration. Dracula can be seen as the beast within, so precariously contained, or he can represent what we might become after cultural degeneration: the sad end of a declining civilisation. Charles Blinderman[52] provides a challenging analysis of *Dracula*'s interaction with evolutionary theory, reading the text as an exposition of Darwinist materialism and Dracula as a soulless onanistic ape of prodigious sexual appetite, parasitically feeding on human protoplasm in order to maintain life. Dracula represents sex without responsibility, without morality, conscience or guilt – sex for its own sake – and seeks to establish his empire of sexual beings without souls. However, Blinderman does not confront the problem of the gender-ratio of vampires in this novel: there are four female vampires to one male vampire. Whilst Dracula is the primary degenerate invader of this text, the principal problem for the team of investigators is *female* contagion: if Dracula is not stopped the world will be overrun with such predatory and impure women, who carry the degenerate strain.

Various young sciences of the late nineteenth century, working from the discoveries of evolutionary theory, postulated theories about the relative position of women on the evolutionary ladder. Vogt, one of the principal exponents of craniology (the measurement of cranium sizes) sought scientifically to prove Spencer's theories of Social Darwinism, developed in *First Principles*.[53] This 'proof' amounted to a classification of the levels of development reached by various races, and such classification depended on brain measurement (or craniology). This investigation provided useful data to justify the biological inferiority of certain races, and the natural inferiority of women. Craniology discovered that women's brains were smaller than men's (no adjustment was made for the smaller physical stature of women) and closer to the brain-size of children and savages:

> We may therefore say that the type of the female skull approaches in many respects that of the infant and in a still greater degree that of the lower races.[54]

Later, women were said to resemble not only children and savages but even animals, thus taking the place of the 'missing link' between the human and the animal worlds:

> We may be sure that whenever we perceive an approach to the animal type, the female is nearer to it than the male, hence we should discover a greater simious resemblance [in studies of the 'missing link' between animals and humans] if we were to take the female as our standard.[55]

Darwin himself tentatively endorsed Vogt's discoveries about the evolutionary development of women in *The Descent of Man*: 'the formation of her skull is said to be intermediate between the child and the man'.[56] As such, then, the scientific discoveries of Darwinism and craniology provided a scientific method for the measurement (and proof) of various degrees of atavism and regression believed to be characteristics of women, children and 'savages'. These marshalled cultural prejudices. Criminology, another young science related to evolutionary theory and to anthropology, was to discover that, bearing readable bodily signs or 'stigmata', certain women were more atavistic and inherently criminal than others. Yet this extract from the work of Lombroso and Ferrero testifies to the inherent criminality of *all* women and children:

> What terrific criminals would children be if they had strong passions, muscular strength and sufficient intelligence; and if moreover their evil tendencies were exasperated by a morbid psychical activity! And women are big children; their evil tendencies are more numerous, and more varied than men's but generally remain latent. When they are awakened and excited they produce results proportionately greater.[57]

Such theories were more widespread than one might imagine. Stoker himself provides a long discussion of the evolutionary development of Dracula's brain in the text, mixing the language of criminology and craniology. Leonard Wolf demonstrates that the following passage spoken by Mina Harker and recorded in Seward's diary, is quoted almost verbatim from Lombroso's *The Criminal Man*:

> The Count is a criminal and of criminal type. Nordau and Lombroso would so classify him and qua criminal he is of imperfectly formed mind . . . . Then as he is a criminal he is selfish; and

his intellect is small and his action is based on selfishness, he confines himself to one purpose.[58]

Bearing what Mina describes as a 'childbrain' (as opposed to the 'manbrain' of the collective alliance) Dracula's position in the evolutionary scheme is made explicit: as a 'child' he is much closer to the brain sizes of a woman or a savage than to a white man. Mina thus assures the alliance that, being more evolutionarily developed in intellect than Dracula and by making themselves familiar with scientific knowledge of this kind, they must win their battle against the monster.

In *The Lair of the White Worm*, scientific knowledge is considered to be a vital part of the campaign against the female white worm who, like Dracula, has been alive for thousands of years, living in a hole in the ground. Here the evolutionary debate is taken up again:

> what could be a more fitting subject than primeval monsters whose strength was such as to allow a survival of thousands of years. We do not know yet if the brain can increase and develop independently of other parts of the living structure. In an age of investigation like our own, when we are returning to science as the base of wonders . . . we should be slow to refuse to accept facts however impossible they may seem to be . . . in process of time . . . (might not) that rudimentary intelligence have developed? There is no impossibility in this; it is only the natural process of evolution. (*The Lair of the White Worm*, p. 106)

The fear here is that the female worm will have a *developed* intellect (in this sense it is the obverse of the anxiety articulated in *Dracula*: the group discover that Dracula has an *underdeveloped* intellect), but no controlling conscience or morality 'and therefore no acceptance of responsibility'.

While the white worm can be taken to represent womankind in the abstract, Lady Arabella March represents womankind in particular: she is the human manifestation of the white worm. She is a snake and commands snakes; her initials spell LAM or Lamia. She is both evil and animal-like. Moreover, there is a strange eroticism and linguistic understanding between Arabella and the black servant, Oolanga (Oo-langour?), who makes love to her. Stoker makes the contrast of their social positions clear in order to indicate the *underlying* evolutionary status, atavism and lack of morality of the woman:

The circumstances were too grotesque, the contrast too violent for subdued mirth. The man, a debased and primitive specimen and of an ugliness which was simply devilish; the woman of high degree, beautiful, accomplished. (*The Lair of the White Worm*, p. 74)

The progress of the investigation is towards an understanding of the atavistic parallels between the predatory woman and the black servant. In a penultimate apocalyptic scene, Arabella lures Oolanga into her home and draws him into the slimy pit beneath her house:

In another instant she had seized Oolanga, and with another swift rush had drawn him, her white arms encircling him, down with her into the gaping aperture . . . which seemed to go down into the very bowels of the earth . . . that fathomless pit, whose entrance was flooded with spots of fresh blood. (*The Lair of the White Worm*, pp. 96–7)

At the core of the degenerate criminality of Lady Arabella and Dracula, as we might expect, is an 'abnormal' sexuality. Lady Arabella's pit signifies both her sexuality and the primal slime from which mankind had dragged itself. To be lured back into this pit is to regress and to die; vampirism is another form of sexual and evolutionary regression. The visual art of this period teems with images of predatory women threatening to carry their male victims 'over the edge' into an abyss or into the depths of the sea.[59]

In *The Lair of the White Worm* Sir Nathaniel de Salis warns that the group strategy must be to play the masculine against the feminine nature. It is the only hope of progress, for given any opportunity, such atavistic women will drag men back to the primal abyss, to sexuality, to irresponsible bestiality. Likewise, Auguste Forel warns in 1906 that pleasure-seeking women may be responsible for the collapse of civilisation:

The modern tendency of women to become pleasure-seekers and to take a dislike to maternity leads to degeneration of society. This is a grave social evil which rapidly changes the qualities and power of expansion of a race and which must be cured, or the race affected by it will be supplanted by others.[60]

Once again such cultural diagnosis is couched in metaphors of disease and its treatment. This extract implies that the 'grave social evil', the disease that must be 'cured', is an hereditary disease: it must be stopped before the 'race affected by it [is] supplanted by others'. Such arguments are eugenicist in origin. Here the seeking of pleasure is bound up with the rejection of maternity, so we can assume that 'pleasure' signifies non-procreative female sexuality. Such women are traps for the male soul, they lie in wait for their victims. They are hungry:

> She [Lady Arabella] tore off her clothes with feverish fingers, and in full enjoyment of her natural freedom, stretched her slim figure in animal delight. Then she lay down on the sofa to wait for her victim! Edgar Caswall's life blood would more than satisfy her for some time to come. (*The Lair of the White Worm*, p. 145)

While the source of disease in *Dracula* is male, women are the carriers of moral and sexual degeneracy. The work of the novel, its strategies of surveillance and vigilance, are to prevent the invasion of foreign degeneration and disease, to ensure the continuous super-vision (protection) of Woman, and above all to mount a witch-hunt where the disease has caught hold, to ensure an emergency quaran-tine of the contagious and to carry out, finally, a cathartic expulsion of the invader of such female bodies.

**Sexual expenditure**

The team of investigators in *Dracula* and in *The Lair of the White Worm*, engaged in the identification of the symptoms of abnormality, are overtly conscious of blood-loss and blood-expenditure. As Dracula is the chief vampire, one would imagine that all the blood-routes lead to him, whereas the final receptacle of the blood in the novel is a woman, Mina Harker.[61] Mina produces the only child of the novel, who bears the names of all the band of men.[62] He is the social production of the alliance. He contains the mixed blood of the alli-ance and the blood of Dracula also. Just as all contribute to the body of the text by producing discourse, all similarly contribute to the body of the child by producing blood.

There is, of course, a sexual undercurrent in all these blood-circulations. 'In the unconscious mind', writes Ernest Jones, 'blood is commonly an equivalent for semen' and time and time again, as C. F. Bentley has shown, the sexual symbolism of the text substitutes blood for semen.[63] The most obvious instance, perhaps, is to be found in Mina's account of Dracula's nocturnal visitation recorded once again by Seward, the familiar compiler of case-histories and the doctor of the insane. As Mina describes her attack Bentley points out that the scene begins to sound like a description of enforced fallatio:[64]

> and with his long sharp nails [he] opened a vein in his breast. When the blood began to spurt out, he took my hands in one of his, holding them tight and with the other seized my neck and pressed my mouth to the wound so that I must either suffocate or swallow some of the – Oh my God, my God! – What have I done?' Then she began to rub her lips as if to cleanse them from pollution. (*Dracula*, Seward's diary, p. 288)

However, the blood/semen overlap is at its most complex in the account of the blood-transfusions initiated by Van Helsing. Blood is frequently referred to as 'manhood' by the alliance. The doctor is careful to establish a hierarchy of suitable blood-donors, insisting that whilst *all* the men are keen to give blood, Arthur, as Lucy's fiancée, must be the first. If Arthur were to discover that other men had donated blood it would 'enjealous' him (*Dracula*, Seward's diary, p. 128), Van Helsing warns. Van Helsing is similarly careful to regulate the *amounts* of blood entering Lucy: for instance, Arthur, as Lucy's fiancée, is allowed to give the most blood, which Seward, as second donor, seems to resent. Seward himself gains obvious satisfaction from the transfusion: 'No man knows till he experiences it, what it is to feel his own life-blood drawn away into the woman he loves' (*Dracula*; Seward's diary, p. 128) and he resents being made to stop by Van Helsing, who watches him 'critically':

> 'That will do' he said. 'Already?' I remonstrated. 'You took a great deal more from Art.' To which he smiled a sad sort of smile as he replied: 'He is her lover, her fiancée.' (*Dracula*; Seward's diary, p. 128)

Within a few days Lucy has absorbed the blood of four men, although Arthur still believes that he has been the single blood-donor. Furthermore Arthur believes that his transfusion of blood into Lucy has consummated his 'marriage' to her, which Van Helsing finds amusing:

> If so that, then what about the others? Ho! Ho! Then this so sweet maid is a polyandrist and me, with my poor wife dead to me . . . even I . . . am bigamist. (*Dracula*; Seward's diary, p. 176).

Van Helsing's tone implies that this is more than a joke: Lucy is indeed a polyandrist having received the blood (semen) of the four men whom she desires.

In Stoker's *The Lair of the White Worm*, female desire is often expressed in economic terms. Even the two innocents, Lilla and Mimi (note the similarity of names to Lucy and Mina in *Dracula*) are husband-hunting although not with quite the voraciousness of Lady Arabella. With a paucity of financially eligible men in the district, all three women are in competition. Lady Arabella March is pursuing Caswall, for Caswall is the best financial 'catch' around as Sir Nathaniel informs Adam Salton:

> Caswall is a rich man. Her husband was rich when she married him – or seemed to be. When he committed suicide, it was found that he had nothing left, and the estate was mortgaged up to the hilt. Her only hope is in a rich marriage. (*The Lair of the White Worm*, p. 25)

This, of course, culminates in the sexual scene already quoted, with Arabella lying naked on her couch waiting for Caswall: 'Edgar Caswall's life-blood would more than satisfy her for some time to come.' Edgar's 'life-blood' is, of course, his *money* which she will consume like blood, as she had already consumed the blood/money of her husband, leaving him mortgaged 'up to the hilt'. Once drained of financial resources he is no longer useful; now financially impotent, he is found mysteriously shot in the head.

Lucy, too, is a husband-hunter, hunting not just for herself but also for her friend, Mina. Lucy herself is being courted by Seward as she is being courted by two others: Arthur Godalming and Quincey Morris. All three propose and Lucy must choose between them. She chooses the richest of the three and the suitor with the title. The triple proposals give her obvious satisfaction, expressed in a letter to Mina:

> But for goodness sake, don't tell any of the girls or they would be getting all sorts of extravagant ideas and imagining themselves injured and slighted if in their very first day home they did not get six in the least. Some girls are so vain. (*Dracula*, letter from Lucy to Mina, p. 56)

It is in this same letter that Lucy laments her restriction to one man although aware that what she is saying is 'heresy'. However, in one sense, Lucy is allowed to have all three men: she absorbs the blood of, not three, but four men.

In the long description of the blood-transfusions there are constant references to manhood, strength and energy. Lucy's energy and that of the men who transfuse blood into her, is being slowly drained. Van Helsing insists on the 'manhood' of each donor for it is strong male blood that will restore Lucy's health, which he can see instantly in Arthur: 'as he took in the stalwart proportions and recognised the strong young manhood which seemed to emanate from him, his eyes gleamed'. (*Dracula*; Seward's diary, p. 121) Each of the four men, after the transfusions, are debilitated. They must rest and restore strength. There is correspondingly a preoccupation about the amounts of blood being transfused and mysteriously disappearing:

> The whole bed would have been drenched to a scarlet with the blood which the girl must have lost to leave such a pallor as she had before the transfusion. (*Dracula*; Seward's diary, p. 123).

Stephen Marcus has written of the application of an economic principle to sex[65] in the work of the late nineteenth-century sexologists. Energy was believed to be expendable, and as energy is bound up with manhood and virility, these become expandable too. Masturbation, particularly, came under attack; it was an irresponsible waste of (national) resources. The young male masturbator would use up his vital supplies of semen and find himself reaching early impotence. Semen, like blood, was to be treasured and not wasted. Peter Gay quotes Tissot:

> Physicians of all ages have unanimously believed that the loss of one ounce of that humor [semen] is more weakening than of forty ounces of blood.[66]

To have an orgasm was colloquialised in the nineteenth century as 'to spend'. Just as Lady Arabella's thirst for money is described in terms of life-blood which she dries up in her husband, Lucy's thirst for blood is similarly insatiable, as Morris exclaims:

> that poor pretty creature that we all love has had put into her veins [within ten days] the blood of four strong men. Man alive, her whole body wouldn't hold it! (*Dracula*; Seward's diary, p. 151)

The fear is, of course, that her body *would* hold it and consume it, leaving the men weak and debilitated. Lucy becomes the conspicuous consumer of high capitalist culture, the vampire of high capitalist culture. She consumes blood, money and sex: vital resources. Such conspicuous consumption identifiable in Lucy becomes another means for reading her abnormality and another justification for her 'treatment'.

Late nineteenth-century case-studies of nymphomania all point to severe, often fatal, exhaustion, as the final outcome of such abnormality. Total physical debilitation was also seen to be the key symptom of the female masturbator. Nicolas Cooke dedicated a good part of his life to rather suspect research into female masturbation, published in the 1870s as *Satan in Society*. He catalogues the symptoms of a female masturbator:

> languor, weakness, loss of flesh, absence of colour, sad expression, panting at the least exertion and the appearance of incipient consumption.[67]

Most masturbators, Cooke believed, were boarding-school girls (like Lucy and Mina) who had picked up the habit from others, for masturbation, like vampirism, is 'the contagious vice'. All forms of excessive sexuality, the sexologists believed and, in the case of women, any form of sexuality outside occasional, enforced, conjugal sex, might lead to anaemia or consumption:

> The frequent exercise of the act of copulation leads directly to anaémia, malnutrition, asthma of the muscles and nerves and mental exhaustion. Immoderate persons are pale and have long, flabby, or sometimes tense features. They are melancholic and not fit for any difficult and continued corporeal or mental work.[68]

Lucy suffers from anaemia, of course, and gets progressively weaker, more melancholic and pale. Her insatiability, her immoderation are causing mental and physical exhaustion. Such women will, of course, like Lucy, reject motherhood and this rejection has a biological cause, for excessive sexuality will use up the vital energies needed for reproduction:

> Sensuality has multiple and imperious needs which absorb the mental activity of a woman and by rendering her selfish, destroy

the spirit of self-abnegation, inseparable from the maternal function.[69]

*Dracula* articulates some of these obsessions. Like sexology itself, it is rather confused in its discourses. *Dracula* articulates both fear of and desire for active female sexuality. The sexualised female vampires are seductive, vital and fascinating, whereas Mina and the early Lucy are somewhat insipid and transparent in comparison. The same is true of Lady Arabella, drawn with such strength and vitality. Yet these monsters must be destroyed before they can assist Dracula in creating a new empire of semi-demons: an empire of unlimited desire, peopled presumably by women such as these. Even the ageing Van Helsing finds himself uncertain when he is faced with the sleeping female vampires, faced instead with the textual ambivalence about the fate of these new creatures, these New Women:

> Yes, I was moved – I, Van Helsing, with all my purpose and motive for hate – I was moved to a yearning for delay which seemed to paralyse my faculties and to clog my very soul. (*Dracula*; Van Helsing's memorandum, p. 370)

**The channelling of sexual energies**

One of the strategies by which the men in the novel seek to control such dangerous sexual energies is through the translation of desire into work. The investigative procedures of the novel are in themselves a means to control the anarchic and chaotic sexuality at loose in the text. Seward renounces his desire for Lucy, to take up a cause – work – which will be to stamp out Dracula or desire:

> Oh, Lucy, Lucy, I cannot be angry with you, nor can I be angry with my friend whose happiness is yours, but I must only wait on hopeless and work. Work! Work! If I could only have as strong a cause as my poor mad friend there, a good, unselfish cause to make me work, that would indeed be happiness. (*Dracula*, Seward's diary, p. 71)

'Lucy' is quite explicitly replaced by 'work' ('Lucy, Lucy' – 'Work! Work!'). The alliance of men in *Dracula* excludes women and puts emphasis on work and progress through the elimination of Dracula as desire. In a sense, then, the work of the novel is the work of restoring cultural 'potency' and it is opposed to the degenerate effeminacy of Dracula and the vampire women. The text deploys strategies of investigation, diagnosis and treatment to translate the Unknown and the Abnormal into the Known. The records of the text, the multiple case-histories upon which it is built, are the means by which threatening sexual Otherness is translated into Knowledge.

## CATHARTIC EXPULSION

When other strategies have been tested by the team of now-seasoned campaigners for social and sexual purity and have failed, they must revise their strategies and find new ones. I have shown how the team deploy various strategies for controlling the outbreak of disease (vampirism) in England. Their first attempts are those of surveillance and the patrolling of women. More complex means are introduced by Van Helsing: those of group interrogation and the persistent conversion of the secret lives of women into case-studies. When such strategies are proved to be too tame to control the outbreak, more extreme measures must be deployed. The inquisitors finally resort to a form of cathartic expulsion by which the invader of the female bodies can be expelled.

There is an extraordinary sexual violence latent in Stoker's texts. Such violence is usually a reaction to the fear of uncontrolled and contagious female sexuality. The investigators in *The Lair of the White Worm* are finally led to the slimy hell-hole concealed beneath Lady Arabella's house. This is the location of the antediluvian white worm. Having failed to eliminate Lady Arabella the investigators realise that they must resort to extreme measures. They pack the pit with explosives which, activated by providential lightning, create craters in the ground far around the hole itself. The investigators return to witness the effect of the blast:

> The Saltons could now look through to the room beyond where the well-hole yawned a deep narrow circular chasm. From this the agonised shrieks were rising, growing ever more terrible . . . . Once in a sort of lull or pause, the seething contents of the hole arose after the manner of a bubbling spring and Adam now saw

part of the thin form of Lady Arabella . . . several times some masses of enormous bulk were forced up with inconceivable violence . . . . The ground for far around quivered and opened in long deep chasms . . . it brought relief – relief from the presence of the fear of all that was horrible – relief which seemed perfected when the red rays of sunrise shot up over the far eastern sea, bringing a promise of a new order of things with the coming day (*The Lair of the White Worm*, pp. 151–2)

Such violence is, then, the destruction of an evil female sexual power and a confirmation of virility. It brings relief of a sexual nature. *Dracula*, too enacts its own expulsion on the body of the sexualised Lucy Westenra and the operators experience similar relief 'of the fear of all that was horrible'. Similarly the expulsion results in a purification of nature, a return to a purer nature. Both expulsions are performed as acts of high social duty. Once sexualised Lucy must be cured, and her purification will cleanse the natural world which has been contaminated by her disease. This cure is performed like an operation to restore her purity (or 'pacification program' in Christopher Craft's words). The men visit Lucy's tomb some days before the operation, to examine their patient (or victim):

Holding the candle so that he [Van Helsing] could read the coffin plates and so holding it that the sperm dropped in white patches which congealed as they touched the metal, he made assurance of Lucy's coffin (*Dracula*, Seward's diary, p. 197).

'Sperm', of course, refers here to the sperm candle (which used ointment from the sperm whale) in use in the nineteenth century, but it has a double signification here and alerts the reader to the concealed sexual impulses of the male 'operators', united in their common desire for Lucy.

Several days of investigation follow, during which the men see the now wholly sexualised Lucy about her new 'career': 'the career of this so unhappy lady is but just begun' (career: prostitution?), remarks Van Helsing, sympathetically. She is now a 'Medusa' with a look that 'could kill'. Gone is the flirtatious, two-dimensional and empty-headed girl of the earlier chapters. The girl has become the woman: voluptuous, languorous and fully sexualised. After this scene Seward speaks for the alliance: 'At that moment the remnant of my love passed into hate and loathing; had she then to be killed, I could have done it with savage delight' (*Dracula*, Seward's diary, p. 211). He does not have to wait long to satisfy this fantasy, for the men return the following night (significantly the night after Lucy's intended wedding) to complete the task. Van Helsing brings the stake 'some two and a half inches thick and about three feet long . . . sharpened to a fine point'. To Seward, Van Helsing's medical preparation is both 'stimulating and bracing'. Arthur, of course, as Lucy's fiancée, is the only 'proper' agent for this 'sexual' operation. The other men stand around voyeuristically, chanting a missal, emphasising the ritualistic nature of the operation and of the 'rape':

> he placed the stake over the heart . . . as I looked I could see its dint in the white flesh. Then he struck with all his might.
> The Thing in the coffin writhed; and a hideous blood-curdling screech came from the opened red lips. The body shook and quivered and twisted in wild contortions; the sharp white teeth clamped together till the lips were cut and the mouth was smeared with crimson foam. But Arthur never faltered. He looked like a figure of Thor as his untrembling arm rose and fell, driving deeper and deeper the mercy-bearing stake whilst the blood from the pierced heart welled and spurted up around it . . . . Finally it lay still. (*Dracula*, Seward's diary, p. 216)

The rhythm of the passage betrays Seward's voyeuristic and sadistic 'delight', which moves towards a relieved quietening in the words 'Finally it lay still'. The text displaces the enjoyment of such violent sexuality by insisting that the 'operation' is performed by men of high honour and social standing and that it is *professional*: a medical operation led by the renowned Van Helsing, free from desire.

Such ritualistic killing echoes the ritualistic killings of Jack the Ripper, the Whitechapel Murders which took place in London around 1888. These too were performed as medical operations, the killer carefully and methodically operating on female bodies (prostitutes), a violent disembowelling and a laying still of the threatening Other of female sexuality. Catherine Clément has linked the ritualistic expulsions of Freud and Charcot to the exorcisms of medieval witch-trials as attempts to expel a threatening and sexualised Other from the female body and to pacify that body. These are also pacification programmes not unlike the operation performed upon Lucy Westenra:

One makes the demon come out by pressing on it, as Freud presses on the forehead, as the malodorous remedy will press the stomach to make it vomit. After he has subdued the possessed woman's body, Father Lactance, the exorcist of Loudan, makes her take various acrobatic positions, 'ravishing' the spectators; but suddenly the demon kicks up and lets out a curse against God, which the possessed woman expressed 'in a hideous voice'. 'On seeing this, Father Lactance threw the possessed woman's body harshly to the ground, trampled on her with great violence, then, one foot on her throat, repeated several times: "Super aspidem et basiliscum ambulabis et conculcabis leonem et draconem".' ('You will walk on the asp and the basilisk, and you will trample on the lion and the dragon.')[70]

The concealed fear of *Dracula* seems to be not that of the Transylvanian vampire, Dracula, but of what he might do to 'our women' and the cultural implications of such sexualisation. Strategies of vigilance must be deployed first as a preventative measure (frontiers of morality will ensure that the invader remains outside), secondly to ensure the sealing of women, and thirdly to expel the sexual invader when contagion has taken place. The text forms a kind of collage, a 'record', of turn-of-the-century conceptions of female sexuality made up from fragments of evolutionary theory, sexology and cultural prejudices. The 'mass of type-writing' is a hotch-potch of such beliefs knitted together to form one of the most prevailing and obsessive of our modern literary myths; a text which is a product of a unique historical moment which saw the birth of the definition and construction of female sexuality, and its institutionalisation.

# 4
# Rider Haggard's Black Widow

## EROTIC AFRICAN LANDSCAPE

in the hush that had fallen suddenly upon the whole sorrowful land, the immense wilderness, the colossal body of the fecund and mysterious life seemed to look at her, pensive, as though it had been looking at the image of its own tenebrous and passionate soul.[1]

(Conrad, 1899)

This is Africa, man-eater, soul-destroyer, wrecker of men's strength, mother of fever and death, mysterious ghost which for centuries has sucked the blood of Europeans, draining them to the very marrow, or making them mad .... The innumerable inlets breathing pestilence, which hide in the sickly shades of the mangroves are the ever-open eyes of Africa, like Sirens ready to engulf those hardy spirits who affront her.[2]

(Paul Vigné d'Octon, 1900)

the 'dark continent' trick has been pulled on her: she has been kept at a distance from herself, she has been made to see (= not-see) woman on the basis of what man wants to see of her, which is to say, almost nothing .... One can teach her, as soon as she begins to speak, at the same time as she has been taught her name, that hers is the dark region: because you are Africa, you are black. Your continent is dark. Dark is dangerous. You can't see anything in the dark, you are afraid. Don't move, you might fall. Above all, don't go into the forest.[3]

(Hélène Cixous)

The conflation of Woman and Africa as Dark Continent in this period is not limited to Freud's infamous equation of female sexuality with the 'dark continent', but seems to be implicit in much imperialist fiction of the late nineteenth century: mysterious and unmapped Other Woman is the Dark Continent and the Dark Continent is female. Late Victorian explorers used metaphors of penetration into 'virgin' territory freely and unselfconsciously. Stanley described himself in his bestseller *In Darkest Africa* of 1890 as an intrepid explorer who 'marched, tore, ploughed, and cut his way for one hundred and sixty days through this inner womb of the true tropical forest'.[4] To confront the 'blank' spaces of Africa is to map the supine body (inscribe it); yet it is also to fear the power of this sleeping and acquiescent body, a power imagined as a desire to arise and take vengeance upon its violators.

Public attention had focused on Africa during the last decades of the nineteenth century and more so as the major European powers began the famous Scramble for Africa in the 1890s. Yet in *The Image of Africa*[5] Philip Curtin argues that it was the missionary travelogues (in particular Livingstone's report of his missionary journey into Africa of 1857) which had captured and retained the public imagination. With the political unrest caused by the first Kaffir wars, then the Zulu War and the first Boer War, whereby Britain was forced to the retrocession of the Transvaal after its annexation three years earlier, public interest was focused on Southern and Eastern Africa rather than Western Africa. Popular magazines of this period, such as the *Illustrated London News*, catered for public demand with years of continual reporting of 'savage' African life using visual images supplied by travelling artists.

Haggard's career as a successful novelist began soon after his return from South Africa, where he had lived in the years 1875 to 1881. He had been intimately involved in the political struggles in South Africa during these years, as secretary to the Lieutenant-Governor of Natal and had been on the team that accompanied Shepstone, the special commissioner of the Home Government, in the march on Pretoria in January 1877, which engineered the subsequent annexation of the Transvaal.[6] The six years which Haggard spent in Africa were years of perpetual fear of native and Boer uprisings, years in which imperial influence and control were continuously under threat.

Haggard's literary career began in the 1880s, when public interest in South Africa had reached a peak. By setting his major works in Africa he was able to exploit such fascination, and his fiction became part of a growing genre of colonial and imperialist fiction. Indeed R. F. Patteson credits the beginnings of this particular genre (the imperialist romance) entirely to Haggard's *King Solomon's Mines*.[7] In such novels, Africa becomes the testing ground for white male adventure. Lawrence Millman, in his thesis on Haggard,[8] suggests another, wider term for such colonial fiction. He terms it the 'male novel', to be defined as that which is 'written by men, for men or boys, and about the activities of men'. He sees this genre as a 'conservative backlash to an overwhelming association of the Victorian novel with women, often made by people who neither liked novels nor women'. As a reaction to the 'forces of feminism and radicalism' this genre celebrates homosocial bonding and male adventure.

## THE QUEST

In Haggard's imperial romances, usually a band of men must journey into the centre of Africa in search of something or someone. They travel into unknown territory and into certain danger. Their physical and moral strengths will be tested at every point of the quest in a series of trials. Importantly with regard to the conflation of Africa and Woman, Haggard insisted in his autobiography: 'the quest for the divine . . . must (for the purposes of the story) be symbolised by a woman. You see, the thing must have a heart, mere adventures are not enough.'[9] The secret-to-be-discovered is thus the woman – the object of the quest, the heart of the story, the centre of Africa. Although we can see that Ayesha is the respective 'heart' of *She*, there is a lack of central female characters in Haggard's adventure fiction such as *King Solomon's Mines* and *Allan Quatermain* – none that can be said to be at the 'heart' of the story. Yet women are at the heart of Haggard's fiction as Africa itself.

The narrative structure of Haggard's *She* has a layered quality. The editor receives the manuscript from Horace Holly. Holly in turn has received the preliminary information from Leo Vincey's father, who had received it from his father and so on. The narrative revolves around the opening of the box which contains the 'history' of Ayesha, left in trust for Leo, to be opened on his twenty-fifth birthday when he reaches manhood. There is an increasing tension and suspense in the text as the day approaches. The box has an explosive quality: '"Now are you both ready?", I said, as people do when they are about to fire a mine'.[10] Once opened, the box reveals a series of other boxes each inside the first and, finally, the information they need for the quest to begin. The box tells of Ayesha who is to become the object of the quest, yet the box also contains a warning: 'He who would tamper with the vast and secret forces that animate the world may fall victim to them' (*She*, p. 212). At the centre of this series of boxes within boxes is Ayesha herself. This destructive desirable being *must* be approached in this way, *must* be contained within various enforced strongholds. To reach her is to unveil her in many complex ways but it is also to unveil oneself and to release her. The 'death' scene completes the unveiling, for Ayesha is stripped to her essence in the centre or womb of the world and the man unveil the truth of her being and the horror of it.

Imperial quests for the source of the Nile and other unknown origins of rivers or lost civilisations were rife throughout the nineteenth century. Captain Richard Burton was a key figure in such exploration and one of the founders of the new science of anthropology. He was to fictionalise himself as a romantic figure on a perilous crusade into the Unknown. *Pilgrimage* (1855) tells of his quest, travelling in Asia, disguised as a Muslim pilgrim, to penetrate the most sacred of sacred places, forbidden to the Westerner: the Kaabah at Mecca. On reaching this inner space and kissing the stone, Burton's excitement is a strange mixture of sexual pride at his illicit 'penetration' of a sacred space and scientific curiosity:

> There at last it lay, the bourne of my long and weary Pilgrimage, realising the plans and hopes of many and many a year. The mirage medium of Fancy invested the huge catafalque and its gloomy pall with peculiar charms . . . and how few have looked upon the celebrated shrine! I may truly say that, of all the worshippers who clung weeping to the curtain, or who pressed their weeping hearts to the stone, none felt for the moment a deeper emotion than did the Haji from the far-north. It was as if the poetic legends of the Arab spoke truth, and that the waving wings of angels, not the sweet breeze of morning, were agitating and swelling the black covering of the shrine.[11]

Patrick Brantlinger comments that Burton casts upon the black stone 'the panoptical gaze of western science' which seeks to penetrate the deepest, most sacred mysteries of every culture'.[12] Burton, one of the founders of the colonising science of anthropology, was to lend his panoptical gaze to its investigations: it is also the gaze characteristic of Haggard's fictional imperialist explorers.

Haggard emphasises throughout his imperial romances the danger of the quest: there is a persistent fear expressed about what will be found once the centre is reached and the veil lifted. The female heart (Freud's 'dark continent'), the object of Haggard's quests, is itself dangerous as the authorial voice warns in Haggard's early novel *Jess*, completed a month before Haggard began to write *She*. Here the heroine is described as 'uncanny', a 'riddle', 'Egyptian Sphinx' and as an inscrutable veiled woman. The hero comes across Jess sleeping, half-hidden by foliage and, as he gazes at her, the authorial voice intervenes with a warning:

> From here and there there is a human heart from which it is not wise to draw the veil – a heart in which many things slumber . . . . Draw not the veil, whisper not the word of life in the silence where all things sleep, lest in the kindling breath of love and pain dim shapes arise, take form, and fright thee.[13]

In *Ayesha or the Return of She*[14] (1904), Leo and Holly are warned about unveiling the mysterious Hes (Ayesha) by Oros the high priest:

> you and your companion come . . . of set purpose, seeking to lift the veil from mysteries which have been hid for ages . . . . But if this veil is lifted, it may chance also that you will find what shall send your souls shivering to despair and madness. Say, are you not afraid? (*Ayesha: The Return of She*, p. 100).

Compelled towards fatality, Holly curses in *She*:

> the fatal curiosity that is ever prompting man to draw the veil from woman, and curses on the natural impulse that begets it! It is the cause of half – ay, and more than half, of our misfortunes. (*She*, p. 309).

Desire, the natural impulse that begets curiosity to lift the veil on the mysteries of Woman and the mysteries of Africa or the Unknown, is the compulsion behind the quest and a compulsion which leads dangerously towards fatality.

## KING SOLOMON'S MINES

Haggard's *King Solomon's Mines*[15] is dedicated to 'all the big and little boys who read it' and we are assured in the first chapter by the hero, Allan Quatermain: 'I can safely say that there is not a petticoat in the whole history' (*King Solomon's Mines*, p. 14). This will be a novel of heroism set in a male world of scrupulous camaraderie and adventure: a truly man-centred novel. It is to be a story free from women and the 'romantic' plot yet while Quatermain insists there are no petticoats in the story, *King Solomon's Mines* does have its female body. That body is that of Africa herself, waiting to be explored and conquered. Africa is at the heart of the quest.

Like Stevenson's *Treasure Island*, *King Solomon's Mines* has its crucial treasure map. Allan Quatermain obtains the map from a descendant of the map-maker, Silvestre, who had drawn the map in his own blood as he died from starvation beside the 'nipple' of the legendary 'Sheba's Breasts', a pair of mountains in Africa. Such an extraordinary motif – death from starvation beside the primary source of sustenance, the breast – sensitises the reader to the harshness and cruelty of this African landscape (body). It is a land that refuses to nurture and refuses sustenance to man. The map (see Plate 2), drawn as it is in blood, underscores the sexual nature of the quest. It forms an image of a headless female body turned upside down. The explorers must travel through 'Sheba's Breasts', down 'Solomon's Road' to a triangle of mountains, called the 'Three Witches', where they must descend into the earth, into a pit, to find the treasure.[16]

Quatermain, Curtis, Good, and Umbopa reach a desert in their travels where 'the burning sun seemed to be sucking our blood out of us' (*King Solomon's Mines*, p. 52). Almost dying from thirst, the men come up over a ridge and perceive Sheba's Breasts glittering in the distance. This scene forms one of Haggard's 'aerial views'.[17] These, according to Peter Pierce, operate as part of an imperialist structure: a group of explorers look down on to the land that they are about to enter. The land stretches out before them invitingly and the men contemplate their fantasy of an acquiescent Africa for, at this early stage in their expedition, the body promises to be taken, promises to sustain their fantasies. Here Sheba's Breasts are seen by the explorers in the distance, inviting and promising sustenance (see Plate 3). Quatermain remarks:

I am impotent before its very memory [mammary?] . . . . These mountains placed thus, like the pillars of a gigantic gateway, are shaped after the fashion of a woman's breasts, and at times the mists and shadows beneath them take the form of a recumbent woman, veiled mysteriously in sleep. Their bases swell gently from the plain, looking at that distance perfectly round and smooth;

and upon the top of each is a vast hillock covered with snow,
exactly corresponding to the nipple on the female breast . . . .
Sheba's Breasts had scarcely vanished into cloud-clad privacy
when our thirst – literally a burning question – reasserted itself.
(*King Solomon's Mines*, pp. 56–7)

Thus if the 'aerial view' is the imperialist gaze of desire, its object
here is the vision of a gigantic recumbent woman, veiled in sleep and
complete with breasts and snow-covered nipples. The fantasy of the
men who *look down* is that of a passive body, naked beneath the thin
veil, and invitingly half-asleep. The body described here is clearly a
white female body (corresponding to a late nineteenth-century definition of white middle-class female sexuality), veiled and passive:
the male fantasy of submissive female sexuality. Yet 'Africa' offers
sexual invitation and in her nakedness and recumbent position hints
at a concealed sexuality that may prove to be 'non-white'.[18]

These confident early aerial views are replaced by a closer confrontation with the body which is Africa. They are to move inside the
body. The heroes are finally taken to the underground location of
Solomon's treasure: led by the black 'witch' Gagool they are taken
down a huge pit with sloping sides to the treasure chamber.[19] Only
she knows the secret of the stones, the treasure to be found in the
mines beneath the mountains. Centuries old, she is the initiator and
the initiated, the hag-like brothel-keeper, the 'madam'. There is no
entry without her as only she knows how to operate the hidden lever
which will reveal the treasure chamber. She leads the white men to
their confrontation with the body which is Africa, to their initiation
into manhood, and (she believes) to their death. They are tricked:
Gagool seals them into the chamber and is herself crushed to death.
The men prepare to die in the perfect silence and darkness of their
underground tomb. Eventually, however, they find a labyrinth of
hidden passages and, taking what little treasure they can carry, they
struggle up and out through the huge pit, returning to England.

Greene writes of *King Solomon's Mines* as being an inner journey
into the heart of darkness,[20] and Margaret Atwood describes it as
'the journey into the unknown regions of the self'.[21] However much
this journey may represent a journey into man's soul, it also declares
itself to be a journey across and into a woman's body. The fantasy is
that the body will be passive (as the explorers survey Sheba's Breasts),
but a nightmare erupts as that body *awakes* and threatens death by
trapping the heroes inside the treasure chamber.

## DANGEROUS AWAKENINGS

Penetration threatens to release the dormant sexuality hidden in the female body (Africa) – this is itself a projection of the fear that for the white male explorers, confrontation with barbarism in Africa may release primitive impulses in themselves. The brutality apparently brought out in the white man in Africa (there was a mythology about such men, men such as Conrad's Kurtz who revert') was more easily attributed to the evil of Africa itself rather than to the evils of imperialism. Patrick Brantlinger argues that 'the potential for being "defiled", for going native, led [the late Victorian explorers] again and again to displace these impulses onto Africans, as well as onto other nonwhite peoples'.[22] In Haggard's imperialist fiction there is anxiety about penetration itself and the violation of the body (the theft of treasure) which expresses itself in the nightmare of the violated body revenging itself by trapping the penetrators. There seems to be also anxiety about sexual disease – the fear of the penetrated foreign body bringing death to the penetrators. The solution is to escape the foreign body before it consumes its white male prey.[23]

Most of the action in *Allan Quatermain* and *King Solomon's Mines* takes place in the open, allowing for a number of 'aerial views'. Yet Peter Pierce notes that the domain of Ayesha is underground: the burial chambers of Kor. There are almost no 'aerial views' in *She*. Pierce adds:

> From the time Holly announces that 'we are entering the bowels of the great mountain', he and Leo lose their sense of location in its dark, confusing recesses. Their wandering in the hot, circuitous passages of the mountain is the correlative of their search for an understanding of the veiled white queen.[24]

Pierce only hints at the sexual content of this correlation, yet the journey of the three white heroes towards the sacred place which is both Ayesha and the centre of Africa is a journey inside a female body. The early part of their journey is navigated across rotting swamps and they enter the domain of Ayesha, the burial chambers of the 'Kor' (Core), through an ancient drainage channel.

When Ayesha takes them on another journey they emerge from the 'long confinement in the caves' (*She*, p. 377), travel through the ruined temples of Kor and into another underground opening. The cave slopes 'inwards like the petal of a flower' and seems to have been 'blown bodily in the mountain'. It is 'pitted with deep holes, in which it would have been easy to break a leg'. They enter a chasm 'jagged and torn and splintered in a far past age by some awful convulsion of Nature' (*She*, p. 387). The chasm is bottomless. A spur juts out across the chasm, vibrating 'like a living thing'[25] and a light penetrates the gloom: 'I presume that there was a cleft or hole through which it pierced . . . . Right through the heart of darkness that flaming sword was stabbed' (*She*, p. 388). This is the Place of Life, the 'womb of the world'. Having experienced the horror of Ayesha's devolution, they escape, again through subterranean labyrinths, and return to the support of Billali, who offers a moral: 'Venture no more into lands that ye know not, lest ye come back no more' (*She*, p. 418). Billali's words echo the statement made about the dead Silvestre, whom the explorers of *King Solomon's Mines* find petrified within the 'nipple' of Sheba's breasts: 'a sad momento of the fate that so often overtakes those who would penetrate into the unknown' (*King Solomon's Mines*, p. 64).

Just as the explorers experience the transition from sleeping and acquiescent Africa to an awakened and vengeful Africa in *King Solomon's Mines*, the fantasy of *She* of a passive and inviting African queen is initially sustained and then violently disturbed. Horace Holly, a pronounced misogynist, having reached the centre of Africa and the home of Ayesha, with his ward Leo, is invited to attend Ayesha in her inner sanctuary, her private and exotically furnished apartments. He hears a silvery voice and sees the veiled figure of Ayesha emerging from behind a curtained recess. This is their first interview and one in which Holly insists upon her unveiling, although she warns him of the dangers involved (the curse of her beauty):

She lifted her white and rounded arms . . . and slowly, very slowly, withdrew some fastening beneath her hair. Then all of a sudden the long, corpse-like wrappings fell from her to the ground, and my eyes travelled up her form, now only robed in a garb of clinging white that did but serve to show its perfect and imperial shape . . . . On her little feet were sandals . . . Then came ankles more perfect than ever sculptor dreamed of. About the waist her white kirtle was fastened by a double-headed snake . . . above which her gracious form swelled up in lines as pure as they were lovely, till the kirtle ended on the snowy argent of her breast

. . . . I gazed above them at her face and . . . shrank back blinded and amazed . . . . How am I to describe it? I cannot – simply, I cannot! (*She*, p. 304)

Phiefer L. Browne remarks that the setting of this scene is 'like an expensive bordello' and that Holly's lengthy description of her unveiled figure (of which I quote only part) presents the various features of her body 'for the delectation of the reader'.[26] Thus Holly becomes the client inspecting the 'goods', but also surveying the landscape of desire and eroticism. We may go so far as to compare it with an extract from the Victorian pornographic magazine, the *Pearl*, first published in London in 1879 and disappearing in 1880. Here the hero, in search of a harem, arrives at the capital of the Turkish empire. Ibzaidu, a Circassian beauty, is brought before him for inspection:

> She was enveloped in a piece of fine Indian muslin and had a veil over her face.
> I raised the veil and started back in amazement at the dazzling beauty of her face.
> I then caught hold of the drapery in which she was enveloped and gently drawing it from her clasp, I threw it on one side and gazed with admiration on the most ravishingly beautiful face and figure I ever beheld. Hers was one of those oval, majestic faces, such as poets and mythologists attribute to Juno. I much admired her rich jet-black hair . . . contrasting singularly with the dazzling whiteness of her skin . . . . Her breasts, luxuriously large . . . tipped with deliciously small nipples, of that fine pink colour which so strongly denotes virginity in the possessor.
> Her waist was gracefully elegant and tapering; her belly fine, round . . . soft as the finest down. Her lips were very large and wide . . . her buttocks swelling out behind two hillocks of snowy white flesh . . . ankles tapering and a foot delicately small.[27]

Admittedly Haggard's description contains less overtly sexual detail, but both passages share the same delight in the opportunity to gaze at the unveiled female form which promises unlimited pleasures. The male gaze travels up or down the object: Holly travels 'up-country' and the Frenchman travels 'down-country'. This is the imperial gaze, the gaze that delights in the passivity of its object, the gaze that *maps* ('two hillocks of snowy white flesh'), the gaze that *travels* ('my eyes travelled up her form'), and the gaze that *explores* ('I raised the veil'): the gaze of the connoisseur and the imperialist. It corresponds to the imperial gaze that Pierce[28] outlines in his analysis of Haggard's 'aerial views': the surveying of the land stretched out before the eye: veiled, mysterious, tantalising and above all, passive, waiting to be taken.

Corresponding to Haggard's portrayal of Africa (from passive to awakened and menacing landscape), this fantasy of Ayesha as passive object is disturbed when Ayesha's desire is awakened. Ayesha has extraordinary sexual powers and plays with her two admirers with great pleasure, even her beloved Leo. Over the corpse of Leo's murdered 'wife', she chooses to demonstrate these powers:

> 'Look now on me Kallicrates!' and with a sudden motion she shook her gauzy covering from her, and stood forth in her low kirtle and her snaky zone . . . rising from her wrappings, as it were, like Venus from the wave . . . or a beatified spirit from the tomb. She stood forth, and fixed her deep and glowing eyes upon Leo's eyes, and I saw his clenched fists unclasp, and his set and quivering features relax beneath her gaze. I saw his wonder and astonishment grow into admiration, and then into fascination, and the more he struggled the more I saw the power of her dread beauty fasten on him and take possession of his senses, drugging them, and drawing the heart out of him . . . .
> · Once more she stretched out her arms to him and whispered 'Come', and then in another few seconds it was over. I saw him struggle – I saw him even turn to fly; but her eyes drew him more strongly than iron bonds, and the magic of her beauty and concentrated will and passion entered into him and overpowered him – ay, even there, in the presence of the body of the woman who had loved him . . . but he cannot be blamed too much . . . the temptress who drew him into evil was more than human. (*She*, pp. 357–8)

There is a role-reversal here, similar to the scene in *Dracula* in which Harker is approached and caressed by the three vampire sisters who similarly drug his senses. Here Ayesha enters into and overpowers Leo, taking possession of him with her eyes in a powerful inversion of the earlier scene in which Holly's desiring and panoptical gaze maps Ayesha's body. Here it is Ayesha's returned gaze, her eyes, which penetrate Leo and draw the life and heart from him. It is precisely Ayesha's sexual awakening, through her recognition of her reincarnated lost lover, Kallicrates, in an inverted version of the Sleeping Beauty myth, that will release her potency and her danger for the West.

## 'THE YELLOW PERIL': THE INVASION OF AYESHA/ASIA

'the East, which has slept so long, shall awake'

In *She*, Ayesha with her lost lover returned to her, details to Holly an invasion campaign of the Western nations which will give Leo and herself 'dominion over the sea and earth . . . dominion over the world' (*She*, p. 396). Holly remarks with horror and fascination:

> The terrible She had evidently made up her mind to go to England, and it made me absolutely shudder to think what would be the result of her arrival there . . . . It might be possible to control her for a while, but her proud ambitious spirit would be certain to *break loose and avenge itself* for the long centuries of its solitude . . . what was there to stop her? In the end she would, I had little doubt, *assume absolute rule over the British dominions and probably over the whole earth*, and though I had no doubt that she would speedily make ours the most glorious and prosperous empire the world has ever seen, it would be at the cost of a terrible sacrifice of life. (*She*, p. 376; emphasis mine)

At this stage, 'caught in the web of her fatal fascinations', Holly believes that Ayesha is being used by Providence: 'as a means to change the order of the world and possibly . . . to change it for the better' (*She*, p. 376). Yet Ayesha's sacrificial 'death' corrects Holly's optimism: 'Providence' removes Ayesha as a social anomaly by means of natural selection.

Ayesha's invasion threat is considerably more detailed and realisable in the later novel, *Ayesha: The Return of She*. Cultural anxieties about invasion had increased by this date, the peak of Samuel Hynes's category[29] of invasion literature: 1904. Here several chapters describe the careful planning of invasion detailed by Ayesha. She is to begin in China this time (see Plate 4):

She took a map of the Eastern Hemisphere which I had drawn, and, placing her finger upon Pekin, said:

'There is the place that shall be our home . . . . I have chosen the Chinese because thou tellest me that their numbers are unaccountable, that they are brave, subtle, and patient, and though now powerless because ill-ruled and untaught, able with their multitudes to flood the little Western nations . . . '.

'And if the "little Western nations" will not wait to be flooded?' suggested Leo. 'If they combine with Russia, for instance – in whose territory we may be at this moment, for aught I know – and attack thee first?'

'Ah!' she said . . . 'I have thought of it, and for my part hope that it will chance, since then thou canst not blame me if I put out my strength. Oh! then the East, that has slept so long, shall awake – shall awake, and upon battlefield after battlefield . . . thou shalt see my flaming standards sweep on to victory. (*Ayesha*, pp. 158–159)

Ayesha's plan is, then, to take over the rule of China and from there to conquer the 'little Western nations'. Tibet and China were crucial territories in the first decade of the twentieth century; Persia, Afghanistan and Tibet were the countries that separated the respective empires of Russia and Britain, which explains Leo's confusion as to which territory they occupy. Similarly China and Japan embodied another threat to the Western world, nicknamed the 'yellow peril'[30] (see the French cartoon of 1904 in Plate 5). The so-called 'peril' of China and Japan was perceived to be an influx of cheap labour, the successes of Japanese production techniques, and the sheer scale of population combined with technical advances which might enable them to repossess the East to reclaim it. It is precisely this repossession of the East that Ayesha vows to spearhead and thus She-Who-Must-Be-Obeyed becomes the modern weapon necessary for this invasion – indeed she becomes Asia/Ayesha. She proposes to waken the nations of the East and flood the little Western nations with the numerical superiority of the Chinese peoples. The possibility of these Western nations joining forces with Russia to oppose the 'yellow peril' was a very real one in 1904. Russia was at war with Japan in the years 1904–5, and 1907 saw the Anglo-Russian Convention which 'organised' the territories in Afghanistan, Persia and Tibet. Kipling, in praising Japanese art before Japan's victory over Russia in the war of 1904–5, nonetheless hints at a fear of what was to come: 'Mercifully she has been denied the last touch of firmness in her character that would enable her to play with the whole round world.'[31] Ridley argues that after the war of 1904 Kipling was never to lose his fear for the future of the world when the East 'really wakes up'. Ayesha too proposes 'to play with the whole wide world' by enabling the East to awake under her leadership.

The gap between Burton's confident and daring trespass into the sacred place of the East – Mecca, 1855 – and the experience of Haggard's explorers in reaching the inner space of Africa (1880s) and then Tibet (1904) is a significant one. While Burton experiences fear as he kisses the Kaabah, it is precisely this fear that drives him and that adds to his excitement. He has demonstrated his cunning and his power to penetrate the forbidden places of an alien culture. He has reached the centre of the culturally unknown and colonises it by his presence. Haggard's heroes experience no such simple victory. Reaching the sacred place (the womb of Africa) is to risk the retribution of the invaded body. Ronald Robinson and John Gallagher have shown that by this point, the period of 'conscious imperialism', imperial policy is primarily motivated by fear of native uprisings on the edges of the empire and by the prospect of not being able to maintain colonial power.[32] In the gap between Burton's arrival at Mecca disguised as a pilgrim and the publication of Haggard's two novels, the Empire had experienced the Indian Mutiny of 1857 and the Transvaal rebellion of 1880, of which Haggard was an eye-witness. The Victorians were becoming aware for the first time of the disturbing effects of one culture on another,[33] and of the perilous nature of its colonies. The adventure fiction of this period is characterised by a preoccupation with the destructive magic of the Orient and of Africa – magic statues, talismans, curses from violated tombs – the avenging and supernatural powers of the colonised culture.[34]

British imperialism, as fictioned in the imperial romance, expresses an anxiety of possession (perhaps exacerbated in Haggard's case by his firsthand experience of the Boer uprising in 1880). The quests described in the last decades of the nineteenth century are in themselves more treacherous and the consequences of penetration more likely to prove fatal. What is perhaps more interesting is that the experience of such dangers is fictioned in the contrast between the tiny male explorers and the colossal and menacing female body of Africa, which holds out its arms invitingly like the female vampires of *Dracula* and carries death in its embrace. It is a body which is littered internally with the petrified bodies of its victims (dead rulers, dead explorers, past civilisations). I have argued that there is an increasing fatality about the Empire in the late Victorian period (a sense of declining power) but in the imperial romance of Rider Haggard this fatality is located in (projected on to) the body of Africa itself as the *femme fatale*/the Dark Continent.

## A MEANS OF INVESTIGATION: ANTHROPOLOGY

Whilst the investigative processes of *Dracula* seem to couple occult knowledge (garlic, stakes, Holy Wafer) with the techniques of elementary psychoanalysis (such as confession, hypnosis, the case-study and the recording of hysterical or neurotic discourse), the primary investigative mode of Haggard's novels is that of anthropology. Both are engaged in similar processes of mapping the Unknown but they adopt different yet complementary scientific models of investigation. The 'experts' who coordinate the detection are trained in different areas: Van Helsing is a medical man, a specialist in obscure diseases and psychic phenomena, whereas Haggard's explorers are amateurs in popularised comparative anthropology.

In his study of the representation of the 'savage' in the imperial romance[35] Brian Street argues that from the 1870s onwards the Victorian novel spawned a genre which can loosely be termed the ethnographic novel which drew upon contemporary anthropological debate. Street's survey of the late nineteenth-century imperial romance attests to the 'wide use made of anthropological theory in work directed at the general public'[36] in this period. While there is disagreement and debate in these novels about the nature of 'barbarism' and 'civilisation', the hierarchical ranking of races, about the opposing theories of polygeny versus monogeny, degeneration and progress, few imperial romances question the superiority of the white races or question the hierarchical model inherited from the medieval 'Great Chain of Being'. Literature was to make such theories accessible and to provide a means for the reading public to keep up with the rapid advances of science. It also afforded a reassuring confirmation of ethnocentric assumptions of white superiority and a means to justify widespread imperial expansion into unexplored continents. Popular fiction became a forum for the debate of anthropological theories and their implementation, theories which were in themselves very much in the public eye:

*The Popular Magazine of Anthropology* which set itself up as an intermediary between science and the 'people', and the Anthropological Society of London, with its open meetings and political debates, were passing on these ideas . . . to a large and very interested audience.[37]

The anxieties caused by the writings of the evolutionists were wide-reaching. Leo Henkin writes that the late nineteenth century saw the 'invasion' of such theories into popular consciousness:

By 1910 evolutionary theory had invaded every branch of science, ethics, philosophy and sociology. As such it had entered so generally into the warp and woof of modern thought as to be indistinguishable as an independent factor.[38]

The anthropologists were to tailor and adapt evolutionary theory to a more accessible and less troubling shape for the general public. Anthropology both played to (and played out) the widespread alarms caused by the 'discovery' of the common ancestor of man and the ape and alleviated such fears by confirming at every point the evolutionary superiority of the white races.

*The Origin of Species* was published in 1859, three years after Haggard's birth, so that, as Alan Sandison[39] points out, Haggard would have grown up in an intellectual climate charged with the fierce debate which the evolutionary doctrine had excited. Brian Street argues that it was Haggard's unique experience of and interest in the social, sexual, political and religious customs of African tribes and his friendship with the anthropologist and writer Andrew Lang that were to account for the detailed anthropological knowledge displayed in his fiction.[40]

Haggard uses footnotes, fictitious editors, lost manuscripts and a type of narrator familiar with anthropological discourses to lend authenticity to his narratives and to give them a scientifically empirical flavour. His footnotes borrow ethnographical details from traveller's tales to explain native customs described in the text and in *Allan Quatermain* Haggard devotes an entire chapter to detailing the customs and history of the Zu-Vendis tribe. Allan Quatermain is the most notable of Haggard's narrators, mediating, translating and interpreting the Unknown in his characteristically sardonic manner. Quatermain is very much the amateur anthropologist relying on his inside knowledge of various African tribes to make contrasts and value-judgements about tribal customs as a means to place and rank racial groups. He is not an academic nor a scientist but a valuable observer who collects data and understands and is trusted by the natives. For *She* Haggard created a new type of narrator, Horace Holly, the university man, the scholar. Street has shown how academic explorers are generally satirised in the imperial romance.[41] In Conan Doyle's *The Lost World* of 1912, for instance, two professors, scientifically curious but unfit to survive the rigours of the primitive jungle, must be constantly saved from perilous situations by the 'real men'. Holly, however, is both 'real man' and scholar; hairy and apelike, he is the most fit to survive the dangers, heat and mosquitoes of Africa.

Holly collects his data and information for a specific purpose and for a specific audience – his university colleagues. It is to these scientific scholars that the text is to be given, the manuscript which Holly believes constitutes an extraordinary history, a 'gift': 'and that is the end of this history as far as it concerns science and the outside world' (*She*, p. 419). Furthermore its publication and editing are the responsibility of another member of the university, an anthropologist, we assume. The text is the property of the university, to be edited and transcribed by academics and it is for these 'consumers' that Holly includes all the anthropological data: the customs and beliefs of the Armahagger tribe, the information about the ancient race of Kor. Like Harker, he incorporates the foreignness, the strangeness, through this process of collecting and recording information. This recording process extends to even the smallest of botanical details. Holly notes, for example, the existence of certain waterlilies: 'few of the flowers were perfect, owing to the prevalence of a white water maggot with a green head which fed upon them' (*She*, p. 245).

Such small details form part of a larger pattern: the presence of a Darwinian consciousness in the recording voice of the text, a pessimistic sense of the struggle of all things for existence in the brutal landscape of Africa. Holly is witness to, for example, a struggle to the death of a crocodile and a lion which he describes as a 'duel to the death' (*She*, p. 243). The white men enter a Darwinian world of eat-or-be-eaten, kill-or-be-killed. They are the predators invading and killing the big game of Africa, but they are also the preyed-upon, the prey of the bloodthirsty mosquitoes. Haggard's story, then, is filtered through a mind sensitised to new evolutionary science, a scholarly mind which orders and arranges its material conscious of the watchful eyes of the 'colleagues', conscious of the scientific implications of its data.

As Quatermain chronicles the Zu-Vendis tribe, Horace Holly, as investigator, collects information about the Armahagger tribe, a debased and 'bastard' stock, descendants of the ancient race of Kor, whose ruins are to be seen in Ayesha's domain. A self-declared misogynist, Holly is fascinated by the customs of the matriarchal Armahagger community and describes their social organisation in great detail. Much of the anthropological framework of *She* is concerned with female power and its organisation. The hot-potting custom of the Armahaggers, used as a means to exact female vengeance, alerts the reader to what Holly and his companions are to receive at the hands of the mighty She herself, the ruler of the race. Holly's panoptical gaze is peculiarly alert to instances of female atavism, cruelty and vengeance. In these novels the outstretched arms of the sexually predatory female invariably bring death to the seduced male – a pattern which is to be repeated until the moment of Leo's death in the sequel to *She* in which Leo dies in Ayesha's killing embrace. Ayesha, though she is of Oriental rather than African origin, and superficially extremely 'civilised', is shown through the anthropological comparison with the Armahaggers to share a kinship with her people of sexual cruelty and degeneracy. Thus, much of the anthropological investigation undertaken by Haggard's narrators is directed towards the supposed barbarism and cruelty of native or primitive women, enabling the reader to 'know' the 'symptoms' of savagery, to know, like Allan Quatermain, that these signs are not only to be found in the Dark Continent but at the very heart of civilisation.

## WHAT WE SAW: THE UNVEILING

Once the three men have entered the 'bowels' of Ayesha's domain, Holly's anthropological hunt begins in earnest. While his ward lies in a fever, Holly undertakes a series of interviews with the fully-veiled and alluring white queen and chronicles what he discovers: her racial origin, her beliefs, her languages and her knowledge. Holly observes her at night uninvited as she lets 'loose her passion' upon the dead Kallicrates. He is compelled by the duality of Ayesha's nature: her evidently civilised nature in contrast to her surroundings and the side of her which he has observed in her midnight tryst with her embalmed lover – her dark malevolence and barbaric passions. His research is increasingly directed towards the darker side of her nature, 'the depths of her dark soul'. The text is a record of 'what we saw': a voyeurism disguised as scientific empiricism.

Throughout his research Holly is preoccupied with assessing Ayesha's anthropological rank by placing her in the context of information about the Armahagger tribe and their ancestors, the ancient race of Kor. He seeks to place her within these two poles: the lost civilisation and their degenerate descendants. He seeks also to place himself as white man in relation to her. In a crucial early scene he attempts to prove his racial superiority by refusing to debase himself before her like Billali, who crawls into her presence on his hands and knees, 'after the fashion of an Irishman driving a pig to market' (*She*, p. 294):

> I was an Englishman, and why . . . should I creep into the presence of some savage woman as though I were a monkey . . . it would have been a patent acknowledgement of my inferiority. (*She*, p. 294)

Yet significantly it is Holly who carries the stigmata of atavism: it is he who is nicknamed the baboon, it is he who is said to resemble an ape so closely as to be living proof of the 'monkey theory'. It is his hairiness which protects him from the dangers of the African terrain, a protection interestingly not afforded to the Aryan Leo, but it also ensures that he will not be the object of the female desire which so often proves to be fatal in Haggard's novels.

Within an hour of his meeting Ayesha she has unveiled and in this unveiling Holly is bewildered and half-blinded by her beauty. He falls to the ground 'babbling confusedly in [his] terror' and in this fall, this debasement, he implicitly acknowledges her superiority. From this point Holly's investigations are directed towards reversing this humiliating defeat, directed towards proving her inferiority by demonstrating her savagery and barbarism, demonstrating that it is Ayesha who is the 'monkey' rather than himself. The text dramatises this struggle for racial superiority between the band of white men and the white queen of Arab origin and the struggle is articulated through a series of evolutionary and anthropological metaphors. The struggle is finally resolved in Ayesha's devolution which confirms the racial supremacy of the white explorers.

In *Darwinism in the English Novel*, Leo Henkin writes that the 'monkey theory', the suggestion that man evolved from the ape, had a particularly dramatic effect on popular consciousness[42] in the late nineteenth century. Two years before the publication of Darwin's *The Origin of Species* of 1859 Huxley had started exploring the links between man and the apes and it was in 1863 that he published these theories in *Evidence as to Man's Place in Nature* which began the 'missing link' hypothesis and caused huge public controversy. By 1871 Darwin felt secure enough to commit himself to publication on the same subject, producing *The Descent of Man*. Henkin attributes the main controversy over evolutionary theory to this particular part of the debate: man's proposed shared ancestry with the apes was the single greatest obstacle to the public acceptance of evolutionary theory.

Haggard's fascination with the beast in man, the savage under-side of civilisation, is evident throughout his writings, voiced in particular by his narrator Allan Quatermain. In the introduction to *Allan Quatermain*,[43] written in 1887, the same year as *She*, Quatermain lays out his theories:

> Ah, this civilisation, what does it all come to? For forty years and more I lived among savages, and studied them and their ways; and now for several years I have lived here in England . . . and what have I found? A great gulf fixed? No, only a little one . . . . I say that as the savage is, so is the white man, only the latter is more inventive and possesses the faculty of combination . . . . It is a depressing conclusion, but in all essentials the savage and the child of civilisation are identical. (*Allan Quatermain*, p. 429)

Quatermain proposes that the child of civilisation is made up from twenty parts: 'nineteen savage and one civilised' (*Allan Quatermain*, p. 430) and that it is these savage parts that we must look to if we are to understand ourselves, whilst the one civilised part is spread over the other nineteen parts like the blacking on a boot or the veneer on a table: 'It is on the nineteen rough, serviceable savage portions that we fall back in emergencies, not on the polished but unsubstantial twentieth' (*Allan Quatermain*, p. 430). Quatermain's conclusions are typical of late Victorian writing on 'savagery' and 'civilisation'. In Mark Rutherford's *Deliverance* of 1885, for instance, William Hale White states: 'our civilisation is nothing but a thin film or crust lying over a volcanic pit'.[44]

Quatermain finds this a 'depressing conclusion': we are *no better* than savages, and savages are brutal, barbaric, unevolved. What is significant in Quatermain's introduction is his singling-out of Woman as his chosen representative of the latent savagery of civilisation. Whilst he attacks the 'superfine, cultured idler scientifically eating a dinner at his club the cost of which would keep a starving family for a week' (*Allan Quatermain*, p. 429), this is the only mention of the civilised *male*. The focus of Quatermain's discourse is directed at the civilised *female*:

> I dare say that the highly civilised lady reading this will smile at an old fool of a hunter's simplicity when she thinks of her black, bead-bedecked sister . . . and yet my dear lady, what are those pretty things round your own neck? – they have a strong family resemblance, especially when you wear that *very* low dress, to the savage woman's beads. Your habit of turning round and round to the sound of horns and tom-toms, your fondness for pigments and powders . . . the quickness with which your taste in feathered head-dress varies – all these suggest *touches of kinship*, and remember that in the fundamental principles of your nature you are quite identical . . . . (*Allan Quatermain*, p. 429; emphasis mine)

'Touches of kinship', 'family resemblance': the nature of woman and the nature of the savage are 'quite identical'. Moreover, they belong to the same family. Whilst Haggard exposes the beast in man in his novels, the 'bloodlust' that can overcome even the most civilised of men, it is not the beast *in* women that compels him but *the woman as beast*. Quatermain's tone is that of the 'expert' whose exploration and knowledge of foreign races enables him to *read the signs* of atavism within civilisation. His aim is to undermine the smug Western confidence in racial superiority and to warn of the dangers of complacency, but in doing so once again Haggard singles out Woman as the site of a particular investigation into atavism.

One of the preoccupations of late nineteenth-century science, particularly craniology and criminology, was to find evidence to support the woman-as-savage or woman-as-evolutionary-throwback hypothesis. To find Woman as the crucial link between Man and his savage ancestors was to *project* fears of the barbarism *in* man on to the barbarism of certain types of women. Craniology had established, or was in the process of establishing in this period that women, by virtue of their stunted brain-sizes, were closer to the evolutionary state of animals, savages and children. Hottentot women, particularly, were considered a curious phenomenon and even *displayed* as 'freaks' or missing links throughout Europe in this period.[45]

George Cuvier, for instance, a French scientist, wrote in 1878 of the 'Hottentot Venus' (who died in Paris that year):

> she had a way of pouting her lips exactly like that we have observed in the orang-utan. Her movements had something abrupt and fantastical about them, reminding one of the ape. Her lips were monstrously large. Her ear was like that of many apes, being small, the tragus weak and the external border almost obliterated behind. These are animal characters. I have never seen a human head more like an ape than that of this woman.[46]

On this issue, the fascination with women, particularly black women, as 'missing links', the discourses of craniology and criminology were to fuse. Criminology sought to define the criminal type ('the evolutionary throwback in our midst' in Lombroso's words)[47] not just by brain-size, but also by facial and bodily features. With such theories, the criminal could be conceived of as a *type*, or even a separate *species* because he/she can be demonstrated to have facial and bodily features (termed *stigmata* by the criminologists) which resemble those of the ape. Such types can be 'read' by experts versed in the discourses of biological determinism. Both criminology and craniology worked to provide a system of signs (a language) whereby the atavistic type could be identified as an evolutionary throwback or missing link.

This drive towards measurement and classification can be seen as a response to the fears caused by the discovery of the common ancestor, the ape. Science could demonstrate, empirically, that such an ancestry could be 'detected' in certain anti-social individuals, thereby ensuring its 'containment'. The stigmata, the clues by which such detection or diagnosis could take place, became all-important in this period, with scientists engaged in the study of atavism competing to find systems of signs to read the human body and the human face.[48] Cesare Lombroso and William Ferrero's *The Female Offender*,[49] published in England in 1895, for instance, provided a series of photographed faces of female criminals which are offered as a kind of 'map' for reading. Lombroso and Ferrero attend to each face in turn, identifying various stigmata: primarily negroid features, large jaws, unusual facial hair, cranium size, shape of the earlobe and even unusually sharp teeth. They demonstrate the atavism of each face, the ape hidden beneath the skin. Biological determinism of this kind was not restricted to rarefied academic journals and specialised publications, but could be translated into wider social contexts.[50] The discourses of biological determinism are present in many debates about higher education for women in this period, for instance, and are used to underpin both arguments for and against the education of women.[51]

This search for the 'missing link', the search for the signs of atavism in the social anomaly, and the search for a system of signs by which to read and identify the evolutionary throwback, were to become fertile themes in the anthropological romance. Leo Henkin writes that a common theme of such novels was the discovery of a 'missing link, not in fossil form but alive'.[52] Typically explorers, often with anthropological knowledge, discover an individual or even a whole tribe in Africa whose development has been arrested and who become a means of investigation into the atavism of man. Occasionally these 'freaks' are shipped back to England to become the subject of scientific experimentation. The 'missing link' theme extends to a fascination with hypothetical species and mutations – the discovery of a reverted type living in civilisation who, like the criminal, can *only* revert to type.[53]

## HAGGARD'S MONKEY WOMAN

Henkin makes no mention of Haggard's fiction in his study of the 'missing link' theme in English fiction. Yet Haggard's work incorporates three 'monkey women': Gagool in *King Solomon's Mines* (1885), Hendrika in *Allan's Wife* (1889) and Ayesha herself, who reveals herself to be a monkey beneath her enticing flesh in *She*. Hendrika is said to be a 'missing link' and by implication this description extends to Gagool and Ayesha, through their 'touches of kinship' with this baboon-woman.

In Haggard's *Allan's Wife*,[54] published only two years after *She*, Quatermain 'accidentally' discovers his lost childhood sweetheart, Stella, in deepest Africa where she has grown up with her father. Quatermain is both repelled and fascinated by Stella's companion and servant, Hendrika, whom he describes as:

> young, of white blood, very short with bowed legs and enormous shoulders. In face she was not bad-looking, but the brow receded, the chin and ears were prominent. In short she reminded me of nothing so much as a very handsome monkey. She might have been the missing link. (*Allan's Wife*, p. 79)

This description parallels that of the 'Hottentot Venus' (cited above), except that here the woman is white. Stella explains the mystery: Hendrika has been reared by baboons who live in the rocks behind Stella's father's house. Stella had rescued her and tamed her. Hendrika has 'long sinewy arms', is able to shin up trees, swing from limb to limb, and loves her white mistress with a passionate intensity. She both speaks and understands the baboon language.

When Allan falls in love with and proposes to Stella, Hendrika warns him off with a declaration of her love for Stella. She warns him that his desire leads him dangerously near the 'pit' or abyss of her revenge:

> 'do I not love her also? . . . I am a woman as she is, and you are a man, and they say in the kraals that men love women better than women love women. But it is a lie . . . . She used to kiss me sometimes . . . but those who loved her before you came are forgotten. Be careful, Macumazahn, be careful, lest I am revenged upon you . . . . Walk softly, Macumazahn, or you will fall into a pit . . . '. (*Allan's Wife*, p. 108)

Allan fears her jealousy and is intrigued by it and it is at this point that anthropological discourses are motivated in his attempt to *translate* her aggressive behaviour (and his fear of her behaviour) into scientific, objective terminology that confirms his racial superiority:

> the lower one gets in the scale of humanity, the more readily this passion thrives; indeed it may be said to come to its intensest perfection in brutes . . . . Now Hendrika was in some ways not far removed from the animal, which may account for the ferocity of her jealousy of her mistress' affection. (*Allan's Wife*, p. 109)

Allan Quatermain is *ranking* Hendrika here as the lowest scale of humanity and in so doing confirming his superiority in the battle for Stella. This is the same Haggardian hero who, in the introduction to *Allan Quatermain*, had attested to the 'touches of kinship' between the civilised woman and the savage and he is privileged here to have his theories substantiated by the opportunity for close observation of a baboon woman. Hendrika tries to gain superiority by rallying her baboon kin to kidnap Stella, yet Stella is to be the victim of this struggle for supremacy between Quatermain and the menacing monkey woman: Stella dies as Hendrika reverts to type and confirms Quatermain the tragic victor. Hendrika's story confirms

Quatermain's suspicions about the savage in the white woman, for although Hendrika is white she has been nursed on baboon's milk and no amount of education, love and nurture can protect her from her savage self, for this is fixed. As a predatory and sexual woman whose sexual inclinations are towards other women and whose crime is a crime of passion she displays all the degenerate symptoms necessary to confirm her atavism.

Yet the text also moves towards a yet more complex unveiling. The two women, the civilised and the savage, are inseparable and have known only each other's love. The text establishes Hendrika's savagery in unveiling her and Stella dies, a victim in the struggle for supremacy. Yet Hendrika is also revealed as the darker underside of the impossibly angelic Stella, just as the vampire Lucy lurks beneath the innocent, pure Lucy: the beast within the civilised white woman. Significantly it is not until the appearance of Quatermain and his passion for Stella and marriage to her that the savagery of Hendrika is unleashed. Quatermain realises that he cannot have Stella's innocence without the accompanying savagery of her companion. The two must die together, they cannot be separated, for Hendrika is the 'bead-bedecked sister', the bead-bedecked Other: she is the apelike underside of the civilised and superficially innocent white woman.

Gagool and Ayesha display 'touches of kinship', touches of sisterhood, with this apewoman Hendrika, through the series of links and shared metaphors used to describe them. Gagool is the wicked sorceress of *King Solomon's Mines* (1885) and, like Ayesha, she is immortal. She is less athletic than Hendrika: a wizened, shrivelled-up version of the same fictional type. Allan Quatermain has a second opportunity to observe at close quarters a female 'missing link' (he seems to be unable to escape from these figures):

> I observed the wizened, *monkey*-like figure creeping from the shadow of the hut. It crept on all fours, but when it reached the place where the king sat it rose upon its feet, and throwing the furry covering from its face, revealed a most extraordinary and weird countenance. Apparently it was that of a woman of great age so shrunken that in size it seemed *little larger than the face of a year old child* . . . . Set among these wrinkles was a sunken slit, that represented a mouth . . . . There was no nose to speak of; indeed the whole visage might have been taken for that of a sun-dried *corpse*, had·it not been for a pair of large black eyes still full of fire and intelligence, which gleamed . . . like *jewels in a charnel-house*.

1   Philip Burne-Jones, *The Vampire* (ca. 1897)

3  Sheba's Breasts. Illustration by Walter Paget from the 1898 edition of Rider Haggard's *King Solomon's*

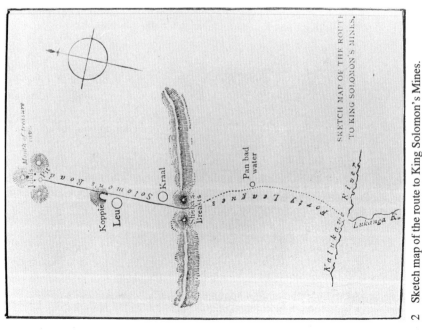

2  Sketch map of the route to King Solomon's Mines. Illustration by Walter Paget from the 1898 edition of

4   She took a map, and placing her finger upon Pekin, said 'There is the
place that shall be our home.' Illustration by Maurice Grieffenhagen
from the 1905 edition of Rider Haggard's *Ayesha: The Return of She*

5   French cartoon (1904) of the 'Yellow Peril' as seen in Europe

6   Sketch by Conrad (Manuscripts Department, Lilly Library, Indiana University, Bloomington)

7   Stanley Resisting Temptation from J. W. Buel, *Heroes of the Dark Continent* (1898)

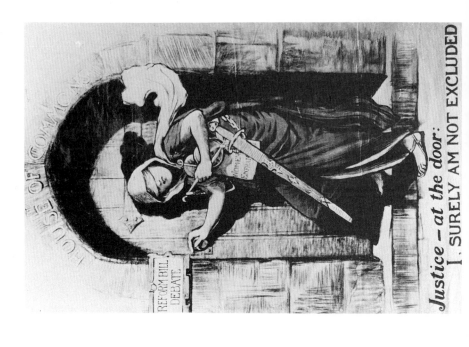

*Justice — at the door:*
I. SURELY AM NOT EXCLUDED

FRANCHISE VILLA

JOHN BULL "HOW LONG ARE YOU GOING ON MAKING THAT NOISE OUTSIDE?"
MRS BULL "TILL YOU LET ME IN JOHN!"

'We Want the Vote'

'Hear Some Plain Things'

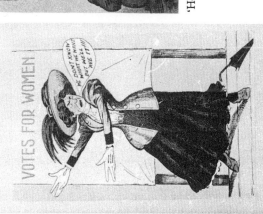

'Votes for Women'

9   Anti-Suffrage posters and postcards

BERLAND

THOMAS

10  French and Russian female offenders from Cesare Lombroso and
William Ferrero, *The Female Offender*, 1895

The head itself was perfectly bare, and yellow in hue, while the naked, wrinkled scalp moved and contracted like the head of a *cobra*. (*King Solomon's Mines*, p. 112; emphasis mine)

This description of Gagool includes all the iconography of the Haggardian 'monkey-woman': monkey, snake, corpse, child and savage. There are also touches of the vampire about her:

Rivers of blood; blood everywhere. I see it, I smell it, I taste it . . . . Blood is good, the red blood is bright; there is no smell like the smell of new-shed blood. (*King Solomon's Mines*, p. 161)

Gagool is the perpetrator of the witch-hunt, which Quatermain and his companions witness and in which she is joined by her 'daughters', the 'horrid ministers' or 'vultures'. Together they dance themselves into a frenzy and select the members of the tribe who are to be sacrificed. Gagool is said to be in a 'frenzy of excitement'; foam flies from her 'gnashing jaws', her flesh quivers, her eyes start from her head. When Quatermain describes her dancing as *waltzing*, the whole scene becomes a grotesque parody of the civilised Victorian ball, and reminds us of Quatermain's jibe at the civilised woman in the introduction cited earlier when he refers to the white woman's 'habit of turning round and round to the sound of horns and tom-toms' (*Allan Quatermain*, p. 429).

When Gagool is forced to take them to Solomon's treasure chamber later in *King Solomon's Mines*, she flits like a 'vampire bat' through the underground passages, and then creeps like a 'snake' out of the treasure chamber. Once again this text pairs the apewoman with an 'innocent' woman (although here not white) for whom Captain Good has an attachment. Foulata struggles with the escaping Gagool and the scene parallels the descriptions of the Darwinistic struggles between animals that the Haggardian hero is forever witness to, such as the fight between the crocodile and the lion that Leo and Holly witness in *She*. Here Gagool fights 'like a wild cat' and twists 'like a snake' and finally Foulata is fatally stabbed as Gagool is crushed under the closing wall of the chamber. Now she is no more than a 'bloody ooze', and the men in the darkness accidentally step in her . . . .

Gagool, like Hendrika, can also be seen to signify the dangerous underside of her innocent double. Foulata and Gagool, too, die together – the virgin and the beast – they must die together. Foulata's death saves Good from an inter-racial marriage. Her death is 'fortunate' which she herself admits in her dying words. *King Solomon's Mines*, then, finds its own solution to the 'woman problem' as does *Allan's Wife*: the women annihilate each other and free the men from responsibility for their removal and from the risk of confronting the barbarism in Woman. Gagool is the dark, aggressive underside of Foulata's deceptive beauty and purity; she is the animal beneath her skin. Holly and Leo, too, are doubled as Beauty and Beast with Holly's bestiality significantly confirming his superiority over Leo in terms of his ability to survive the climatic dangers of Africa, his strength and his stamina. They too are inseparable, a doubling of intelligence and beauty which Ayesha finds compelling, a union of father (Holly) and son (Leo) which Holly is dedicated to protecting and which will not be broken until Ayesha receives Leo's spirit in *Ayesha: The Return of She*.

Gagool is in many ways only the prototype of Ayesha. Norman Etherington writes that Ayesha is 'Gagool tarted up to be sexually devastating',[55] but she also represents the successful integration of the polarity of the Haggardian woman; the poles represented by the pairs: Hendrika/Stella and Gagool/Foulata. Hence the ambiguity of response. She is both the object of desire and the object of fear and loathing. She is surrounded by and associated with symbols of evil, yet she is also the object of the lifelong quest. While the text struggles with this ambivalence, it moves towards unveiling the dark underside of Ayesha's nature, it moves towards revealing the 'Gagool' beneath her skin. Ayesha's flesh is stripped away by the Pillar of Life in the extraordinary and pivotal devolution scene at the climax of the novel. It is here that her true skin colour is revealed: 'her skin changed colour, and in place of the perfect whiteness of its lustre, it turned dirty brown and yellow . . .' (*She*, pp. 402–3). The 'black' woman and the 'yellow' woman (Ayesha as Asia – the yellow peril) are revealed beneath the perfect white skin of the white woman which is peeled back in this devolution.


## RETROGRESSIVE EVOLUTION

This 'death'-scene can also be seen to be a dramatisation of the evolutionary concept of retrogressive evolution, a savage devolution which unveils the truth and origin of Woman. Ayesha shrinks, her hair falls out and then her hands metamorphose into claws. When she is no bigger than a two-month-old child she shrieks and in her final death-throes manages to raise herself on all-fours and look around her blindly 'as a tortoise does . . . her whitish eyes were covered with horny film'. Finally she 'dies' reduced to 'the hideous little monkey frame . . . covered with crinkled parchment that once had been the glorious She' (*She*, p. 403). The glorious She has been reduced by degrees to a baboon, a child, a tortoise and finally again a monkey, yet Holly remarks with horror at the revelation that 'it was the same woman', just as Jekyll and Hyde share the same body, the same set of clothes. For this is another Jekyll and Hyde transformation: in Stevenson's *The Strange Case of Dr Jekyll and Mr Hyde* Jekyll's alchemy releases the apelike troglodific Hyde beneath the skin of the civilised Jekyll, just as Ayesha's desire, her determination to possess Leo, releases the Gagool beneath her skin.

In this metamorphosis Ayesha passes through retrogressive evolution and demonstrates the concept of recapitulation: 'the idea that higher creatures repeat the adult stages of lower animals during their growth'.[56] Cope, one of the principle exponents of this branch of evolutionary theory, defines retrogressive evolution in 1896 as that which:

> may be accomplished by a retardation in the rate of growth of the taxonomic characters, so that instead of adding and accumulating them, those already possessed are gradually dropped, the adults repeating in reverse order the progressive series, and approaching more and more the primitive embryonic stages. This process I have termed 'retardation'.[57]

Retardation, he adds, terminates in extinction. Ayesha is retarded to the point of extinction. She approaches the primitive embryonic stages (no larger than a two-month-old child), and the origin of the human species (no larger than a baboon). Although Haggard's knowledge of evolutionary discourse may not have extended to the finer details of recapitulation theory, by 1887 the transformation myths of Darwinian theory (particularly shrinkage and growth) had entered into popular fiction.[58]

Holly's research has been persistently thwarted by his desire for Ayesha. He has been 'caught in the web of her fatal fascination' and, bound there confused and disorientated, he has been unable to decide whether Ayesha is an evil anomaly or a means to a better world. This unveiling scene takes Holly as investigator to the heart of the matter and resolves his doubts and confusions. The scene provides him with the final signs to read this previously unreadable woman and confirms his sense that she must be eliminated. Yet Holly's confusion about Ayesha, his expressed regret at her removal, reveals a double register of fear and desire: the fantasy of the desire to be seduced and the fear of its consequences – that of being consumed and bestialised by Woman. The 'unveiling' scene, in which Ayesha is revealed as what she really is and must be – some kind of antediluvian relic, a beast and a hag – parallels the discovery of the 'reality' of Lady Arabella March in Stoker's *The Lair of the White Worm*. Lady Arabella, the beautiful and sophisticated, yet predatory widow of Diana's Grove, is shown to be the manifestation of some antediluvian white worm, another sinister and hideous relic from the past, waiting to consume men, heavily disguised as an attractive young woman.

Criminology incorporated 'retardation' into its theories, arguing that the criminal as evolutionary throwback had been retarded in the normal processes of growth. Biological determinism of this kind began to be used as a platform for the arguments of those who wanted to promote capital punishment or even genocide. Criminology was to fuse on this issue with the evolutionary theory of artificial selection which connects it inevitably with eugenics. Ferri demonstrates how these discourses fuse in 1897:

> It seems to me that the death penalty is prescribed by nature, and operates in every moment in the life of the universe. The universal law of evolution shows us also that vital progress of every kind is due to continual selection, by the death of the least fit in the struggle for life. Now this selection in humanity as with the lower animals may be natural or artificial. It would therefore be in agreement with natural laws that human society should make an artificial selection, by *the elimination of anti-social and incongruous individuals*.[59]

Ayesha and Dracula are 'incongruous individuals' and thus must be eliminated for the protection of society. Holly remarks after Ayesha's 'death' that he perceives 'the finger of Providence in the matter' (natural selection), for Ayesha:

> strong and happy in her love, clothed in immortal youth and godlike beauty and the wisdom of centuries *would have revolutionised*

*society* and even perchance have *changed the destiny of mankind.*
(*She*, p. 405; emphasis mine)

Ayesha is sacrified to and by Providence and the responsibility for
her death lies with Providence, Holly insists. She has been 'naturally' deselected, eliminated as an anomalous female power of great
strength of arms and intellect. Holly realises that to countenance her
invasion of the Western world would be to barbarise the race and to
allow a 'retrogressive' revolution, not unlike the social apocalypse
which the *Saturday Review* predicted in 1871 would be the outcome
of the enfranchisement of women:

> Far from undervaluing the part played by woman in the history
> of our race, we think them more powerful than men to disturb the
> deeper foundations of order . . . . To discourage subordination in
> women, to countenance their competition in masculine careers by
> way of their enfranchisement, is probably among the shortest
> methods of barbarising our race . . . .
> Slight checks may seriously affect the prospects of a race in the
> severe struggle of humanity, and if our better halves alter the
> conditions which have raised us from the conditions of orang-
> utans, a relapse into savagery is quite possible.[60]

Changes in women's place in society would represent a retrogressive evolution – a return to savagery and barbarism. Ayesha, as
modern woman, also threatens the invasion of a closed brotherhood.
If her effect on the men of England is to parallel her effect on Holly
and Leo, she will turn the men into beasts, turn them against themselves and each other, infiltrate into and destroy the closed circle of
the brotherhood.


## CATHARTIC EXPULSION

Holly and Leo, finding themselves entombed underground with the
alluring and snake-like Ayesha, just as Quatermain and his companions find themselves walled into the treasure chambers of the mountain in *King Solomon's Mines*, must find a way to push out of the
threatening enclosures of this powerful and fatal woman. They must
escape this space as the location of defilement and contamination –
both Africa and Woman (the object of the quest and a death-trap).

The quest itself prepares the heroes for the final sexual arena, the final conflict with the *femme fatale* in which their manhood will be confirmed or forever lost. On this quest the men are 'educated' through trial and observation; they observe and record instances of female power which weaken and emasculate male victims and are given prophetic warnings by those who have gone before and lost: the body of a petrified explorer entombed forever in a stone 'nipple' (*King Solomon's Mines*), a lama rendered spiritually impotent by carnal desires (*Ayesha: The Return of She*), a man hot-potted by a vengeful woman (*She*), lovers 'wedded in death' (*She*) – all these are the signs and portents of endangered masculinity.

*King Solomon's Mines*, dedicated to 'all the big and little boys who read it', fantasises a world of male adventure and camaraderie, yet also inscribes those signs which educate the Haggardian explorer. It is itself a warning from one who has gone before, a Cassandra-like cry from an adventurer who has seen and recorded the dangers of making Woman (or Africa as Woman) the object of the quest. Contact with Woman, even where she is desired, effeminises the adventurer and saps his moral strength, just as Africa will trap the explorer and render him impotent if he does not resist its power of defilement. Over and over again in Haggard's novels female power subjugates, demoralises and degrades the male adventurer, weakening the brotherhood of men, breaking up the bands of loyalty which unite them. In *Allan Quatermain*, Captain Good comes under the influence of Sorais and, 'bewitched by her beauty', cannot distinguish good from evil. This enchantment unmans Good and makes him a woman: 'now had Bougwan become a woman, and no longer knew the good from the evil' (*Allan Quatermain*, p. 580). In *Ayesha: The Return of She*, Leo too begins to metamorphose – Holly cannot recognise him as the 'deep-chested, mighty-limbed . . . traveller, hunter and fighting-man' (*Ayesha*, p. 184) that he had known. He becomes more ethereal, more like Ayesha herself. There is a profound distrust of female power here, disguised beneath a mantle of scientific objectivity and liberalism: all the powerful women in these texts, Circe-like, use their power against men by systematic emasculation. Only virilent masculinity can succeed against these unmanning women.

One of the most resonant prophetic voices of Haggard's texts is that of the lama of *Ayesha: The Return of She* (1904). Holly and Leo rest in a lamasery, high in the Himalayan mountains, where they find a group of celibate lamas who have denounced the company of women in their attempts to reach Nirvana. Here they befriend a lama haunted by Ayesha herself, who had unveiled herself to him in a previous incarnation, leaving him contaminated with desire. Another bewitched man tells of a demonic woman exercising her power for the sake of proving her superiority; yet another of Ayesha's unmanned victims warns the adventurers of their threatened masculinity. She has been a 'hindrance', 'delaying me on my journey to the other side, to the shore of salvation' (p. 22), he laments. He describes this as a kind of 'slipping backward': 'that woman lit a fire in my heart which will not burn out' (p. 22). He warns Leo and Holly not to continue on their quest but to remain in the lamasery to fulfill their spiritual rather than carnal desires. The spiritual quest or the quest for eternal brotherhood freed from desire is a quest in opposition to that of the search for the fulfilment of desire. The lama warns them that to continue would be to repeat his fall, to slip backwards:

> Then brethren, go keep your tryst; and when you have reaped its harvest, think upon my sayings, for I am sure that the wine you crush from the vintage of your desire will run red like blood
> . . . .
>     Rather should you desire to live alone in holiness until at length your separate lives are merged in the God unspeakable, the eternal bliss that lies in the last nothingness. (*Ayesha*, p. 30)

Man attempts to climb the ladder of the spirit but will be forever dragged back by Woman, by sexuality, carnality and desire. Ayesha has invaded the all-male world of the lamasery and, like an infestation, she cannot be 'put out'. While Ayesha appears to be the seductive object of the quest, she also, paradoxically, must be resisted, for as desire she is the single most powerful obstacle to Man's struggle to reach his *spiritual* goal.

Michael Millman establishes that one of the characteristics of the 'male novel' is the fear of female sexuality and the consequent need for men to band together in order to protect themselves. Women, he says,

> become the enemy; so threatening are their attempts to compromise the essential maleness of adventuring . . . . In a world where women exist, there is an urgent need for a kinship among men that will combat the forces of femininity . . . men must love one another or die at the hands of the woman.[61]

Male kinship structures which attempt to expel or exorcise female influence are well-established in *She* long before the quest for Ayesha begins. On inheriting his charge, the baby Leo, Holly determines to protect his relationship with Leo from women in his refusal to employ a female nurse: 'I would have no woman to lord it over the boy and steal his affections from me' (*She*, p. 205). Holly experiences female authority at this early stage as rivalry for the affection of his 'boy'. His struggle against female authority succeeds for, in the absence of women, Leo becomes everything to Holly: son, friend, companion, fellow-traveller. As Leo reaches manhood the quest is laid before them: Leo's manhood will be confirmed in an elaborate initiation ceremony which necessitates a violent combat with the object of desire and which will, under Holly's guardship, ensure the elimination of carnal desire.

The quest of *She* is initially clearly a revenge quest. The mandate inherited at Leo's arrival at manhood instructs them to: 'Seek out the woman and learn the Secret of Life, and if thou mayst find a way slay her' (*She*, p. 214). Amenartus, the dead Kallicrates' wife, had named her son Tisthenes, or the avenger. In the records of lineage the name has changed to 'Vindex' 'which seems to have been adopted by the family after its migration to Rome as an equivalent to the Greek name Tisthenes'. Vindex becomes De Vincey which becomes Vincey. Holly notes: 'It is very curious to observe how the idea of revenge, inspired by an Egyptian before the time of Christ, is thus, as it were, embalmed in an English family name' (*She*, pp. 219–20).

Revenge is both the *raison d'être* of this patriarchal lineage and the name ascribed to it. Leo has inherited an ancestry committed to revenge. He can neither escape this ancestral mandate nor the name ascribed to him. Holly's reason for accompanying his ward is similarly an aggressive one: 'I do not believe in the quest, but I do believe in big game . . . . I've always wanted to kill a buffalo before I die' (*She*, p. 227). The quest in these early stages is clearly a hunt with Ayesha as 'big game' yet, as the quest continues, the men, caught in the queen's web, become forgetful of their purpose and come close to collaborating with her plans to invade Western Europe.

Of the three men, it is Holly as narrator and as the bearer of the stigmata of the ape, who continues to be mindful of the real purpose of the journey: the Secret of Life must be stolen and its possessor slain. Holly has perhaps more pressing motives for revenge: his ugliness has left him deeply distrustful of women. Holly's reasons for joining the quest are clear: for him this is a 'hunt'; his quest, a spiritual quest, is in opposition to the carnal quest of his youthful and naive ward. Unlike Leo, he seeks to cast off carnality and the flesh in a search for a higher truth. Consigned by his ugliness to eternal chastity he seeks to 'loose the prisoned pinions of the soul and soar to that superior point . . . to cast off this earthly robe . . . to have done forever with these earthly thoughts and miserable desires'. Like the lama weakened by desire, he attempts to reverse the sexual power which has debased him and left him gibbering confusedly, and he employs a variety of methods to regain his endangered and bestialised masculinity. Initially he has confidence in the strength of male bonding, that union between himself, his ward and his servant. It is a union which has had notable successes in the course of the quest – the men have fought together and survived together. 'Yet every rope has its breaking strain', Ayesha warns in *She*, and Holly to his despair witnesses the systematic breakdown of his relationship with his ward, a situation he has feared since Leo's infancy. Holly's defensive strategies of allegiance prove to be inadequate in the final conflict as he is left struggling alone with the mighty She for the affection and masculinity of his ward. Unlike the men of *Dracula*, who against all odds maintain their alliance under Van Helsing's leadership, working together to expel Dracula as desire and to protect themselves and the world from the advance of the vampire women, Holly is left fighting a lone battle and a confused one.

## THE EXPULSION

The two opposed quests converge in the sacred inner sanctuary of Ayesha's world (the source of Ayesha's immortality) where the final ceremony of Leo's initiation and Holly's revenge is to take place. In this apocalyptic chapter, the core of the novel, Haggard's prose acquires extraordinary energies.[62] This ceremony for Leo is to be a betrothal ritual in which, having first acquired immortality in the flames, his carnal quest will be finally realised. Earlier Ayesha had warned that until Leo becomes immortal they cannot 'mate':

> As yet I cannot mate with thee, for thou and I are different and the very brightness of my being would burn thee up and perchance destroy thee (*She*, p. 392).

Yet it is Ayesha who is burned up and it is Ayesha who is destroyed. The title of the chapter 'What we saw' emphasises the voyeurism of the writing, the male gaze. Ayesha is naked: 'there she stood before us as Eve might have stood before Adam, clad in nothing but her abundant locks' (*She*, p. 401). The two men, as the sons of Adam, are to act out a long-awaited vengeance upon Eve. The pillar of flame can be heard in the distance:

> On came the crashing, rolling noise and the sound thereof was as the forest being swept flat by a mighty mountain, and then tossed up by it like so much grass . . . . Nearer and nearer it came . . . and now the edge of the pillar itself appeared. Ayesha . . . stretched out her arms to greet it . . . . I saw the fire lap up her form . . . I even saw her open her mouth and draw it down into her lungs, and a dread and wonderful sight it was . . . .
>
> The mysterious fire played up and down her . . . locks, twining and twisting . . . it slid along her pillared throat and delicate features . . . . But suddenly . . . a kind of change came over her face: she was shrivelling up . . . and she shrieked – ah, she shrieked! – she rolled on the floor and shrieked! . . .
>
> At last she lay still, or only feebly moving . . .
>
> She was dying: we saw it and thanked God . . .
>
> Overcome with the extremity of horror, we too fell on the sandy floor of that dread place, and swooned away. (*She*, pp. 401–3)

The prose suggests cathartic release culminating in the swooning of the two voyeurs (or participants?) as if in total exhaustion. The pillar of fire plays with Ayesha and then moves away leaving her dying, her shrieks (repeated three times) echoing the 'hideous blood-curdling screech' of Lucy in the staking scene of *Dracula*. Similarly both bodies writhe and contort. Both bodies finally lay still – *Dracula*: 'Finally it lay still' and *She*: 'At last she lay still' – this is the laying still of the vampire woman, literally: *making still by laying*. Both novels record considerable relief at this point and it is only in the laying still that the excited prose calms itself. Both novels involve a group of male spectators who record the scene in immaculate detail. Both scenes take place on the 'marriage night': Lucy's staking takes place on the night after the planned wedding and Ayesha's 'death' on the eve of the planned consummation of the two lovers.

Millman argues that:

> Viewed in a slightly different light, this description suggests the mingled qualities of rape, carnage and satisfaction and those final

shrieks, wherein Ayesha's immorality is at last conquered, are like the terrible shrieks of pleasure.[63]

Ayesha, as monkey with claws, foaming and gnashing, swaying her head like a tortoise (these are the animal analogies used), becomes an image of the sexually aroused, yet thankfully dying female. This is the final sex/death equation of the book and this climax completes the purpose of the quest: revenge. Ayesha had warned that consummation of desire may result in Leo's death yet in this scene it is she who must die under the patriarchal mandate of revenge, but she must die in a particularly sexually sadistic manner to suit her crime as object and subject of desire. Sandra Gilbert sees this novel as:

> one of the century's literary turning points, a pivot on which the ideas and anxieties of the Victorians began to swivel into what has come to be called the 'modern'.[64]

She sees this scene ('the ceremonial sexual act that brought about Her "reduction" or "devolution"') as the forerunner of a number of similar scenes in turn-of-the-century and modernist tales: Wilde's *Salome* (1894), MacDonald's *Lilith* (1895), Stoker's *Dracula* (1897), T. S. Eliot's 'The Love Song of St. Sebastian' and D. H. Lawrence's 'The Woman who Rode Away':

> In all these works, a man or a group of men must achieve or at least bear witness to a ceremonial assertion of phallic authority that will free all men from the unmanning enslavement of Her land.[65]

The voyeuristic ceremony, the imperial gaze. In *Dracula* the band of men collect around the contorting figure of Lucy chanting a missal. In *She* the ceremony of betrothal is immediately followed by the ceremonial and sexually sadistic 'death'. The prose exposes its voyeuristic complicity in its excited rhythms and will not be satisfied until it can record the words of relief and release from female power: 'at last [finally] she [it] lay still'. Cathartic expulsion, the ritual in which threatened manhood is recovered, is a repeated pattern in many late nineteenth-century texts: Ayesha must be 'blasted', just as Lady Arabella's hell-hole must be detonated. The ends, of course, justify the means for civilisation, the brotherhood, the empire, must be protected. Ayesha is harmless while she waits for Kallicrates to return, while she is passive and docile, contained in the centre of unexplored Africa, but once she has realised her desire with the reincarnation of Kallicrates, she becomes active and threatens invasion. It is at this point that she must be annihilated, for her awakened desire is malevolent and life-threatening.

Lawrence Millman points out that Haggard's novels are:

> the medium of an extraordinary psychic violence which includes the killing off of nearly every female character by the end. These killings are part of the adventure ritual; in them Haggard's usually tepid prose acquires energies one never would have thought it had.[66]

This is the sublimated revenge of the brotherhood: not just to resist but to *kill* or to remove. In *Beatrice* the heroine commits suicide. In *Cleopatra* the heroine commits suicide. In *Marie* the heroine is murdered, disguised as Allan Quatermain. In *Allan's Wife* the heroine and her *alter ego* Hendrika, the baboon-woman, die simultaneously as do Foulata and Gagool in *King Solomon's Mines*. Ayesha, the most powerful of Haggard's heroines, is less easy to expel, for her 'deaths' are not absolute and her return necessitates a repeated quest and expulsion, just as Haggard had experienced the Boer uprising as a problem that would return repeatedly. Her return forms an index of turn-of-the-century invasion scares: her reappearance in Asia, the site of her planned invasion of the West through the awakening of the East, coincides with profound European fears of Eastern invasion.

Sandra Gilbert writes that the preoccupations with the all-powerful New Woman in the literature of this period:

> were symptoms of a complex of late Victorian socio-cultural and sexual anxieties that have until recently been ignored or even overlooked by critics and historians alike.[67]

To ignore or overlook these anxieties is to overlook the complexity and range of the discourses, discourses which are patterned by such sociocultural anxieties, discourses which interact and intersect, discourses which surround and define the Haggardian woman. The fabrication of Ayesha enables an intersection of diverse cultural concerns, a means of expression of cultural imaginings rooted in a widespread sense of British decline and fall. *She*, like *Dracula*, is a complex historical document which displays a rich fabric of inter-secting discourses. The *femme fatale*, the predatory female, is located at the intersection of such discourses, woven of male sexual anxieties and a profoundly ambivalent response to her predatory sexuality. To treat these discourses as separate threads, as critics have done in their search for an appropriate 'interpretation' of the riddle of *She* and Ayesha herself, is to miss the centre and to miss the heart. In the centre of these intersections is Ayesha herself – 'all the rest shaped itself round this figure' – the centre of the text, the centre of Africa, the heart of darkness. As a 'popular' novelist and as a significant contributor to the development of the genre defined by Millman as the 'male novel', with its preoccupation with male adventures in a hostile, threatening environment such as Africa, Haggard has cre-ated a unique and enduring myth expressed through a *horror* of the predatory female as invading Other. She, the woman, is Other, for-eign, alien, exotic territory: 'for thou and I are different'. The male must dare to travel into foreign territory and must risk being con-sumed by this new terrain: an imperialist fantasy expressed in terms of the female body? Or anxiety about the dangers of the female body expressed in terms of imperialism? Here we encounter the intersec-tion: neither *causes* the other, they are both part of the same socio-cultural fabric or collage of discourses.

Haggard anticipates Conrad, whose *Heart of Darkness* involves a familiar Haggardian plot: the male journey into the heart of dark-ness, the centre of Africa. At this centre or heart is to be found the unnamed horror – Kurtz's final words 'the horror, the horror, the horror'. It is here in the heart of darkness that Haggard's heroes witness the horror of Ayesha's devolution, the horror that lies at the heart of Woman as the Dark Continent, where: 'overcome with the extremity of the horror, we, too, fell on the sandy floor of that dread place and swooned away' (*She*, p. 403). Haggard's novels exploit the notion of a dark Otherness, a heart of darkness which is invariably also Woman as Other, as temptress, as foreign territory, as missing link, as active sexual being, but above all as a matrix of horror and fear: an all-encompassing and fearful darkness – the black widow.

# 5

# The Shadowy Embrace: Conrad

In Conrad's *An Outcast of the Islands*[1] (1896), a white trader in exile, marooned on the shore of a Malayan island, takes a canoe upriver in 'search of some solitary spot where he could hide his discouragement and his weariness' (*An Outcast*, p. 61). The 'capricious promise of the track' takes him into a clear space traced with sunlight through foliage and it is here that he is to have the first glimpse of the Arab–Malay woman, Aissa:

> At the end of the first turning Willems saw a flash of white and colour, a gleam of gold like a sun-ray lost in the shadow, and a vision of blackness darker than the deepest shade of the forest. (*An Outcast*, p. 62)

Under Willems' gaze the flash of white and colour, seen through the checkered gloom of the forest, shapes itself into a woman whose returned gaze seemed to him to be 'silent and penetrating like an inspiration' (*An Outcast*, p. 63) and which awakens in him 'new fears, new desires'. Willems, scorched by a wind that seems to 'be driven by her moving figure', must look to the forest itself to explain the silent mystery of her appearance:

> Who was she? Where did she come from? Wonderingly he took his eyes off her face to look around at the serried trees of the forest that stood big and still and straight, as if watching him and her breathlessly. He had been baffled, repelled, almost frightened by the intensity of that tropical life which wants the sunshine but works in gloom; which seems to be all grace of colour and form, all brilliance, all smiles, but is only the blossoming of the dead; whose mystery holds the promise of joy and beauty yet contains nothing but poison and decay . . . but now as he looked at that life again, his eyes seemed to pierce the fantastic veil of creepers and leaves, to look past the solid trunks, to see through the forbidding

126

gloom – and the mystery was disclosed – enchanting, subduing, beautiful. He looked at the woman. Through the checkered light between them she appeared to him with the palpable distinctness of a dream. The very spirit of that land of mysterious forests, standing before him like an apparition behind a transparent veil – a veil woven of sunbeams and shadows. (*An Outcast*, p. 64)

In answering the questions: 'Who was she? Where did she come from?', Willems must look to her source: the forest, for she has not only emerged from the forest but is also 'the *very spirit* of that land of mysterious forests', an apparition produced by the light itself. The forest is active, the trees stand 'as if watching him and her breathlessly', watching Aissa's effect on Willems, watching to see if he will be caught by the temptation it offers him. To decipher Aissa is to decipher the forest, to disclose a dual and united mystery and to do so Willems must 'pierce the veil', 'a transparent veil . . . woven of sunbeams and shadows' which comes between them and which in its piercing reveals the mystery of the woman and the jungle as one.

A colonial encounter in a forest glade: a white man perceives the apparition of a native woman. This scene is one of many such colonial and sexual encounters in Conrad's early novels, in which the white male colonial gaze peers into the gloomy foliage which constitutes an Otherness, and there in the confusion of foliage, his searching eyes make out the form of a native woman. For Willems, the flash of white and colour, the gleam of gold and the vision of blackness will become a revelation of meaning and an awakening as it forms itself into the object of desire. Willems' vision, 'the gleam of gold like a sun-ray lost in shadow' will not signal a spiritual conversion, but instead the beginning of a demonic enchantment.

Joanna de Groot argues that this correlation of Orient and woman is a nineteenth-century phenomenon:

Since European commentators endowed the Orient they had created with qualities with which men of the period also endowed females, they came on occasion to characterise the Orient as essentially or generally 'feminine'. The use of the phrase 'mysterious Orient', like 'mysterious female', indicated that both were seen as hard for western men to understand; references to the irrationality and emotional extremes to which 'orientals' were inclined carried the implied comparison with similar tendencies attributed to women.[2]

Willems, in his attempt to comprehend the incomprehensible Oriental landscape of the Malay jungle, characterises its mystery as erotically feminine but also poisonous and deadly. In Conrad's early Malayan tales and in *Heart of Darkness*, the native women are framed and held by the jungle but are also inseparable from it; they are like carnivorous jungle plants – *fleurs du mal* – alluring and deadly. The contours of these women, pictured or framed against a 'riot of foliage', in twilight or in checkered green sunlight, dissolve into the erotic confusion around them. Conrad describes Willems looking at Aissa a few days after their initial encounter:

> And he looked at her, standing above him, her head lost in the shadow of the broad and graceful leaves that touched her cheek; while the slender spikes of pale green orchids streamed down from amongst the boughs and mingled with the black hair that framed her face, as if all these plants claimed her for their own – the animated and brilliant flower of all that exuberant life which, born in gloom, struggles forever towards the sunshine. (*An Outcast*, p. 69)

Aissa's head is *lost* in the shadows created by the foliage in which she is placed. The foliage and flowers interpose into the plane of vision: they come between her and the eyes that see her, as if she were part of the foliage, just as the checkered light had stood between Willems and his vision in the earlier passage, like a *veil*.

The jungle offers Aissa up as image of itself and as a sexual temptation of the white man but it will also tantalise him by withdrawing her back into its depths, concealing her and laughing at him:

> While he [Willems] sat in the tremor of that contact she ran off with startling fleetness and disappeared in a peal of laughter, in the stir of grass, in the nod of young twigs growing over the path, leaving behind only a vanishing trail of motion and sound. (*An Outcast*, p. 70)

These women, their contours dissolving, can disappear at will, back into the darkness or into the forest, back into the Other world. They will veil themselves from the male gaze: 'It was as if she had drawn slowly the darkness round her, wrapping herself in its undulating folds that made her indistinct and vague' (*An Outcast*, p. 130). As the white man gazes into this riotous and troubling Otherness of the jungle space, he must be able to sharpen his sight in a perpetual attempt to decipher the meaning of the jungle, and to make out its signs and its warnings in the gloom, for it is deceptive and dangerous.[3]

Conrad's Marlow, travelling not through the Malay jungle but into the darkness of the Congo, similarly suffers from a 'confusion of seeing' in the so-called Grove of Death passage in *Heart of Darkness*:

> Black shapes crouched, lay, sat between the trees, leaning against the trunks, clinging to the earth, half coming out, half-effaced within the dim light, in all the attitudes of pain, abandonment and despair . . . nothing but black shadows of disease and starvation, lying confusedly in the greenish gloom . . . . These moribund shapes were free as air – and nearly as thin. I began to distinguish the gleam of their eyes under the trees. Then glancing down I saw a face near my hand. The black bones reclined at full length with one shoulder against the trees.[4]

Like Willems, Marlow struggles to make out shapes in the gloom of foliage, but careful looking will reveal fragmented limbs, eyes, appearing to loom out of the earth, foliage, trees themselves: 'clinging to the earth, half coming out, half-effaced within the dim light'. Marlow's eyes range over the grove and suddenly perceive 'a face near my hand' and 'black bones' reclining against a tree. The tree becomes the bones and shadows of a black man, just as for Willems the light and foliage of a forest clearing become the hair and features of a black woman. Throughout *Heart of Darkness* black bodies are fragmented into and out of landscape:

> But suddenly as we struggled round a bend there would be a *glimpse* of rush walls, of peaked grass – roofs, a burst of yells, a whirl of black *limbs*, a mass of *hands* clapping, of *feet* stamping, of *bodies* swaying, of *eyes* rolling, under the droop of heavy and motionless foliage . . . a black and incomprehensible frenzy. The prehistoric man was cursing us, praying to us, welcoming us – who could tell? (*Heart of Darkness*, p. 37; emphasis mine)

A glimpse of movement and savagery through the trees, these inhabitants of a prehistoric earth are indistinguishable from their surroundings, seen in fragments to the white gaze which must look carefully in order to see them at all, for they form an organic unity with the forest itself.

The Conradian wilderness has a menacing and brooding energy; it moves through its black bodies:

> the crowd, of whose presence behind the trees I had been conscious all the time, *flowed out* of the woods again, *filled* the clearing, covered the slope with a *mass* of naked, breathing, quivering bronze bodies. (*Heart of Darkness*, p. 66; emphasis mine).

The energy of the wilderness becomes intensified as Marlow travels to the centre, to the Central Station, to Kurtz and the 'unspeakable rites'. The energy is concealed behind foliage, veiled, threatening and potentially violent. Marlow looks again and a veil is lifted to disclose the life force of the wilderness:

> I saw a face amongst the leaves on the level with my own looking at me very fierce and steady, and then suddenly, as though a *veil* had been removed from my eyes, I made out deep in the tangled gloom, naked *breasts, arms, legs*, glaring *eyes* – the bush was *swarming with human limbs in movement*, glistening, of bronze colour. (*Heart of Darkness*, p. 46; emphasis mine)

Although the 'mass of human bodies' fills the clearing, it is Kurtz's 'savage mistress' who is the 'eddy in the mass' and its helmeted figure-head: 'the woman with helmeted head and tawny cheeks rushed out to the very brink of the stream. She put out her hands . . .' (*Heart of Darkness*, p. 66). Like Aissa, the wilderness offers her up as a 'savage and superb . . . apparition' and as the image of itself, manifested into woman:

> And in the hush that had fallen suddenly upon the whole sorrowful land, the immense wilderness, the *colossal body* of the fecund and mysterious life seemed to look at her, pensive, as though it had been looking at the image of its own tenebrous and passionate soul. (*Heart of Darkness*, p. 60; emphasis mine)

The savage mistress, holding out her arms to the dying Kurtz as he sails down-river away from her, becomes an emblem of death itself. Kurtz will not be allowed to leave the wilderness – it has embraced him as its own and will not relinquish him. The savage mistress will bring down death with her outstretched arms as easily as she will bring down the twilight:

> Suddenly she opened her bared arms and threw them up rigid above her head, as though in an incontrollable desire to touch the sky, and at the same time the swift shadows darted out on the earth, swept around on the river, gathering the steamer in a shadowy embrace. (*Heart of Darkness*, pp. 60–1)

Like Aissa, the savage mistress is enveloped by the wilderness once more and the last that Marlow sees of her is of her eyes gleaming in the foliage, watching: 'She turned away slowly, walked on following the bank and passed into the bushes to the left. Once only her eyes gleamed back at us in the dusk of the thickets before she disappeared' (*Heart of Darkness*, p. 61).[5]

Whereas black bodies, and particularly female black bodies, are pictured in Conrad's fiction enveloped in twilight, foliage and wilderness, fragmented and dissolved by the light, Jim from *Lord Jim*[6] is always firmly outlined against the twilight wilderness that is Patusan. He is substantial, white and clearly-outlined, seen almost in silhouette:

> That was my last view of him – in a strong light, dominating, and yet in complete accord with his surroundings – with the life of the forests and with the life of men. (*Lord Jim*, p. 175)

> In the midst of these dark-faced men, his stalwart figure in white apparel, the gleaming clusters of his fair hair, seemed to catch all the sunshine that trickled through the cracks in the closed shutters of that dim hall . . . . He appeared like a creature not only of another kind but of another essence. (*Lord Jim*, p. 229)

Marlow, observing Jim, notes how 'in the midst of these dark-faced men' Jim is marked out distinctly, his colour emphasised by the white clothes and fair hair. He seems 'like a creature not only of another kind but of another essence', not only because of his colour, the fact that he catches light rather than dispels it (like the savage mistress), but because this light makes him distinct, clearly outlined:

'distinct . . . planted solidly' (*Lord Jim*, p. 176). These clear contours, moreover, mark his isolation and dominance over this twilight world: 'He was protected by his isolation, alone of his superior kind', 'in a strong light, dominating'.

If clear contours signify isolation from the twilight worlds of Conrad's jungle settings and signify dominance and racial superiority, then Lord Jim in Patusan, although Marlow claims he is 'in complete accord with his surroundings', is culturally isolated, always distinct (presumably Jim as white man, is 'in complete accord with his surroundings' because he has retained his distinction, his superiority – that he is precisely *Lord* Jim in this jungle world; we might add that he is in complete 'biological'/hierarchical accord with his surroundings). Jewel, Jim's native mistress, however, is described as insubstantial and shadowy, threatening his distinctness:

> the ghostly figure swayed like a tender tree in the wind, the pale oval of the face drooped; it was impossible to distinguish her features, the darkness of the eyes was unfathomable; two wide sleeves uprose in the dark like unfolding wings, and she stood silent, holding her head in her hands . . . .
>
> it had grown pitch-dark where we were so that without stirring she had faded like the intangible form of a wistful and perverse spirit. (*Lord Jim*, p. 308)

Jim, unlike Kurtz, escapes, his distinctness intact, but he must extricate himself first from Jewel's arms, from her shadowy embrace.

One of the effects of the debate about Conrad and literary impressionism[7] has been to open up questions about Conrad's portrayal of the effects of the jungle on the white male explorer. Critics have argued that within literary impressionism characters tend to be described as in a continuous state of flux, subject to delusion and fantasy and to an impression of their world distorted by fear and fantasy. Other critics have argued that while Conrad may not be called a 'literary impressionist' in the strictest sense of the term, he uses a technique called 'delayed decoding' whereby the primary sense-impressions of the protagonist are described before they have been translated into secondary, intellectualised impressions.[8] Such critics tend to regard Conrad as attempting to portray psychological realism by foregrounding the psychological experience of the coloniser and by portraying the effects of colonisation on the white man. However, in 1975 Chinua Achebe spawned a crucial critical debate about Conrad's racial stereotypes which has called into question such critical assumptions about Conrad's portrayal of the colonial encounter.[9]

Conrad does achieve a 'freshness of sensory perception' in his descriptions of the barrage of sense-impressions created by the encounter with the native female. Conrad's women, we could argue, are shadowy and indistinct apparitions made up from fragments of the jungle because Conrad's interest is in the effect-of-native-woman on the white male. However, there is clearly much more to Conrad's elusive prose than this. In the passages which describe the dissolving contours of the native woman, the text offers the *reader* a dense web of signifiers (a barrage of sense impressions), so that the dissolution of the woman is as much due to the *prose* as to the jungle into which she disappears. The prose offers an obscuring veil between the reader and the described object: a textual jungle. Willems looks to the jungle (as we look to the prose) to make out Aissa's meaning. He looks to her source, as we must look to her source: the language from which she emerges. He is led inexorably towards that 'deep, black hole full of decay' into which he must inevitably fall. As Conrad's readers, this, too, is our fate: to follow the 'capricious promise of the track' (the text), to move through the textual jungle (language itself) towards the deep black hole into which we and Marlow and Willems must all inevitably fall (the textual void). It is not just, then, that the prose describes the process of dissolution, but that the prose is continually dissolving and reconstituting *itself*, offering the reader glimpses of his/her destination and of a tantalising object towards which the text moves, and simultaneously dissolving that object and that centre. Conrad's prose holds us in its shadowy embrace.

## THE JOURNEY TO THE INTERIOR

Conrad's journeys into the 'interior' begin on the exterior, in which the 'interior' is seen in map form. The blank space beckoning the explorer represents 'unsolved mystery' and promises initiation into manhood. Like Haggard's map in *King Solomon's Mines*, it forms a representation of an inviting and tantalising landscape. The white child (Conrad himself[10] and the fictional Marlow) with audacity and assurance places his finger over that space with a gesture of defiance and dominance:

> Now when I was a little chap I had a passion for maps. I would look for hours at South America, or Africa or Australia and lose myself in all the glories of exploration. At that time there were many blank spaces on the earth and when I saw this one that looked particularly inviting on a map (but they all look like that) I would put my finger on it and say: 'When I grow up I will go there.' (*Heart of Darkness*, p. 11)

Marlow is fascinated by the Congo, it was 'the biggest – the most blank, so to speak – that I had a hankering after (*Heart of Darkness*, p. 11). It is this space that is to ensure his transition to manhood with its 'emblem' of an 'immense snake uncoiled', the mighty river.

At closer range, while Marlow is still 'outside', still distanced from the African wilderness rather than enclosed within it, the land continues to beckon:

> Watching a coast as it slips by a ship is like thinking about an enigma. There it is before you – smiling, frowning, inviting, grand, mean, insipid, or savage and always mute with an air of whispering – 'come and find out.' (*Heart of Darkness*, p. 16)

But already the whisper of invitation has a veiled menace and holds out a more serious challenge to the explorer 'to come and find out', to be tested. In 'Youth'[11] the young Marlow describes his first voyage, an initiation into manhood in its own way. Still on the 'outside' he approaches the East which, like Africa, signifies sensual and exotic promise. Just as Marlow had sailed along the coast of Africa and heard the whispering of its invitation, the younger Marlow approaches the East by sea. To see the land of desire from middle-distance is to smell and feel the erotic invitation and to experience its effect on the senses. No longer a blank space, its promise is more intoxicating and more dangerous:

> I have seen its secret places and have looked into its very soul; but now I see it always from a small boat, a high outline of mountains . . . A red light burns far off upon the gloom of the land, and the night is soft and warm . . . suddenly a puff of wind, a puff faint

and tepid and laden with strange odours of blossoms, of aromatic wood comes out of the still night – the first sigh of the East upon my face. That I can never forget. It was impalpable and enslaving, like a charm, like *a whispered promise of mysterious delight . . . The mysterious East* faced me, perfumed like a *flower*, silent like *death*, dark like a *grave*. (Conrad, 'Youth', p. 41, emphasis mine)

On entering these mysterious landscapes the explorer moves from an exterior conception of white blankness to a profusion of sense impressions. The jungle landscape, seen from within rather than long-distance (the map) or middle-distance (the views from the sea) becomes a confusion of seeing, a sensory experience. Conrad presents us with a Darwinian model of nature as a grim process of beauty and decay, struggle and corruption.[12] His flowers are the *fleurs du mal*, simultaneously beautiful and corrupt, promising joy which masks poison and death. Conrad's jungle-landscapes draw their inspiration from the work of the naturalist and anthropologist A. R. Wallace, whose study of the Malay Archipelago, published in 1869[13] presents a similar model of the fecund decay of the tropics and which draws exquisite pictures of the parasitical beetles found in this area which swarm over and feed off the rotting vegetation and fallen trees. Conrad adds man to this decaying landscape, makes him the subject of the beetles' bite, replaces the fallen trees with the fallen Willems imaging his own death:

He would be stretched upon the warm moisture of the ground, feeling nothing, knowing nothing; he would lie stiff, rotting slowly; while over him, under him, through him – unopposed, busy, hurried – the endless and minute throngs of insects, little shining monsters of repulsive shapes, with horns, with claws, with pincers, would swarm in streams, in rushes, in eager struggle for his body; would swarm countless, persistent, ferocious, greedy – till there would remain nothing but the white gleam of bleaching bones in the long grass . . . . (*An Outcast*, p. 268)

## REVENGE BY ASSIMILATION

Haggard's heroes are subject to the attack of bloodthirsty mosquitoes who, it is said, have awaited the superior blood of the white man for thousands of years (just as Ayesha herself has awaited the

return of Kallicrates). Conrad's jungle is described as passively awaiting vengeance for its invasion:

> And outside, the silent wilderness surrounding this cleared speck
> on the earth struck me as something great and invincible, like evil
> or truth, waiting patiently for the passing away of this fantastic
> invasion. (*Heart of Darkness*, p. 26)

A few pages later the patience which Marlow describes has become an 'ominous patience': his sense of the potential power and
violence of this landscape intensifies as he moves closer to the Inner
Station. This ominous patience, this threatening stillness, is repeatedly expressed by the term 'brooding':

> And the stillness of life did not in the least resemble a peace. It
> was the stillness of an implacable force *brooding* over an inscruta-
> ble intention. It looked at you with a vengeful aspect. (*Heart of
> Darkness*, p. 36; emphasis mine)

The stillness and passivity which characterise Marlow's initial
impressions of this landscape become increasingly more oppressive
(fecund and heavy), until 'stillness' becomes 'force', passive becomes
active, as he moves inwards. Conrad, like Haggard, initially describes a distanced landscape which promises passivity and whispered delight; but at close range it closes in, seductively, for the kill.
Brooding suggests both the action of incubating or hatching ('brooding over an inscrutable intention'), moody mental contemplation
('ominous patience'), and also that which hovers closely around or
overhangs, as a bird over her brood. Thus the stillness which is
described as an 'implacable force brooding over an inscrutable intention' describes the passive imminence of revenge, a revenge of
enclosure and assimilation. Marlow comes to witness the half-con-
sumed Kurtz, withered and consumed by the caresser, a devilish
initiation and a 'terrible vengeance':

> The wilderness had patted him on the head, and behold, it was
> like a ball – an ivory ball – it had *caressed* him and – lo! – he had
> *withered*; it had *taken him, loved him, embraced him, got into his veins,
> consumed his flesh* and sealed his soul to its own by the inconceiv-
> able ceremonies of some devilish initiation. (*Heart of Darkness*, p.
> 49; emphasis mine).

It is the final embrace of the cannibalistic jungle that has sealed Kurtz's fate, just as it is Aissa's embrace that seals Willems'; both are the agents of death and decay; both consume flesh. Willems, too, feels the encroachment of the wilderness, imprisoned as he is on his river post, as the erotic caress and embrace of death:

He saw the horrible form [of death] among the big trees, in the network of creepers, in the fantastic outlines of leaves, of the great indented leaves that seemed to be so many enormous hands with broad palms, with stiff fingers outspread to lay hold of him; hands gently stirring, or hands arrested in a frightful immobility, with a stillness attentive and watching for the opportunity to take him, to enlace him, to strangle him, to hold him till he died; hands that would hold him dead, that would never let go, that would cling to his body for ever till it perished – disappeared in their frantic and tenacious grasp. (*An Outcast*, p. 268).

In his late essay 'Geography and Some Explorers',[14] Conrad writes:

Regions unknown! My imagination could depict to itself there worthy, adventurous and devoted men, *nibbling at the edges*, attacking from north and south and east and west, conquering a bit of truth here and a bit of truth there, and *sometimes swallowed up by the mystery* their hearts were so persistently set on unveiling. ('Geography and Some Explorers', pp. 19–20; emphasis mine)

The adventurers attack and conquer, and this is seen in terms of consumption: 'nibbling at the edges', until the mystery of the land swallows *them*: the unveiled consumes the unveiler. Likewise Kurtz's imperial fantasy of swallowing the world (Marlow describes Kurtz opening 'his mouth wide – it gave him a weirdly voracious aspect, as though he had wanted to swallow all the air, all the earth, all the men before him', *Heart of Darkness*, p. 59) is reversed in his encounter with the devouring femininity of the jungle so that he, the man who seeks to consume, is himself consumed.

Devouring femininity is a characteristic of Conrad's work, as Meyer's biography of Conrad persistently demonstrates,[15] but it is not so much the gleam of female teeth[16] that is emphasised but the brooding and maternal tenacity of the female embrace such as that of Lord Jim's native mistress, Jewel:

Her tenderness hovered over him like a flutter of wings . . . . Her vigilant affection had an intensity that made it almost perceptible to the senses; it seemed actually to exist in the ambient matter of space, to envelop him like a peculiar fragrance, to dwell in the sunshine like a tremulous, subdued and impassioned note. (*Lord Jim*, p. 283).

Jewel clings to Jim ('Thou art mine!') and must be cut away from him before he can escape from her embrace. This clinging, caressing, cloying quality of the jungle and of the native women is likened to the great jungle vines which cling to the giant trees, felling them by erotic strangulation. As Aissa clasps her hands about Willems' neck and hangs upon him, he stands 'unyielding under the strain, as solid and motionless as one of the big trees of the surrounding forests' (*An Outcast*, p. 120). Within days his solidity is threatened as he topples over like a forest tree towards the decay which he most fears: 'He struggled with the sense of certain defeat – lost his footing – fell back into the darkness . . . he gave up . . . because death is better than strife' (*An Outcast*, p. 72).

Throughout the description of the courtship of Dain and Nina in *Almayer's Folly* the text threads a leitmotif of falling and withering trees caught in the stranglehold of tangled creepers:

On three sides of the clearing, appearing very far away in the deceptive light, the big trees of the forest, lashed together with manifold bonds by a mass of tangled creepers, looked down at the glowing young life at their feet with the sombre resignation of giants that had *lost faith in their strength*. And in the midst of them the *merciless creepers* clung to the big trunks in cable-like coils, leaped from tree to tree, hung in thorny festoons from the lower boughs, and, sending slender tendrils on high to seek out the smallest branches *carried death to their victims in an exalting riot of silent destruction.*[17]

The alien threat of jungle spaces is perceived as feminine and maternal (brooding, clinging, caressing) and the native women themselves are described as enacting the vengeance of the jungle, even as extensions of the jungle itself, felling the imperial trees, threatening their mastery and exalting in a riot of silent destruction. As agents of decay, these women are also agents of a Darwinistic conception of tropical nature, incubating and destroying in the same moment.

## THE RETURNED GAZE OF THE JUNGLE

When Willems meets Aissa for the first time in the jungle clearing, 'the serried trees of the forest seemed to be *watching* him and her breathlessly' (*An Outcast*, p. 64). They continue to watch, to *witness* his decline, as he approaches his death imprisoned on the river and he sees them as 'a great crowd of pitiless enemies pressing round silently to *witness* his slow agony', *An Outcast*, p. 266; emphasis mine). Marlow, too, will experience the returned gaze of the forest as something malevolent and oppressive: 'The woods were unmoved like a mask – heavy like the closed door of a prison – they looked with their air of hidden knowledge, of patient expectation, of unapproachable silence' (*Heart of Darkness*, p. 56). For Marlow the effect of the jungle gaze is to make him question for the first time the balance of power – does the jungle have the power to destroy the white man? is this sexual invitation or menace?

> I wondered whether the stillness on the *face* of the immensity *looking at us* two were meant as an appeal or as a menace. What were we two who had strayed in there? Could we handle that dumb thing, or would it handle us? I felt how big, how confoundedly big was that thing that couldn't talk and perhaps was deaf as well. (*Heart of Darkness*, p. 29; emphasis mine)

The returned gaze of the forest challenges the invader, makes him the object of the gaze, but while the jungle itself looks on still and implacable, it will also look at the white man through the eyes of its human representatives, the natives: 'the jungle of both banks [was] quite impenetrable – and yet eyes were in it, eyes that had seen us' (*Heart of Darkness*, p. 44). Marlow and his companions, to Marlow's horror, become the object of a returned gaze – they are transformed from spectators to spectacle. The natives are *veiled* in foliage, concealed from the white gaze, but with only their eyes visible the menace of the native gaze is intensified. In a study of the eroticism of the Algerian colonial postcard, *The Colonial Harem*,[18] Malek Alloula suggests that as the omnipotence of the colonial gaze demands transparency, the veil refuses that transparency and that, by presenting only the tiny orifice for the eye, the feminine returned gaze (like the eye of a camera) dispossesses the colonial eye of its mastery.

Willems is filled with rage when Aissa veils herself and her refusal to be perpetually transparent to him makes him feel 'exasperated, amazed and helpless' (*An Outcast*, p. 110), able to see only her eyes 'sombre and gleaming like a starry night'. Later he turns furiously upon her, tearing off her face-veil, trampling on it 'as though it had been a mortal enemy' (*An Outcast*, p. 119). The veil, as a demarcation of private space, forces Willems to question his mastery, just as Aissa's perpetual and brooding gaze compels him to reassert his white identity in a hysterical outburst to Lingard:

> Always watching, watching . . . for something. Look at her eyes. Ain't they big? Don't they stare? You wouldn't think she could shut them like human beings do. I don't believe she ever does. I go to sleep, if I can, under their stare, and when I wake up I see them fixed on me and moving no more than the eyes of a corpse . . . . The eyes of a savage: of a damned mongrel, half-Arab, half-Malay. They hurt me! I am white! I swear to you I can't stand this! Take me away. I am white! All White! (*An Outcast*, p. 222)

Willems is transformed from subject to object under Aissa's gaze, and thus must remind himself and Lingard of his whiteness, that he must be colonial *subject*, not the object of the gaze of a mongrel woman[19] just as the returned gaze of the wilderness makes Marlow wonder: 'Could we handle that dumb thing or would it handle us?' (*Heart of Darkness*, p. 29)

## 'COULD WE HANDLE THAT DUMB THING OR WOULD IT HANDLE US?'

> The images of Otherness and subordination . . . need to be understood as ways for men to explore and deal with their *own identity and place in the world* as sexual beings, as artists, and intellectuals, as imperial rulers, and as wielders of knowledge, skill and power.[20]

Conrad's presentation of the colonial encounter questions the power relations between man and jungle; his sexual encounters question the power relations and struggle for racial superiority between man and native woman (could we handle *her* or would she handle *us*?). Both such encounters and the confused and threatened identity of the white man are for Conrad, I would argue, deeply bound up with ontological uncertainties about the nature of language: are we the subject or object of language, do we master it or does it master us?

The Conradian text plays with the reader, offering the promise of a centre to the text (the heart of darkness) but continuously and simultaneously postpones the arrival at this textual centre, denying its very existence. Positing meaning and ceaselessly evaporating it, the refusal to fix meaning constitutes a denial to the reader of the transparency of *language*. Our experience in reading Conrad's prose is precisely that of Willems' experience with the veiled Aissa. As he looks to the jungle to pierce its fantastic veil, to disclose its mystery, to disclose Aissa's mystery, we look to the language which in turn both refuses to disclose its secret (and denies that there is any secret at all) and offers a secret (the promise of textual centres, resolutions, hidden knowledge).

For Conrad, we must remember, English was a *foreign* language – not his first language, and he was engaged in a perpetual struggle with that foreignness, as he described it to Marguerite Poradowska (in *French*): 'l'Anglais m'est toujours une langue étrangère qui demande un effort formidable pour être manée.'[21] Throughout his letters and essays Conrad describes this formidable struggle in terms of sexual encounter and in terms of mastery. Moreover, Conrad seems to have been fascinated and compelled by the *blurred* meanings and contours of the English language as Ford Madox Ford described it:

> Conrad's indictment of the English language was this, that no English word is a word: that all English words are instruments for exciting blurred emotions. 'Oaken' in French means 'made of oak wood' – nothing more. 'Oaken' in English connotes innumerable moral attributes . . . . The consequence is, that no English word has clean edges: a reader is always, for a fraction of a second, uncertain as to which meaning of the word the writer may intend. Thus all English prose is blurred. Conrad desired to write a prose of extreme limpidity . . . .[22]

Conrad's conception of the instability of language and the endless deferral of meaning could be seen to anticipate post-structuralism and the proposition that meaning is scattered along a whole chain of signifiers as a 'constant' *flickering* of absence and presence'.[23] Yet in his writings on the struggle with language, Conrad seems also to yearn for 'le mot juste', the elusive word in which meaning is fixed and 'limpid', the uniquely correct expression. To accept a model of language as a blurred and web-like complexity, an open-ended play of signification (Eagleton's terms) is also to question the meaning of self, the whole fiction of self as a stable unified entity, since language constructs that self. Martin Ray explores Conrad's paradoxical concept of language (his yearning for 'le mot juste' and his polyglot awareness of language as blurred and elusive) and concludes that Conrad's multilingual background and his decision to write in English resulted in an acute detachment, even isolation from his medium, a fundamental *suspicion* of the language he employs and a desire to transcend linguistic precision:

> Conrad's characteristic attempt to transcend merely precise language (which may be seen as the true purpose behind the style which Leavis defines adversely as 'adjectival insistence') leads him to welcome the *mists* and *shadows* which surround every English word . . . .[24]

It is precisely this double awareness of the blurring of language and a belief in 'le mot juste' (the tantalisingly elusive correct expression) that we can see mirrored in Conrad's description of the effect of the jungle/native woman on the white man; the pursuit of the object of desire is coupled with an awareness that the object can never be 'fixed' and a fear that contact with that object will result in a transformation of power whereby the subject (he who desires to master) becomes object (the mastered). In 1895 Conrad advised Edward Noble to:

> search the darkest corners of your heart, the most remote recesses of your brain, – you must search them for the image, for the glamour, for the right expression[25]

and it is in 1896 (the year of the publication of *An Outcast of the Islands*), only a year after Conrad offered this piece of advice to Edward Noble, that Conrad writes of the 'capricious promise of the track' which leads Willems into the darkest corners of the jungle, where he is to glimpse a flash of white and colour and a vision of blackness (the native woman, Aissa) which is soon to disappear with mocking laughter, leaving behind 'only a vanishing trail of motion and sound'.

In 1911 Conrad wrote to Joseph de Smet, 'I wrestle painfully with that language which I feel I do not possess but which possesses me, – alas!'[26] and 12 years earlier, in 1899, Marlow had asked about the colossal body of the brooding jungle: 'Could we handle that dumb thing or would it handle us?' The colonial, sexual and linguistic encounters described by Conrad raise anxious questions about mastery and power, possession and dispossession. Unlike Stoker, whose vampire-hunters police the boundaries of binary oppositions between self and Other, male and female, good and evil, truth and falsity, health and sickness, Conrad writes of transgression, of the blurring of those boundaries and the dissolution of self. Conrad shows us men attempting to police the boundaries of their colonial and sexual identities and shows us too the falsity of such absolute demarcations in a world in which oppositions of this kind (between self and Other) collapse in upon each other in the ceaselessly decaying and simultaneously fecund landscapes of his early fiction.

## 'A DASH OF ORIENTALISM ON WHITE': FROM ORIENTAL TO WHITE WOMAN

> I know the white men, Tuan . . . In many lands have I seen them; always the slaves of their desires, always ready to give up their strength and their reason into the hands of some woman . . . . Let one man destroy another. (*An Outcast*, p. 57)

Aissa is used, perhaps innocently, as the instrument of a double revenge: she is used by the wilderness as a means to ensure its vengeance upon the invaders and as an enticement by Aissa's native kinsmen to ensure Willems' complicity in a native plot to overthrow white imperial control in the area. This native plot begins with the knowledge that white man's weakness is his sexual desire for the native woman; Aissa is to break down the fragile bonds of loyalty between Willems and Lingard, his patron and the ruler of the river, and to set the two men against each other. Willems, caught in a trap of his own making, 'measures' the 'depth of his degradation':

> He – a white man, the admired of white men, was held by those miserable savages whose tool he was about to become. He felt for them all the hate of his race, of his morality, of his intelligence. He looked upon himself with dismay and pity. She had him. (*An Outcast*, p. 109)

Willems' delusions are made manifest here. On his river sanctuary and place of exile he maintains complex fantasies about his past supremacy in the white community from which he has been exiled as a fraud and a thief. Increasingly he 'measures' the depth of his degradation against the native woman who he believes is responsible for his 'fall'; he projects his shame on to her.

Soon after their initial encounter, Willems, having lost his wits, finds himself drinking the muddy water from the river out of the palm of his hand: 'He drank again, and shuddered with a depraved sense of pleasure at the after-taste of slime in the water' (*An Outcast*, p. 66). After their second meeting he begins to feel his strength being drained away:

> he, so strong, so superior even in his errors, realised at last that his very individuality was snatched from within himself by the hand of a woman. (*An Outcast*, p. 70)

The persistent irony used to describe Willems' delusions of moral purity reminds the reader that Willems is already corrupt before he meets Aissa, that he is not 'so strong' nor 'so superior'; that Aissa only speeds up a process already begun. Yet Aissa as native woman has an important part to play in Conrad's story of white man's regression into savagery; it is a story which draws upon powerful sexual and racial stereotypes.

When Aissa finally lays down beside him after days of torment, Willems

> sat up suddenly with the movement and look of a man awakened suddenly by the crash of his own falling house. All his blood, all his sensation, all his life seemed to rush into that hand leaving him without strength, in a cold shiver, in the sudden clamminess and collapse as of a deadly gun-shot wound. (*An Outcast*, p. 70)

The sexual implications of Willems' encounter are self-evident: the sexual debilitation of the male. The hands recall the passage cited above in which Willems, much later in the novel, imagines himself held by the foliage which, like outstretched hands will caress and hold him until he dies. This powerful evocation of the dissolution of self (the falling house) through desire is an image that Conrad frequently draws upon in his letters to describe his struggle with language and writing. Compare for instance another passage from the letter cited earlier in which Conrad had advised Edward Noble (only a year before the publication of *An Outcast*) to pursue the 'right expression' into the darkest corners of his heart:

at the end of your day's work you should feel exhausted, emptied of every sensation and every thought, with a blank mind and an aching heart with the notion that there is nothing, – nothing left in you. To me it seems that it is the only way to achieve true distinction.[27]

While Conrad advises the young writer, Noble, to pursue desire (the right expression) he also warns of the dangers involved in such a quest for the object of desire. Willems, the anti-hero, becomes a powerful dramatisation of Conrad's desire to 'go there', into the darkest corners of his mind, the blank, unexplored places but, in that very quest, virility and identity are threatened in the encounter with the fatal object of desire. Conrad, as exile, seems to identify with Willems' sufferings at the hands of an elusive and self-destroying Other but in his portrayal of the deluded and egotistical Willems he seems to be examining both the dynamics and delusions of mastery.[28]

Under Aissa's seductive spell, Willems begins to feel his gradual slide into destruction as a slippage, just as Haggard's lama cries out in his despair that he is slipping backwards:

Now and then he would grasp the edge of the table and set his teeth hard in a sudden wave of acute despair, like one who, falling down a smooth and rapid declivity that ends in a precipice, digs his fingernails into the yielding surface and feels himself slipping helplessly to inevitable destruction. (*An Outcast*, p. 71)

In this pivotal section of the novel, Willems' 'fall' is described as a loss of self and of *outline*: he feels 'lost amongst shapeless things that were dangerous and ghastly'; struggling 'with the sense of certain defeat', he 'loses his footing' and literally falls 'back into the darkness' (*An Outcast*, pp. 72–3). As he falls, he feels that he has surrendered 'to a wild creature the unstained purity of his life, of his race, of his civilisation'. For Willems this is not a personal fall but a fall for Western civilisation, a terrible regression and a surrender to the forces of barbarism. Regression or 'going native' was often described in the late nineteenth century as a backsliding towards an abyss, as Patrick Brantlinger has argued:

Just as the social class fantasies of the Victorians (*Oliver Twist*, for example) often express the fear of falling into the abyss of poverty, so the myth of the Dark Continent contains the submerged fear of falling out of the light into the abyss of social and moral regression. In both cases the fear of backsliding has a powerful sexual dimension.[29]

Between Parts One and Two of this novel, Willems slips into a textual void. We last see him sliding inevitably towards the precipice of his destruction; and in Part Two, after five weeks in the jungle with Aissa, Willems reappears like a 'ghost' to Almayer sitting on his porch:

> a masquerading spectre of the once so very confidential clerk of the richest merchant in the islands. His jacket was soiled and torn; below the waist he was clothed in a worn-out and faded sarong. He flung off his hat, uncovering his long, tangled hair that stuck in wisps on his perspiring forehead and straggled over his eyes, which glittered deep down in the sockets like the last sparks amongst the black embers of a burnt out fire. An unclean beard grew out of the caverns of his sun-burnt cheeks. The hand he put out towards Almayer was very unsteady. The once firm mouth had the tell-tale droop of mental suffering and physical exhaustion. He was barefooted. (*An Outcast*, p. 79)

Willems, resembling somewhat humorously Conrad's depiction of the burnt-out writer, has 'gone native', reduced even to biting himself (he shows Almayer an arm covered with fresh scars) to forget his pain. Another Circe figure, working with and through the jungle to achieve her ends, Aissa has trapped and consumed her white prey and has begun to draw the life out of it – at least, this is how the men (both white and native) see it. Aissa herself remains largely a blank in the text, used as part of an elaborate male struggle for supremacy and power.

Similarly, Marlow in *Heart of Darkness* sees Kurtz, drawn by 'the heavy, mute spell of the wilderness', crawling through the jungle towards the 'weird incantation' of the savage dance, awakened by 'forgotten and brutal instincts, by the memory of gratified and monstrous passions' (*Heart of Darkness*, p. 65). Kurtz, bestialised, like Willems, by the jungle, crawls towards the centre of the 'inconceivable rites', the vortex of the savagery – the savage mistress. Conrad shows us that the jungle and the jungle woman have *particular* victims, in this case Willems and Kurtz, men who are corruptible, and perhaps vulnerable to the influence of the jungle, because they have the jungle within them. Yet these men revert to bestiality through the agency of a dark Otherness: the correlation of native woman/ jungle.

## CONRAD'S 'MONKEY WOMEN'

While Conrad's texts, deploying complex levels of irony and devices to ensure authorial distance, appear to be concerned with the psychological effects of colonisation upon the white male coloniser, they nonetheless share and draw upon some of the historically and culturally determined stereotypes of Rider Haggard's imperial romances. Conrad, too, doubles alluring native beauty with aged and demonic hag-figures (Haggard's Foulata/Gagool, Stella/Hendrika pairings and the two sides of Ayesha) presenting the hag of this pair as the savage underside or alter-ego of the seemingly innocent beauty. Both Nina and Aissa, the two most finely-drawn native women in Conrad's early fiction, are accompanied by ageing crones: Nina is doubled by her witch-like mother and Aissa by the servant woman who is Willems' only other companion in his river 'prison'.

Aissa's companion, ever-present in the background of Conrad's descriptions of Willems and Aissa's cruel entanglement, and described as 'a shrivelled, an unmoved, a passive companion of their disaster' (*An Outcast*, p. 266), is most often seen bending over the fire, blowing on the embers or stirring food in a pot. As she comes to represent death itself to Willems ('The old woman appeared to him . . . as if in a fog, squatting on her heels, impassive and weird', *An Outcast*, p. 280), the death-in-life state of his existence and the death that awaits him, she becomes increasingly inseparable from Aissa. In one instance Willems hears a low moan in a storm:

> He peered round in the half-light under the roof and saw the old woman crouching close to the wall in a shapeless heap, and while he looked he felt a touch of two arms on his shoulders. Aissa! . . . He turned, and she clasped him round the neck instantly . . . . He stiffened himself in repulsion, in horror . . . while she clung to him. (*An Outcast*, p. 233)

The *sight* of the wizened woman is transformed into the *embrace* of Aissa, which stiffens Willems in repulsion and horror, experiencing the fusion of the two women just as he feels the heavy, fused gaze of the two women following him about the encampment as a threat to his whiteness, his identity and his life. Moreover, the epilogue records more directly their correlation: Almayer, some time after Aissa's murder of Willems, shows the now-aged Aissa to a visitor as 'that doubled-up crone'. Not only is the fate of the native woman to age quickly ('they age quickly here', Almayer states) and to lose beauty, but by implication Aissa is inseparable from the hag-like serving woman who represents her dark, savage interior. The epilogue of *An Outcast of the Islands* records how Aissa's fate is to become Almayer's daughter's serving woman: Nina is to tame her, just as Hendrika had been tamed by Stella in Haggard's *Allan's Wife*. Although the earlier *Almayer's Folly* does not mention Aissa as Nina's nursemaid, she is nonetheless part of Nina's childhood and an important bridge between the two novels.

The half-caste Nina of *Almayer's Folly* is doubled by Aissa but more importantly by her mother who, we are told, had been a beauty, but is now a doubled-up, betel-chewing, witch-like figure: 'her betel-chewing mother, squatting in a dark hut, disorderly, half-naked and sulky' (*Almayer's Folly*, p. 27). She encourages her daughter's affair with Dain, believing him to be a great Rajah and, persuaded by Dain's 'open-handed generosity', she manages to collect together a considerable amount of money in return for her daughter. Nina catches a glimpse of her counting this money hoarded in a treasure chest: 'her mother extracted handfuls of shining guilders and Mexican dollars, letting them stream slowly back again through her *claw-like* fingers' (*Almayer's Folly*, pp. 56–7; emphasis mine). The old serving-woman and Nina's mother share the iconography of the Haggardian monkey-woman. They squat, are doubled-up, they are disorderly, half-naked and impassive. Nina's mother has claw-like fingers, like Gagool, and like Gagool, she squats in a dark hut, sulky and menacing. By giving Nina and Aissa such companions, the text suggests that there are affinities: in Aissa's case this is both what she *is* beneath her beauty (agent of death) and what she will *become*; in Nina's case the savage qualities of her mother make up half of her inheritance as half-caste.

Yet Conrad's use of contemporary anthropological theories of racial and biological determinism is far more complex and contradictory than Haggard's anthropological and racial stereotypes. Nina is half-caste daughter of white man and savage Malay woman, and the traces of her racial mixture are to be seen in her face, of which Conrad offers us a reading:

She was tall for a half-caste, with the *correct profile* of her father, *modified and strengthened* by the squareness of the lower part of her face inherited from her maternal ancestors – the Sulu pirates. Her firm mouth, with the lips slightly parted and disclosing a gleam of white teeth, *put a vague suggestion of ferocity* into the impatient expression of her features. And yet her dark and patient eyes had all the *tender softness of expression common to Malay women*, but with a gleam of *superior intelligence* (*Almayer's Folly*, p. 17; emphasis mine)

The text surveys and maps her face, dividing her features between white and Malay and would appear to be informed by the anthropological studies of A. R. Wallace[30] (who categorises the races of the Malay Archipelago according to facial features and social customs), and anticipates, too, the studies of Lombroso and Ferrero:[31] the stigmata of the native and of the criminal type. Yet by suggesting that the 'correct profile' of her father is 'strengthened' by her maternal inheritance from the Sulu pirates, the text begins to disturb these racial readings.

Nina's story is that of a half-caste woman trapped between two cultures and codes of behaviour. Her father's ambition is to take her to Europe where his money will disguise her colour, while her mother wishes to see her remain true to her Malay inheritance and marry a Rajah. Like Henry James's Maisie, in *What Maisie Knew*, she is the victim of a power-struggle between her parents, who see her development only in terms of gain for themselves. Nina's early exposure to the sleek hypocrisies of white civilisation in the household of Mrs Vinck has shaped a crucial decision for her. She realises that while both cultures share 'sordid greed' and lust for money, her Malay kinsmen have at least shown her a 'savage and uncompromising sincerity of purpose' in contrast to the 'polite disguises' of 'such white people as she had had the misfortune to come in contact with' (*Almayer's Folly*, p. 38). Forced to choose between the two cultures, she becomes 'more contemptuous of the white side of her descent represented by a feeble and traditionless father', and falls more and more under the influence of her mother.

While the text plays with theories of biological determinism in the emphasis placed on Nina's inheritance fixed in her facial features, it also, by placing emphasis on Nina's rejection of her whiteness, implies that Nina makes a *choice* about values. She does not *revert* to savagery in a Haggardian sense (Hendrika and Ayesha), but *chooses* her Malay inheritance because it offers a way of life which is more sincere and less corrupt. In his stress on choice, Conrad may well have been drawing on his own experience of linguistic determinism figured in his choice of language as his artistic medium.[32] Such a passage disturbs the basis of biological determinism: Nina's fate is not fixed, she has a choice. Moreover by making her decision that of choosing sincerity rather than corruption (whiteness), the text disturbs theories of regression.


## THE RAPACIOUS EMBRACE

Almayer and his wife are engaged in a struggle for power and influence over their daughter but also for possession of her as valuable commodity. Mrs Almayer 'sells' her daughter to Dain, whose 'open-handed generosity' buys her protection of the union. Nina's gaze ranges over the erotic richness of Dain's appearance and recognises him as a 'gorgeous and bold being so unlike in appearance to the rare specimens of traders she had seen before on the same verandah' (*Almayer's Folly*, p. 47). The visible richness of Dain's appearance is never seen again in the text's descriptions of him, but terminates in Mrs Almayer's treasure chest (just as the blood circulation in *Dracula* terminates with Mina), and later Nina is to see Mrs Almayer letting the dollars stream through her claw-like fingers. While Almayer's dream is of immense wealth to enable him to take Nina to Europe where money will hide her colour, his dream will never be realised. The visible money/wealth in the novel, the realisation of the commodity (Nina) is obtained by a voracious mother-figure, whose power is enabled by her knowledge of male weakness – desire – just as the success of the native uprising in *An Outcast* is enabled by native knowledge of white man's weakness for the native beauty.

Similarly the movement of ivory in *Heart of Darkness* is out of Africa to *Europe*, Brussels. Kurtz, we are told, had travelled to Africa to improve his status and increase his wealth, in order to be accepted by the family of his Intended.[33] Marlow returns to Brussels and visits Kurtz's Intended and it is *here* in this 'whited sepulchre' of a city that Marlow discovers the destination of the stream of ivory from Africa, and the only place that ivory is seen in the city is in the drawing-room of the Intended, the keys of her grand piano, which stands like 'a sombre and polished sarcophagus' (*Heart of Darkness*, p. 72).[34] Moreover, just as the source of the ivory in the white woman's drawing-room is the darkness of the African wilderness, the source of the white woman herself is the savage mistress, correlated in the final pages through the motif of the outstretched arms of both women. This motif signifies embrace, entreaty, promised passivity, but conceals in Conrad, as it does in the novels of Stoker and Haggard examined, a female rapaciousness, a devouring quality; an embrace which, like Conrad's jungle will embrace and caress the object and hold it until it dies and is consumed back into darkness. Conrad's fusion of white woman with black woman in this final scene completes a pattern of imagery associated also with the jungle itself as devourer of the male subject, with leafy hands outstretched, waiting to trap and consume its prey. It is a gesture rapacious enough to bring back the phantom of Kurtz:

> She put out her arms as if after a retreating figure, stretching them back and with clasped pale hands across the fading and narrow sheen of the window. Never see him! I saw him clearly enough then. I shall see this eloquent phantom as long as I live and I shall see her too, a tragic and familiar Shade, *resembling in this gesture* another one, tragic also, and bedecked with powerless charms, stretching bare brown arms over the glitter of the infernal stream, the stream of darkness. (*Heart of Darkness*, p. 75; emphasis mine)

In *Almayer's Folly*, Dain, under Nina's gaze, feels 'penetrated' and overpowered, yet Conrad terms this 'the look of a woman's surrender'. Willems lies passive in the jungle, 'like death itself', visited by Aissa who approaches nearer every day 'with the slight exaltation of intoxicating triumph lurking in [her smile's] dawning tenderness' (*An Outcast*, p. 69). Willems believes that he is *taming* her ('the gradual taming of that woman', p. 69), with words of love, but it is *his* strength that rushes into *her* hand when she finally touches him. This fascination with the sexual dynamics of power, mastery and role reversal can be seen in a drawing by Conrad (see Plate 6), unfortunately undated. The movement of the drawing is from left to right – the woman moves toward the man with arms outstretched, cigarette in hand. The man moves away, as B. C. Meyer comments: 'his knees pressed firmly together like a well-behaved girl'.[35] The woman is white, her arms appear to be about to envelop the retreating male, her gaze is fixed upon him, her head in profile. At her feet is a tiger skin, laid out from left to right, reflecting the movement of the woman, its head in profile like hers, but ferocious with mouth open, teeth exposed. The woman is clearly white, dressed in Western clothes and smoking a cigarette which identifies her as the 'New Woman' type (a supremely Western phenomenon), yet the tiger skin and the Eastern-looking table with decanter standing upon it, give a touch of Orientalism to the scene. That the tiger should add visual meaning to the scene, should reflect the movement and profile of the woman placed above it (and indicate her sexual voraciousness, her man-eating qualities), underlines Joanna de Groot's contention (cited above) that

> While the Orient came to be explored and characterised through images of gender and sexuality, it is equally important that the 'Oriental' became an image through which gender and sexuality could be defined within European culture.[36]

It is this shift to the Oriental or African as a means to define *Western* notions of gender and sexuality (the superimposition of black woman on white woman – 'a dash of orientalism on white') that Conrad fabricates in his novel set in the darkness of the London underworld, *The Secret Agent*.

## THE WOMAN IN BLACK: WINNIE VERLOC

Conrad once confessed that a 'dash of orientalism on white' was far more likely to excite him than the 'genuine Eastern'.[37] This final part of the chapter will examine some of the vestiges of the native woman to be found in Conrad's representations of white women, in particular Winnie Verloc of *The Secret Agent*[38](1907) who carries some of the iconographic traces of Conrad's early native woman[39] as an atavistic murderess and agent of death.

Conrad documents Winnie's family history and her inherited characteristics, just as he documents Nina's biological inheritance in *Almayer's Folly*. Winnie is the daughter of an alcoholic and sister of a 'degenerate type', Stevie, who is retarded and possibly epileptic. By doing so Conrad sets up both Stevie and Winnie as 'specimens', scientific specimens, and plays with the assumptions of the naturalistic novel, such as Zola's *Nana*, in which Nana (a prostitute) is given a substantial family history (she too, is the daughter of alcoholic parentage). Moreover Winnie is half-French, which suggests that Conrad is perhaps alluding to this notorious naturalistic novel. *The*

*Secret Agent* is full of references to Lombroso and Nordau and their studies of degenerate types (the novel is about anarchists and Nordau has much to say about the degeneracy of anarchists), and criminological speculations become focused on Winnie after she has murdered her husband, through Ossipon's 'scientific gaze'. Winnie becomes progressively the site of Ossipon's investigations into degeneracy.

Conrad began his novel with the story of Winnie: he could not begin the novel, he tells us in the Preface to *The Secret Agent*, until 'the story of Winnie Verloc stood out complete from the days of her childhood to the end'. Yet the critical debate of the last few years about Conrad's debt to Lombroso and Nordau[40] has sadly neglected to study the criminological and degeneracy discourses mobilised by Conrad to describe Winnie Verloc, although the debate itself provides an important confirmation of Conrad's extensive knowledge of criminology and anarchism. It has been shown that Conrad would have had easy access to such scientific discourses either through *Blackwood's Magazine* which ran a series of articles on anarchism between 1899 and 1907, or through Nordau's widely-read book *Degeneration*, published in England in 1895.

Allan Hunter, in his important book *Joseph Conrad and the Ethics of Darwinism*,[41] attests to Conrad's eclecticism on the subject of criminology, yet argues that while Conrad used current scientific discourses, he would rewrite or extend such theories or even use his fiction to reject them entirely. Hunter contends that Conrad's *The Secret Agent* is particularly critical of criminological theory and argues that it is in this novel that Conrad 'rejects scientific and ethical speculation as inadequate to his needs'. The novel applies its ironic mode both to criminological theory and to the anarchists, themselves the site of contemporary criminological investigation. The anarchist Ossipon is used as an ironic mouthpiece for Lombrosan theory and this enables Conrad to distance himself from scientific discourse by satirising its representative and by making him a classic degenerate type, as he would have been read by Lombroso and Nordau. The key episode in which Ossipon, finding himself confronted by the desperate Mrs Verloc and, realising that she has murdered Verloc, attempts to read her face, is treated with savage, ironic scorn:

> He was scientific, and he gazed scientifically at that woman, the sister of a degenerate, a degenerate herself – of a murdering type.

He gazed at her, and invoked Lombroso, as an Italian peasant recommends himself to his favourite saint. He gazed scientifically. He gazed at her cheeks, at her nose, at her eyes, at her ears .... Bad! ... Fatal! ... he gazed also at her teeth .... Not a doubt remained ... a murdering type ... he had in him the scientific spirit, which moved him to testify on the platform of a railway station in nervous, jerky phrases .... He spoke scientifically in his secret fear ... (*The Secret Agent*, p. 259)

Science here provides a language for Ossipon's 'secret fear' (of Winnie's murderous strength), 'a voice [for] his abiding dread' (that she will kill him too) and provides a series of signs (stigmata) whereby Ossipon can 'read' her as criminal anomaly and as 'fatal' woman. Ossipon's first instinct is to 'translate' his fear and dread into scientific discourse to create the illusion of control and moral supremacy. But the prose is not simply describing the effect of a murderess upon the man who confronts her – it is also itself stimulating that effect. It builds up clichés, disrupts syntax, overloads the passage through repetition to the point of rupture. It obscures both Winnie and Ossipon in a dense web of words, a kind of simulated *linguistic* degeneracy. The nervous, jerky phrases are those of the prose as well as of Ossipon. 'Degenerates', writes Nordau, 'utter monosyllabic cries, instead of constructing grammatically and syntactically articulated sentences.'[42] The phrases such as 'scientific gaze', 'degenerate' and 'murdering type' do not only describe the phrases in Ossipon's mind, but testify to a linguistic dissolution and regression.

Martin Ray[43] argues that Conrad's interest in Nordau was particularly in Nordau's reading of the *artist* as a degenerate type (in effect this was Nordau's most important 'contribution' to the study of degeneracy). Nordau makes this point in the dedication to the work:

Degenerates are not always criminals, prostitutes, anarchists and pronounced lunatics; they are often authors and artists. These, however, manifest the same mental characteristics, and for the most part the same somatic features, as the members of the above-mentioned anthropological family, who satisfy their unhealthy impulses with the knife of the assassin or the bomb of the dynamiter, instead of with pen and pencil.[44]

Ray points out that the publication of *Degeneration* in English in 1895 coincided with the beginning of Conrad's literary career, and moreover, that as Conrad suffered from many so-called 'degenerate' characteristics (neurasthenia, irritability, extreme nervous exhaustion, and hypochondria), he may have been inclined to read Nordau's work ironically as confirmation of his own artistic and supremely 'modern' (degenerate) artistic sensibility. That Conrad used Lombroso and Nordau in his writing of *The Secret Agent* is not in dispute, but what is less clear is Conrad's response to such theories. Martin Ray speaks of a kind of 'reflexive irony' whereby Conrad undermines his own authorial assertions by hinting that, as artist, he too is degenerate – the degenerate type writes of the degenerate type. In Nordau's scheme the author, the prostitute, the anarchist, the criminal are all members of the same anthropological family: *The Secret Agent* writes this family.

## THE MURDER SCENE

What matters is the emotional state of the masses. Without emotion there is no action. (*The Secret Agent*, p. 80)

As Winnie delivers her 'plunging blow' and releases 'the first sign of a destroying flood' (the dripping of Verloc's blood), the text offers a criminological reading of her 'emotional' action not unlike the readings of female criminal acts offered by Lombroso and Ferrero in *The Female Offender* (1895):[45]

Into that plunging blow, delivered over the side of the couch, Mrs Verloc had put all the inheritance of her immemorial and obscure descent, the simple ferocity of the age of caverns and the unbalanced nervous fury of the age of bar-rooms. (*The Secret Agent*, p. 234)

Yet this kind of reading is also one that Conrad uses to read his own creative 'nervous fury', for instance in a letter to H. G. Wells in 1903 (to whom he also dedicates *The Secret Agent*): 'for me, writing – the only possible writing is just simply the conversion of nervous forces into phrases . . . . When the nervous force is exhausted the phrases don't come.'[46]

Conrad infuses Winnie's story with the discourses of criminology and biological determinism, just as his own self-readings are infused with these discourses. Yet he is also subverting such discourses by undermining his own readings through oblique references to a text which includes him in the same anthropological family of degeneracy (Nordau's *Degeneration*). Allan Hunter's analysis of *The Secret Agent* concludes:

> Conrad has presented what appears to be a genre-piece, but he has reassessed the formula, whilst at the same time rewriting the major criminologist of his time . . . . *The Secret Agent* is concerned to describe a social problem, to describe the interactions of free-will and social conditions – it resists Lombrosan categorisation.[47]

I would argue that Conrad 'resists Lombrosan categorisation' more in Winnie's case than any other character in the novel in giving her the one 'free action' of the novel and by giving her the (ironic) title 'free woman'. This term is used insistently in the text from the moment that Winnie realises that her 'contract' with Verloc is annulled (by her brother's death) to the point where she attaches herself to Ossipon when the text announces: 'Mrs Verloc was no longer a free woman' (p. 255) and while Conrad seems to be using it to demonstrate the impossibility of Winnie remaining free for very long (she must save herself and needs male assistance to do so), its initial significations are more complex. The phrase primarily carries the resonances of 'New Woman',[48] signifying emancipation from economic and sexual dependency upon men, and rejection of motherhood and femininity. It is important to note, then, that Winnie becomes 'free', not by murdering her husband (although this is part of it), but by her *realisation* that she is freed from her contract (needing to be dependent on Verloc in order to support Stevie). Winnie is released from her ties of duty, from responsibilities, but this is not enough to make her act anarchic; it must be coupled with an atavistic passion (in this case maternal) and it is therefore Winnie, rather than the passionless anarchists, who can act.

Ossipon, horrified by the desperate and fugitive Winnie clinging to his legs, 'entertained delusions' (*delirium tremens*) and sees 'the woman twined around him like a snake, not to be shaken off. She was not deadly. She was death itself – the companion of life' (*The Secret Agent*, p. 255). From the point when Winnie realises that she has been released from her 'contract' with Verloc, when the text describes her as a 'free woman', and throughout the passages which describes her murder of Verloc and her attempt to escape the gallows, Winnie comes to represent death and atavism in the text. Her contours begin to dissolve, like those of Conrad's native women, not against the riotous foliage of tropical landscape but against the all-consuming blackness of the London night.[49]

Winnie is a white woman with dark hair and dark eyes and before the murder she is most often described as in bed, awaiting Verloc, clearly and solidly outlined against the dazzling whiteness of the sheets: 'Her big eyes stared open, inert and dark against the snowy whiteness of the linen' (*The Secret Agent*, p. 172). After the murder she is dressed in black, veiling her face in black and for the first time she is described *outside*, against the blackness of a London night. It is *before* the murder, as a consequence of dressing herself in black, that her contours begin to dissolve:

> *A tinge of wildness in her aspect* was derived from the *black* veil hanging like a rag against her cheek, and from the fixity of her *black* gaze where the light of the room was absorbed and lost without the trace of a single gleam. (*The Secret Agent*, p. 232; emphasis mine)

Winnie's eyes *absorb* the light as she closes her transaction with Verloc, and the 'tinge of wildness in her aspect', her emerging atavism, reminds us of the 'vague suggestion of ferocity' about Nina's face. It is at this point, before the murder and in the dissolution of her contract with Verloc, that the text begins to dissolve her contours, merging her with blackness, dressing her in black, naming her 'free woman' and associating her with darkness and death.

The text continues to mystify Winnie (literally to dissolve her into mist) as these atavistic connections become clearer, dissolving her contours into the absorbing blackness of night:

> her face, veiled in *black* net, in the light of a gas-lamp *veiled* in a gauze of mist.
>
> Near him, her *black form* merged in the night, like a figure *half chiselled* out of a block of *black* stone. (*The Secret Agent*, pp. 246–7; emphasis mine)

In 1908 (the year of the publication of *The Secret Agent*) Conrad wrote to Garnett complaining once again of his terrible struggle with writing: 'I had to work like a coal miner in his pit quarrying all my English sentences out of a black night'[50] and it is in the final chapters of *The Secret Agent* that Winnie is described as a 'black form merged

in the night, like a figure half chiselled out of a block of black stone'
(cited above). Both women and language share a disconcerting atavistic quality; they must be chiselled or quarried out of primeval
darkness and Winnie herself is 'chiselled' from the 'black night' of
Conrad's linguistic struggle.

In the above passage Winnie is described as 'half chiselled out of
a block of black stone' just as the slaves in *Heart of Darkness* had been
described as 'half effaced, half coming out' of the earth. Ossipon
begins furthermore to call her 'this savage woman'. This darkness
begins to constitute her signification of death itself: 'Mrs Verloc
came out, with her veil down, and *all black* – black as commonplace
*death* itself, crowned with a few cheap and pale flowers' (*The Secret
Agent*, p. 258; emphasis mine) Even when she lifts the veil, the face is
stony and remains black, black as the burnt-out holes which would
have been left by the Greenwich explosion:

> She had uncovered a face like adamant. And out of this face the
> eyes looked on, big, dry, enlarged, *lightless*, burnt out like two
> *black holes* in the white shining globes. (*The Secret Agent*, p. 259;
> emphasis mine)

The text insists on Winnie's blackness just as it insists on her being
a 'free woman'. *The Secret Agent* sets up a series of repeated leitmotifs
to contain and frame its characters. In Winnie's case these change
emphasis, moving from 'Winnie believed "things don't stand much
looking into"', to Winnie as 'freewoman' and Winnie's blackness.
Whilst the label of free woman is limited to the period in which she
is free from her dependency on men, the attribution of blackness
begins with the plan to murder Verloc and continues to the end of
the novel, with Winnie's suicide. On the night of Winnie's death the
steward had seen: 'A lady in a *black* dress and a *black* veil, wandering
at *midnight* alongside on the quay' (*The Secret Agent*, pp. 266–7;
emphasis mine) and this is the last that is seen of her, for she disappears altogether: 'when they came back for her in less than five
minutes the lady in *black* was no longer in the hooded seat. *She was
nowhere*. She was gone' (*The Secret Agent*, p. 267; emphasis mine),
leaving only her wedding ring glittering on the seat, the only non-
dissolvable part of herself. Like James Wait, she dissolves into blackness and ultimately into the sea. They are both degenerate agents of
death and dissolve into the dark Otherworld: literally 'nowhere'.

The text mimics a complex Lombrosan reading of Winnie's atavism, by persistent descriptions of Winnie as black, emerging out of the darkness and finally dissolving into it: 'Mrs Verloc, veiled, had no face, almost no discernible form'. As agent of death, Winnie like the native woman (Aissa is also a murderess) is associated in the Conradian pattern of iconography with blackness, not just with the blackness of night, mystery and death, but with the blackness of *body*. Sander L. Gilman's study of the iconography of the black female in the late nineteenth-century art, medicine and literature[51] shows how, in the closing decade of the nineteenth century, contemporary scientific discourse linked the white prostitute with the black woman as types signified by unbridled sexuality and a primitive expression of emotion which marked a regression into a dark, primeval past. These associations between female criminality (or sexual excess) and blackness, endorsed by Lombroso's studies which argued that the prostitute and the female criminal were atavistic, reached its peaked at the turn-of-the-century. Gilman cites Zola's *Nana*[52] as an example of the 'degenerate' blackness that lies beneath the sexualised white woman or prostitute. *Nana* ends with the prostitute, decomposing into darkness and earthy mould, riddled with pox and disease which has lain dormant beneath her beguiling beauty. *Nana*, like Aissa, like Ayesha, like Winnie, like the female vampires, dissolves into a primeval darkness or mud so that her features are no longer discernible.

## BREAKING THE CONTRACT, BREAKING THE FAMILY

Critics have rarely been uniform in assessing Conrad's use of stereotypes, particularly racial stereotypes[53] and although Ian Watt's argument that Conrad is engaged in an exposure of the internal contradictions of the ideology of his period[54] may appear to us, particularly after Chinua Achebe's analysis of Conrad's 'racism', somewhat reductive, Conrad does seem to be disrupting the ideology of criminology with complex levels of irony in *The Secret Agent*. Biological determinism in its various forms is offered up by the text only to be dissolved and disturbed by radical contradictions within it. It is perhaps closer to Conrad's method to propose that the text of *The Secret Agent* in particular mobilises the stereotypes of prostitute, degenerate type, murderess, and the discourses of degeneration (in Lombrosan criminology and in Nordau), pushing them to their utmost point, overloading the text with signifiers of this kind; that it pushes language and ideology of this kind to its point of rupture, and attesting in this rupturing of language to the degeneracy and dissolution of language itself.

The anthropologist and collector of orchids who appears at the end of *An Outcast of the Islands* has no answers for the 'string of questions' with which Almayer assails him. Almayer offers this drunken scientist (who declares to everyone his 'intention of writing a scientific book about tropical countries') the story of Aissa and Willems and asks him to 'read' it: 'You, who say you have read all the books, just tell me . . . why such infernal things are ever allowed', while his own eyes are on the distant hillside 'trying to make out through darkness and distance the shape of [Willems' tombstone]'. The naturalist, 'who ought to have been made a professor', makes a tremendous effort 'to articulate distinctly' (he has read all the books), is silenced by Almayer's questions, the tombstone is unreadable; there is no answer and no meaning within scientific discourse.

Conrad mimics the Lombrosan discourse in his representation of Winnie Verloc as atavistic throwback, but this discourse (translated *via* Nordau) also offers a reading of *him* as degenerate author (especially as a writer experiencing problems with *language*: the inability to construct grammatically-correct sentences was perceived to be a degenerate characteristic) so that the *textual* contract with Lombrosan theory (*via* Nordau) is finally broken, as Winnie's contract with Verloc is broken, pushed to its point of rupture. Winnie Verloc shares touches of kinship with her black atavistic sister, the Conradian native woman, just as Conrad shares touches of kinship with *both*, as degenerate (atavistic) artist; that is, by breaking the textual contract with Lombrosan theory, he dissolves the familial contract with this family and denies that there is any family at all.

In a letter to H. G. Wells, which describes the beginning of his work on *The Secret Agent*, Conrad wrote:

> It is all very monstrous, – my news is. I stick here fighting with disease and creeping imbecility . . . . The damned stuff comes out only by a kind of mental convulsion lasting two, three or more days – up to a fortnight – which leaves me perfectly limp and not very happy, exhausted emotionally to all appearance, but secretly irritable to the point of savagery.[55]

(Sexual) contact with language leaves the writer 'limp', 'exhausted', 'unhappy', but most important of all, *savage*. It coincides with Aissa's effect upon Willems in *An Outcast of the Islands* at the point when Willems emerges from the jungle/Aissa's embrace. Conrad struggles with disease and creeping imbecility; Aissa creeps upon Willems with triumph lurking in her smile. Conrad experiences language as a foreign Other which must be wrestled with in a kind of sexual struggle for mastery which reduces him to exhaustion and to 'savagery'. For Conrad, in these descriptions of the process of writing, language itself is Circe, the *femme fatale* who threatens to reverse roles and to master *him*: 'I wrestle painfully with that language which I feel I do not possess but which possesses me – alas!'[56]

If language is experienced as a feminine Other for Conrad, then the struggle with language involves just this sense of threatened mastery and a crisis of male identity, just as the Otherness of the unexplored jungle threatens imperial identity: this land/this language must be mastered or it will master us. Failure to master language in this (sexual) arena will result in the dissolution and possession of the subject: the transformation of subject (master) to object (the mastered). Nordau's vision of *fin-de-siècle* degeneration in Europe is strikingly similar to both the setting of the Conradian texts examined in this chapter, and to the effects of reading Conradian prose:

> Over the earth the shadows creep with deepening gloom, wrapping all objects in a mysterious dimness, in which all certainty is destroyed and any guess seems plausible. Forms lose their outlines and are dissolved in floating mist.[57]

This description of perceptual uncertainty and the dissolution of form (the merging of forms in twilight) is mirrored in Conrad's description of the struggle with writing (perhaps even deliberately couched in the discourses of degeneration) in a letter to Garnett in 1899 – the *fin-de-siècle* moment:

> All is illusion – the words written, the mind at which they are aimed, the truth they are intended to express, the hands that will hold the paper. Every image floats vaguely in a sea of doubt – and the doubt itself is lost in an unexplored universe of incertitudes.[58]

The loss of self and of certitude in an unexplored universe is precisely the dilemma of the Conradian hero who, threatened with the 'shadowy embrace' of both the jungle and the native woman, experiences a dissolution of self. It is women (as atavistic and degenerate types) who are characterised by the dissolution of contours (looming out of and disappearing back into the jungle/darkness) and who are described as agents of that twilight world, able, like Kurtz's mistress (and Conrad's Circe-like mistress, language itself) to bring down twilight and chaos on to the white male with her 'shadowy embrace'. The triple fusion of Others – the intersecting colonial, sexual and linguistic encounter – is powerfully expressed through a devouring and fatal female sexuality which enables Conrad to explore the complex sexual dynamics of power, mastery and empire.

# 6

# 'Something More To Be Said': Hardy's Tess

Tess is usually regarded as the archetypal victim, even as an exception amongst Hardy's heroines, 'an almost perfect anthithesis of the more usual Hardyan heroine who brings calamity through sex',[1] the anthithesis, indeed, of the *femme fatale*. Unlike Bathsheba Everdene or Arabella, Eustacia or Felice she is not a coquette experimenting with her power over men, but a woman violated and exploited. Yet to read Tess as solely a victim (of herself and others), is to be blind to the contradictions and fissures in Hardy's presentation of her sexuality, for the text keeps reminding us that her beauty and sexual charms are not only tragic but fatal, a fatality inherited with her 'bad blood' and her tendency to violence.

## THE CENSORSHIP OF *TESS OF THE 'D'URBERVILLES*

Hardy's *Tess of the d'Urbervilles*[2] grew out of the author's confrontation with late Victorian censorship. From its conception in 1888 to its final 'definitive' form of 1912, Hardy, in his search for a publisher for his novel, was forced to inflict upon his text an infinite number of modifications, excisions, and revisions, many, but not all, demanded by the strictures of serial publication. The shaping and reshaping of this text for publication is also a search for a 'permissable portrait of a woman',[3] a search for a way of writing Tess, its heroine, that would be acceptable to the morality of its audience.

Hardy realised late in November 1889 that his first manuscript version of *Tess* – begun in 1888 and rejected by publishers in 1889 – would not receive the approval of those guardians of public morality, the editors and proprietors of the Victorian serial magazine, who objected to the eroticism of the novel.[4] It was at this point that Hardy made a 'cynical' decision to adapt his novel and his decision is recorded in the account of his life written by his second wife, Florence Emily Hardy, an account which recent research has shown to be largely written by Hardy himself or compiled from Hardy's private writings and diaries, now edited by Michael Millgate and entitled *The Life and Works of Thomas Hardy*.[5] Chapter XVII of Hardy's *Life*, entitled 'More London Friends and a Novel's Dismemberment', records in detail Hardy's decision to 'dismember' his novel (cut out various episodes and publish them elsewhere until they could be restored in the single volume form of 1891):

> Hardy had never the slightest respect for his own writing, particularly in prose, and he carried out this unceremonious concession to conventionality without compunction and with cynical amusement, knowing that the novel was moral enough and to spare. But the work was sheer drudgery . . . .
>
> However the treatment was a complete success and the mutilated novel was accepted . . . . (*Life*, p. 232)

In the Preface to the First Edition of 1891 in which Hardy was able to restore the passages which had been published separately from the *Graphic* serialisation, Hardy writes:

> My thanks are tendered to the editors and proprietors of these periodicals for enabling me now to piece the trunk and limbs of the novel together, and print it complete, as originally written two years ago.

The cynicism alluded to in the *Life* emerges here in a public preface in which Hardy thanks his editors for allowing him to piece the mutilated 'trunk' and 'limbs' of his novel back together again. Throughout Hardy's descriptions of his experience of censorship (both public and private) he was to use metaphors of mutilation, infanticide and retarded birth to describe this process of enforced revision, a process he regarded with cynical and bitter amusement.[6] The chapter which describes the mutilation of *Tess* (written, of course, retrospectively as Hardy and his second wife look back on that period and assemble diary entries and notes to describe it) is itself crammed with anecdotes, press-cuttings and commentary which draw upon female murders, Jack the Ripper mutilations, severed heads, and public executions.

Buried in this chapter is an extract from *The Times* dated 10 September, read and cut out for his notebook, whilst Hardy was preparing his mutilated text for serial publication. It is an account of the events preceding one of the Whitechapel Murders which Hardy reads as an example of how:

> Destitution sometimes reaches the point of grandeur in its pathetic grimness e.g. as shown in the statement of the lodging-house keeper in the Whitechapel murder:–
>
> 'He had seen her in the lodging-house as late as half-past one o'clock or two that morning. He knew her as an unfortunate, and that she generally frequented Stratford for a living. He asked her for her lodging-money, when she said, "I have not got it. I am weak and ill and have been in the infirmary". He told her that she knew the rules, whereupon she went out to get some money' (*Times* report)
>
> O richest City in the world! 'She knew the rules'.
> (*Life*, p. 223)

The story behind this, related in macabre detail in the *Times* report from which Hardy's quotation is taken, is that this woman, Eliza Sivvy, had been turned out of the lodging-house and then found disembowelled, murdered by 'Jack the Ripper' in the early hours of the morning. Hardy's comment: 'O richest City in the world! "She knew the rules"' seems to be central to Hardy's 'cynical' resolution to dismember his text. Hardy is fascinated by the lodging-house keeper rather than the macabre details of the mutilation, the lodging-house keeper who evicts Eliza Sivvy despite her illness, to expose her to the dangers of a London night. 'The rules' (she must pay for her keep) prevent her from finding shelter and force her outside (presumably to prostitution as she is described as 'an unfortunate') where she is later to be horribly murdered. Hardy too was learning the 'rules', the rules of 'moral purity' enforced by censorship and such rules meant that he must undertake to mutilate his own text. Hardy's identification and compassion is for the 'unfortunate', the outsider whose exclusion from the relative safety of the lodging-house left her vulnerable to terrible savagery. His enmity is directed at those 'inside' who make the rules and who exclude and shut out those unfortunates who do not or cannot abide by them.

## CHANGES IN THE NOVEL UNDER DISMEMBERMENT

One of the most significant permanent revisions, a revision which took place after November 1889 (and therefore coming under the process of dismemberment which Hardy describes in the *Life*) is the addition of most of the blood-red imagery and with it much of the hunted animal/sacrificial victim imagery that surrounds Tess (the White Hart legend, the rat hunt, the trapped animals and birds).[7] Tony Tanner shows that the novel is saturated with blood and the colour red most often emphasised by its contrast with a white background: Tess is splashed with blood from the dying horse, Tess spills the blood of Alec.[8] The text is saturated with blood but it is also a blood-letting text, a violent text, written through and because of Hardy's experience of the violent blood-letting of censorship and, because of this, the text bears a terrible and relentless identification of author with heroine (scarred, cut, bleeding but finally murdering) through the mutilated novel which contains her. It is also at this stage – the revisions following November 1889 – that the authorial intrusions begin to emerge at their most bitter and angry, both the protectiveness towards Tess and the anger of the philosophical commentary which condemns the system that hounds her.[9] It is a novel which condemns the violence done to outsiders by the rule-makers, those outsiders who, like Eliza Sivvy, wander outside looking in for safety and sanctuary, and who like Jude and Tess will be forever outside looking in.

Censorship was a crucial subject of debate in the 1890s, a debate which Hardy joined in January 1890 (during the revisions of *Tess*) when he was asked to contribute to a symposium on censorship published in the *New Review* only a year or so after the publisher, Vizetelly, had been tried and imprisoned for publishing Zola's work in England. Hardy's contribution, published as 'Candour in English Fiction'[10] is a remarkably restrained piece from an author who had suffered so recently from censorship. Much of Hardy's anger, missing from 'Candour', is, I believe, deflected into the novel, *Tess*, which he was revising at the same time. His confrontation with moral censure and double standards was to be subtle and literary – he would defend his text by defending Tess as 'pure' – 'a pure woman faithfully presented' – appended to the novel in the First Edition of 1891. To stamp the word 'pure' on the title-page of his controversial novel was to anticipate the moral censure of the critics who would brand it 'impure', an expression of his belief that the novel was 'moral enough and to spare'. The account of the revisions describes Hardy's 'cynical amusement' in the 'unceremonious concession to conventionality' (*Life*, p. 223) and a kind of cynical amusement must have led him to append the sub-title and then claim to be surprised at the controversy it caused. It was just this controversy, I am convinced, that Hardy expected: a focusing of attention on the moral judgement of both Tess and text for in a letter to his publishers in 1892 he claimed that the sub-title 'pure' was absolutely necessary to 'show its meaning'.[11]

Finally there is one signal in this bloodletting text – a piece of bloodstained paper – which stands as a memorial to the lost and dismembered text, and which repeats Tess's tragic dismemberment. It comes at the point where the destitute Tess makes a trip to Angel's parents to ask for support. Her trip is in vain for once again her potential protectors are absent. While she rests after her fifteen-mile walk:

> A piece of blood-stained paper, caught up from some meat-buyer's dust-heap, beat up and down the road without the gate; too flimsy to rest, too heavy to fly away; and a few straws kept it company. (*Tess*, p. 374).

Tony Tanner[12] has pointed out that the paper is also Tess beaten about, too flimsy too rest, too heavy to fly away. Yet, that bloodstained paper from a meat-buyer's dust-heap seems also to be a remembrance of that bloodstained and mutilated novel, a page from the absent novel which has been so insistently and persistently censored and dismembered (splashed with blood), perhaps even a page from the two episodes that had been removed for serial publication. We must remember that while Hardy *removed* these two passages from the *Graphic* edition in November 1889, it was at this same point that he *added* the detail of the bloodstained paper. The meat-buyer whose 'dust-heap' has produced this bloodstained paper perhaps remembers also those editors and proprietors whom Hardy was later to thank for allowing him to 'piece the trunk and the limbs of the novel together' and the 'meat-buying' circulating-library barons such as Mudie who police the boundaries of moral purity.

## THE DEFENCE OF TESS AND TEXT

'A Pure Woman Faithfully Presented' . . .

Hardy's 'faithful presentation' of Tess's story (the novel) is also a careful presentation of the 'case-history' of a pure woman charged with murder. The text tells her story slowly and painstakingly, taking the reader from the months immediately preceding her seduction to her execution. In his Preface of 1892 Hardy explains that: 'there was something more to be said in fiction than had been said about the shaded side of a well-known catastrophe' (*Tess*, p. 37). The well-known catastrophe alludes to both the seduction and its consequences (Tess's murder and her execution) and Hardy feels that 'there was something more to be said *in fiction* than had been said'. 'Fiction' is to take up her case, is to provide the defence-that-should-have-been, the absent trial of the novel. It is a retrospective defence, told by a author fascinated by murder, particularly female murderesses, by executions, by the workings of the legal system.[13] From the *Life* it seems that Hardy's interest in murder and execution is characterised not so much by a macabre voyeurism but by a profound response to the physical proximity of murder and the way it is presented in journalism and in the law-courts.

During 1890, the year in which he was engaged in the revisions of *Tess*, Hardy was visiting the police courts for 'novel-padding':

> At the police-courts, where at this time he occasionally spent half a hour, being still compelled to get novel-padding, he noticed that the 'public' appeared to be mostly represented by grimy gentlemen who had had previous experience of the courts from a position in the dock; that there were people sitting around an ante-room of the courts as if waiting for a doctor; that the character of the witness usually deteriorated under cross-examination; and that the magistrates' spectacles as a rule endeavoured to flash out a strictly just manner combined with as much generosity as justice would allow. (*Life*, p. 238)

The novel-padding was presumably for *Tess* yet none of this material finds its way into the revised novel in any form. *There is no trial*. There are no police-courts. I would suggest that this research finds its way into the narrative as the voice of Tess's defence and that the double-standard which impresses Hardy so keenly in his visit to the police-courts (the fact that the public who 'consume' the trial are those who have been in the docks themselves) is present in the novel as Angel's judgement of Tess for a 'crime' he had himself committed.

David Lodge identifies two voices in Hardy's fiction: the voice in touch with the agrarian community and the voice that speaks to the metropolitan 'quality', the distanced voice which places the characters in their cosmic, historical and social settings and which contains the mediating accents of philosopher, local historian, topographer and antiquarian.[14] In *Tess* the voice which 'reads' and mediates Tess for us as metropolitan 'quality' is heavily accented with legal discourses, a voice which both tells and explains Tess's behaviour to the ultimate jury who are asked to judge her: the metropolitan 'quality' of his public. The judgement of Tess is spread across the entire novel, articulated by those fictional characters who judge her and *name* her, and the narrative voice. The defence draws upon retrospective testimony from secondary characters: a doctor, otherwise irrelevant to the plot, who had seen Angel and Tess on the night of Tess's confession, recalls the incident 'a long while after' (*Tess*, p. 303) and Mrs Brooks, the eavesdropping landlady, is used as a witness for the prosecution, a witness to murder.

Yet in examining 'the shaded side of the well-known', the novel *exposes* the unknown, the hidden, the unarticulated: the offensive truth. It becomes simultaneously an attack on this 'quality' and a defence of Tess. The great exposé of the late nineteenth century had been W. T. Stead's series of articles published in the *Pall Mall Gazette* in 1885, entitled 'The Maiden Tribute of Modern Babylon', which led to his prosecution under the Criminal Law Amendment Bill and which were read widely in England and in Europe, translated into French, German and Portuguese.[15] In order to strengthen his exposé of the trade in abducted working-class girls to continental brothels, Stead set up a *simulation*, working through an ex-prostitute to purchase a young girl from her mother and then 'export' her. This simulated abduction provided a test-case, proof of the existence of the trade-routes and the ease by which young girls could be purchased by those with the money to pay. The articles themselves, which constituted an attack on those complicit in the trade through all levels of society (including leading members of the morals police in Belgium and France), led to mass demonstrations in London and to the Criminal Law Amendment Bill finally being passed by the Commons. Ironically, it was Stead who was one of the first to be charged under the new Act, charged with the illegal abduction of Eliza Armstrong.

Hardy, too, *selects* a rather unwilling Tess as the subject of the text's exposé of seduction and its effects (also echoing the title of Stead's articles in its movement from 'Maiden' to 'Maiden No More'). Tess is selected from anonymity (a fieldwoman pure and simple) to be an example, like Eliza, of what has happened to thousands more like her. The earliest manuscript version of *Tess* is itself also much closer to the Stead simulation: the villain (then called 'Hawnferne' and no relation of Tess's family) sees Tees at a country dance and visits her mother to 'purchase' Tess for 'employment' at the Slopes. Joan, who even in the final version of *Tess* is worldly-wise and exasperated by her daughter's refusal to put a financial premium on her sexuality (her inability to play her 'trump-card'), mirrors the mercenary mothers of Stead's articles.

Stead's articles initiated a mass demonstration in Hyde Park on 22 August 1885 to pressurise the Commons to pass the Criminal Law Amendment Bill. One speaker was reported as saying:

> The truth must be spoken no matter what interests or class are affected. The chief cause of criminal vice is to be found in our economic system . . . . The same system that cleared the country-side of its labourers filled the brothels with girls . . . and the cause is the possession of the land by a few good-for-nothing aristocrats.[16]

Hardy's Preface of 1891 echoes the tone and interpretation of this speaker:

> I would ask the genteel reader, who cannot endure to have said nowadays what everyone thinks and feels, to remember the well-worn sentence of St. Jerome's: If an offence come out of the truth, better it is that the offence come than that the truth be concealed. (*Tess*, p. 35)

The offensive truth must be spoken. The material in *Tess* which persistently connects Tess's tragedy with the depopulation of the agrarian community and the possession of the land by a few good-for-nothing land-owners (Alec d'Urberville's model farm at the Slopes) sets Tess's tragedy firmly in the same socioeconomic framework articulated by the Hyde Park speaker as the cause of the exploitation of virginity. Yet Hardy was himself publicly reticent about the radical nature of his book. Of his interview with Thomas Hardy, Edmund Blunden recalls:

> When it was forecast that the broad result of the book would be a greater freedom for open and serious discussion of some deep problems of human life, Hardy went slow (he had of course no

desire to set himself up as a protagonist in the manner of W. T. Stead).

'That would be a very ambitious hope on my part. Remember I am only a learner in the art of novel-writing. Still I do feel very strongly that the position of man and woman in nature may be taken up and treated frankly.'[17]

## DO YOU SUPPORT HER OR NOT?

*Tess*, in its volume form of 1891, took London by storm. Hardy's novel, like Stead's articles, brought down the furies of moral and critical censure upon his head. *Tess* and the judgement of Tess became the 'talk' of London as is evident from an anecdote recorded in the *Life*:

> The Duchess of Abecorn tells me that the novel has saved her all the future trouble in the assortment of her friends. They have been almost fighting over her dinner-table over Tess's character. What she now says to them is 'Do you support her or not?'. If they say 'No indeed. She deserved hanging: a little harlot!', she puts them into one group. If they say 'Poor wronged innocent!' and pity her, she puts them in the other group where she is herself (*Life*, p. 258).

One can sense Hardy's delight in this anecdote. His sub-title, an incitement to discourse, was beginning to take its effect at the dinner-tables of the aristocracy. The *judgement* of Tess's character – her estimate – becomes a way of sorting one group from another, a method of judging *society* for this hostess.[18]

There is a group of modern writers on Hardy who respond to the same incitement to judge Tess, to naturalise her and to put her on trial. In fact it is difficult *not* to defend or blame Tess; the temptation to naturalise her is a strong one. Critics often set themselves up as a kind of literary jury not to debate the merits of Hardy's text, but to interrogate and judge the naturalised Tess. Even a generally well-balanced critic such as Daleski, for instance, adopts a censorious tone in his discussion of the seduction: 'There is, after all, a point at which one *allows* oneself to fall asleep'.[19] 'She asked for it.' I do not so much object to the preoccupation with Tess's moral culpability (Hardy, as I have argued, encouraged this) as to the tone of such criticism which often assumes a male audience who know about the wiles of women.)

The anger which we hear in the authorial voice which defends Tess, surfaces through blood, the blood of the ritual mutilation Hardy was forced to suffer upon his own text to satisfy the editorial 'morals police'. It was doubtless this experience – the way in which his text had been a site for a series of interrogations and judgements about moral purity – that determined him to defend the 'purity' of Tess and to put the judges of 'moral purity' themselves on trial. The defence of Tess (and text) stages the trial that should have been (the absent trial of Tess and the trial of the novel *Tess*) and presents the 'something more to be said in fiction' about the policing of purity – more to be said than Hardy was prepared to say in his public article about censorship. That Hardy felt drawn towards the police-courts for 'novel-padding' during his revisions of *Tess* testifies to his quest for a language with which to defend the purity of his novel and the purity of Tess. The voice which speaks her defence bears the marks of this research, defending Tess with rhetorical flourish and a tenderness designed to tug the heart-strings of even the harshest jury:

> It was the third day of the estrangement. Some might risk the odd paradox that with more animalism he could have been the nobler man. We do not say it. (*Tess*, p. 315)

> But might some say, where was Tess's guardian angel? Where was the providence of her simple faith? (*Tess*, p. 119)

> It was a thousand pities, indeed; it was impossible for even an enemy to feel otherwise on looking at Tess as she sat there . . . (*Tess*, p. 140)

> the stopt-diason note which her voice acquired when her heart was in her speech, and which will never be forgotten by those who knew her (*Tess*, p. 145)

We, as jury assembled to interrogate the moral implications of Tess's story, are invited to participate in a continuous process of judging Tess and her actions, and to participate in the absent (and yet continuously present) trial of Tess, which is a trial ultimately about moral purity and its definition. Who defines moral purity? What are the politics of power or class implicit in such judgements?

It is impossible to read Hardy's novel without confronting these questions, impossible to bypass the stamp of purity which Hardy inscribes on its title page and which incites us to discourse on moral purity.

## BAD BLOOD

However, it would be reductive to assume that the narrative voice is consistent and unified throughout. There is nothing so simple in this text. The novel is inconsistent especially in its philosophical intrusions, as almost every commentator on the novel has pointed out. There is a second voice, a voice that persistently stresses Tess's heredity, that insists that she is victim of biological determinism. In a sense this voice still 'defends' Tess in that it argues that she is not *responsible* for her violent tendencies – they are an unfortunate hereditary trait. This voice colludes with Angel's reading of Tess as 'a belated seedling of an effete aristocracy'. It is the voice that explains Tess in terms of *degeneracy*, as when it notes that she is: 'an almost standard woman, but for the slight incautiousness of character inherited from her race' (*Tess*, p. 141), or when she submits to Angel's conditions on leaving her: 'Pride, too, entered into her submission – which perhaps was a symptom of that reckless acquiescence in chance too apparent in the whole d'Urberville family . . . ' (*Tess*, p. 324).

Critics such as John Lucas have been uneasy with such authorial persistency:

> Hardy seems to have taken quite seriously the 'blood taint' of the d'Urbervilles . . . I suppose he hopes by means of it to exonerate Tess, but it has the opposite effect, since it makes her less of a free moral agent and more of a hunted animal . . . . [20]

And more of a degenerate carrying an 'obscure strain of the d'Urberville blood' which leads to the 'aberration' of murder. 'A degenerate of murdering type' echoes back Ossipon from the pages of Conrad's *The Secret Agent*. Conrad's text, of course, was written twenty years after *Tess* and after the publication of Nordau's *Degeneration*, but there is much in *Tess* which anticipates the criminological discourses of Conrad's text and of Nordau's. Much of Ossipon's reading of Winnie is present in the voice that reads Tess as the *fatal woman*, the degenerate with debased (and alcoholic) parentage, the degenerate of murdering type. Winnie's blood line carried *French* blood; likewise Tess's, as Parson Tringham informs John Durbeyfield that his ancestor was one of the twelve French knights who came from Normandy to conquer Glamorganshire with William the Conqueror, Sir Pagan d'Urberville. The bad blood that constitutes Tess's degeneracy is that of a French invader and Hardy had just witnessed the legal censure of another French 'invader' – Zola – whose publisher (in assisting the 'invasion') was being tried and imprisoned as *Tess*, the novel, came into being.[21] French naturalism in this period is persistently described in terms of moral corruption – it must be kept out at all costs to ensure that British fiction and the (British 'Young Person') be kept morally 'clean'.

The emphasis on Tess's heredity (and degeneracy) finds its way into the novel *during* the dismemberment stage – after the rejections of November 1889, and appears to be part of Hardy's growing determination to defend Tess (and text) from charges of moral impurity. But these determinist discourses create significant textual incoherences: is it possible to protest that Tess is 'pure' when her degenerate bloodline is held up so insistently as the explanation for her propensity for both violence and passivity? Is Hardy arguing that Tess is innocent for she is not responsible for the bloodline which compels her to extreme behaviour? Mary Jacobus has argued that the contradictions of Hardy's text arise out of his attempt 'to argue a case whose terms were dictated by the conventional moralists themselves'[22] and that in whitewashing Tess in his revisions, making her more of a victim (of her biology, of Alec, of exploitation), he robs her of her tragic status. Perhaps his own identification with Tess as the 'belated seedling of an effete aristocracy' (the fact that the Hardys too were in decline, were a 'fallen' family)[23] blinded him to the dangers of perceiving biology and race (blood) as determinants of 'fate'. Is Tess 'fatal' (to herself and others) because she cannot escape her fatalistic bloodline or is she fatal because others insist on reading her in these terms and 'construct' her fatality in terms of race or bloodlines? The text does not resolve these questions but holds them open, and in this fissure a process of deconstruction and implosion begins in which Hardy's philosophical intrusions and readings of Tess in terms of moral purity begin to collapse in upon themselves.

The Prefaces of the novel, which Hillis Miller describes as both apologies for and reiterations of the central questions of the text,[24] enact just this implosion of language as Hardy fights his battles with both the critics of Tess and the critics of his novel, whom he denounces angrily as 'manipulators' and 'judges' of Tess and text. In angrily defending his subtitle in the Preface of 1892, he draws attention to the slippage of definition of the word 'pure', unable in this attempt to even write the word, referring only to the 'subtitle adjective'. By the 1912 Preface (by which time he had entirely abandoned writing fiction) he writes with resignation: 'Melius fuerat non scribere', testifying to his awareness of the 'shaping or constraining force of language upon apprehension'.[25] This movement towards silence is another censorship in itself, a final refusal to engage in a debate from which there is no escape within a language and a culture which offers no alternatives to the polarities of clean/unclean, pure/impure, virgin/whore, innocent/guilty.

## THE READING AND WRITING OF TESS

'It is not what is done to us, but what is made of us', she said at last, 'that wrongs us'.
  Lyndall in Olive Schriener's *The Story of an African Farm*, 1883

'It is difficult for a woman to define her feelings in language which is chiefly made by men to define theirs.'
  Bathsheba in *Far From the Madding Crowd*, 1874

'For she you love is not my real self, but one in my image . . .'
  Tess in *Tess of the d'Urbervilles*, 1891

'The social moulds civilisation fits us into have no more relation to our actual shapes than the conventional shapes of the constellations have to real star-patterns.'
  Sue Bridehead in *Jude the Obscure*, 1895

The narrative voice of Hardy's *Tess* both tells Tess's story and reads Tess's story. It speaks for her and about her in an attempt to defend her purity. It is both an exposé of the socioeconomic pressures that exploit and transform women and of the transformative powers of the masculine *reading* of women. John Lucas describes the novel as:

a great novel about a girl who tries to discover, and live into a secure identity, a sense of self than shan't be fixed for her, shan't deny her her own sense of identity. And of course the whole relentless pressure of the novel is towards showing how again and again she has to struggle free of various 'fixed' images of purity and womanhood, how she desperately tries not to be 'owned', 'possessed', how the men in the novel – Alec, Dairyman Crick, Angel, Farmer Groby – do in different ways 'own' her, and how finally they defeat her struggles . . . .[26]

But Hardy himself joins the attempt to 'fix' Tess. He generalises about Tess almost as unquestioningly as Angel does.[27] She is the site for a textual investigation of purity just as Eliza Armstrong had been the site for Stead's discourses upon London and European corruption, just as Hardy's own manuscript had become the site for a judgement about the moral purity of text. Yet as the page upon which so many discourses are inscribed, Tess is discursively overdetermined.[28] Hardy's reading of her through the philosophical intrusions which try to make sense of her story, are inconsistent and often contradictory. The fact that critics are still at odds about *Tess* – is she a victim or *femme fatale*? Was she seduced or raped, did she 'ask for it' by being too passive, too often in reverie? Where is her fatality located: in her beauty or in her degenerate bloodline? – suggests that Tess is still 'on trial', and that there are inconsistencies in her defence. That these questions are still pertinent and often crucial to twentieth-century critics of Hardy's novel suggests, too, that the debates about the purity of a 'fallen' woman still loom large to us. Hardy's 'inconsistencies' in presenting Tess, his portrayal of her as *both* passive victim of an exploitative world and as *femme fatale* with an active and desiring sexuality which proves fatal to herself and to those around her, should perhaps not be seen as disjunctions but as a partial attempt to render Tess not as she should be but as she is: multiple and unfixable.

The first inscription of Tess is enacted on the title-page itself, appended to her name in the subtitle of the book: the 'estimate' of her character as 'pure' by the author. It begins a process of writing on her as blank page which is continued by all who encounter and judge her.[29] Alec's violation of Tess is described as the tracing of a 'coarse pattern' upon 'beautiful feminine tissue, sensitive as gossamer, and practically blank as snow as yet' and as a result Tess is divided from her former 'maiden' self, branded like Hester Prynne, not by the experience itself but by an 'immeasurable social chasm' which will ensure that the coarse pattern will never be removed. She does not, and cannot, write herself but is written upon and constructed by others, itself a kind of violation.

Hardy, too, inscribes Tess with numerous tracings, not least with the discourses of biological determinism, his tracing upon Tess of the degenerate characteristics of her 'race' (family) and its murderous tendencies. When we encounter Tess the text insists that we always take her heredity, her 'race' into account. It explains her reverie, her impulsiveness, her malleability and her violence. As such it too forms a 'coarse pattern' inscribed upon her and in its textual overdetermination perhaps reflects Hardy's growing unease at such methods of measuring women or for accounting for human behaviour,[30] an unease which he records in an account of a meeting with Sir James Crichton Browne in 1893:

> A woman's brain, according to him, is as large in proportion to her body as a man's. The most passionate women are not those selected in civilised society to breed from, as in a state of nature, but the colder; the former going on the streets (I am sceptical about this). The doctrines of Darwin require readjusting largely . . . . (*Life*, p. 275)

Hardy's recognition of the dangers of sexual typing appears as early as 1874 where he criticises Boldwood's habit of 'deeming as essentials of the whole sex the accidents of the single one of their number he had ever closely beheld'[31] (*Far From the Madding Crowd*). In *A Group of Noble Dames*[32] which was written quickly alongside the revisions of *Tess* for a fast financial return, Hardy presents the stories of ten aristocratic women as related by the men of the Wessex Field and Antiquarian Club (Hardy was himself a member of this club) on a night when there was 'a paucity of more scientific papers' (*A Group of Noble Dames*, p. 50). These stories were:

> made to do duty for the regulation papers on deformed butterflies, fossil ox-horns, prehistoric dung-mixens, and such like, that usually occupied the more serious attention of the members. (*A Group of Noble Dames*, p. 48)

Female domestic history becomes the subject of scientific attention, and at the end of each story the men of the club draw generalised moral conclusions from the 'scientific' data presented by the case-histories. Much of the ironic humour of this work has gone unnoticed by critics who tend to regard it as a lesser work, but it was written alongside the revisions of *Tess* for serial publication, and Hardy seems to be drawing attention to the ways in which women are used as a subject or means of investigation for male 'scientific' discourse: the page on which such masculine discourses are inscribed. Yet Tess's story is similarly told by a narrative voice which interrogates her innocence, a voice which both tells and (over)reads her through a series of generalisations.

Yet the Tess presented by Hardy is a figure who eludes categorisation just as she is simultaneously also a continuous site for masculine attempts to fix and name her not only by the men of the novel who attempt to read her but by the critics who have continued that process. Ellen Moers, for instances, challenges Irving Howe's naming of Tess as a 'cultural stereotype' by asking: 'Of what?' 'Which cultural stereotype?'[33] For Moers she is the all-purpose heroine: milkmaid, emancipated woman, good-girl/governess type of heroine, doomed descendant of an ancient race, earth goddess, doomed bride of balladry, prostitute, unwed mother, murderess, princess in disguise . . . . Most importantly she contains both poles of the virgin–whore split: she is both passive (victim, hunted animal, virgin) and active (prostitute, murderess). Ellen Moers concludes that Tess is 'a fantasy of almost pornographic dimensions' but she is also compounded of many contradictory and 'fixed' readings of woman sustained and held within a single body – both virgin and whore simultaneously.

In almost every erotic passage of the novel Tess's dual (active/passive) sexuality and personality is stressed. In the famous garden scene, for instance, she signifies 'fallen' woman in that she is placed on the outskirts of the Edenic garden, aligned with 'fallen' nature. She is a predatory *femme fatale* in stalking the object of her desire, advancing towards him, like a cat. She is associated with anarchic sexuality in that she occupies a part of the garden which is rank, wild and uncultivated. She occupies the twilight – the scene is set at dusk – when things are indistinct and where the darkness is crescent: the nebulous twilight world in which she is figured throughout the novel. Yet she is also a 'fascinated bird', caught in the trap of her own desires, unable to leave the spot. She is not stained by the sticky blights, she stains *herself*:

> rubbing off upon her naked arms sticky blights which, though snow-white upon the apple-tree trunks, made madder stains on her skin; thus she drew quite near Angel Clare, still unobserved of him. (*Tess*, p. 179)

Red on white. The transformation of the colour of the 'sticky blights' from snow-white (on the trees) to 'madder' (a red pigment) as it comes into contact with her skin signals the transformation from passive to active sexuality: Tess is 'mad' with desire. Furthermore, as it is Tess who stains *herself* with natural pigments, her stalking of Angel becomes a primitive ritual: she is the painted hunter stalking her prey, or the cat. Since Angel does not see her in this description, this reading of Tess is that of the authorial gaze, a gaze which can maintain plural (and contradictory) readings.

Later in the confession scene, Hardy shows us Tess's lover, Angel Clare, forced to revise his idealised image of Tess as pure woman by her confession. Angel begins to see her as a different woman and his understanding of her cannot maintain contradictions. For him she must be either 'pure'/virginal, or corrupt/debased. It is a wedding-night confession, a necessary prelude to their consummation and it is on this wedding-night that Tess 'falls' from grace for Angel. The d'Urberville portraits, added at the rewriting stage (after November 1889), part of Hardy's new and expanded heredity theme, become a point of reference for Angel's rereading of Tess. Built into the masonry of the d'Urberville mansion in which they are staying, they provide a means by which Angel can measure Tess's 'degeneracy':

> these paintings represent women of middle age, of a date some hundred years ago, whose lineaments once seen can never be forgotten. The long pointed features, narrow eye and smirk of the one, so suggestive of merciless treachery; the bill-hook nose, large teeth, and bold eye of the other, suggesting arrogance to the point of ferocity, haunt the beholder afterwards in his dreams. (*Tess*, pp. 283–4)

This is the first entrance into the text of the *female* side of the d'Urberville ancestry. Angel discovers that the stigmata of degeneracy (hooked nose, large teeth, bold eye) seen in the female ancestors, and representative of the essence of d'Urberville womanhood – a female bloodline to which Tess belongs – are also to be traced in Tess's face:

> The unpleasantness of the matter was that, in addition to their effect upon Tess, her fine features were unquestionable traceable in those exaggerated forms. (*Tess*, p. 284)

As he gazes at Tess he traces, or *maps* that 'sinister design' on to her face, superimposing the two images in his own mind but it is not until after the confession that he perceives the similarity of *trait*. Ironically, it is Angel himself who *transforms* her (by dressing her and adorning her with jewels as Alec will do later), who brings about a transformation which, with the confession, enables him to reconstruct her as a different woman. About to re-enter her room (for reconciliation?) he is checked by the portrait which reminds him of Tess's physiognomy although Hardy adds significantly: 'So it seemed to him then.' Angel's reading of both Tess and portrait is *distorted* by the effects of her confession, which he perceives as a 'sinister design' and as a 'concentrated purpose of revenge on the other sex'. Tess's confession, her 'revelation' (literally 'unveiling') of her 'fallen' past, lifts the veil from Angel's eyes so that beneath the 'new-sprung child of nature' he can see 'the belated seedling of an effete aristocracy'. The change in his perception of her is so striking that he says to her: 'I repeat, the woman I have been loving is not you' . . . [she is] 'another woman in your shape' (*Tess*, p. 299) echoing Tess's earlier awareness that 'she you love is not my real self, but one in my image' (*Tess*, p. 281).

There are other wedding-night revelations in Hardy's work, notably in *The Pursuit of the Well-Beloved* and in *Jude the Obscure*. In the former the protagonist's wife returns to him after forty years and in unveiling reveals herself as a 'wrinkled crone', a 'Witch of Endor', and as 'a parchment-covered skull', echoing Ayesha's parchment-coloured skin exposed in her devolution. Jude, too is duped on his wedding-night as Arabella removes her false hair in a grotesque unrobing which leaves Jude with 'a feeling of sickness'. Angel, stupefied, marvels that Tess's appearance 'looked absolutely pure. Nature, in her fantastic trickery, had set such a seal of maidenhood upon Tess's countenance' (*Tess*, p. 307). Elaine Showalter interprets these wedding-night revelations as 'transformations' (these women are 'terribly changed, reverting to the beast'),[34] but the emphasis is placed upon a process of *unveiling* rather than transformation, an unveiling which enables the man who surveys to confront the full horror of the Woman, a horror that has previously been concealed from him by the 'fantastic trickery' of Nature.

Yet in *Tess* most of the shrinking and withering which usually takes place in such revelation scenes is significantly displaced on to Angel. It is Angel's persistence in judging Tess and misreading her that withers him:

he was becoming ill with thinking; eaten out with thinking; withered by thinking; scourged out of his former pulsating flexuous domesticity (*Tess*, p. 313).

On his return from Brazil, he is reduced to a 'ghost', a 'yellow skeleton' but nonetheless cured of his moral puritanism by the cursory remarks of a large-minded stranger met with in Brazil who persuades Angel to abandon his parochialism and to adopt a wider view of ethics. It is this revelation of the relativity of ethics that allows Angel to cure himself by readjusting his doctrines and in this process he comes to realise too the falsity of his interest in her bloodline: 'it was a most useful ingredient to the dreamer, the moraliser on declines and falls' (*Tess*, p. 423).

Tess's revelations prove fatal to Angel's moral doctrines and bring about a radical re-evaluation of his philosophical inconsistencies. Tess's passive gaze disturbs and silences, too, the 'pious rhetoric' and fanaticism of the newly-evangelised Alec d'Urberville, whom she encounters preaching in a barn:

> The effect upon her old lover was electric, far stronger than the effect of his presence upon her. His fire, the tumultuous ring of his eloquence, seemed to go out of him. His lip struggled and trembled under the words that lay upon it; but deliver them it could not as long as she faced him . . . This paralysis lasted, however, but a short time; for Tess's energy returned with the atrophy of his, and she walked away as fast as she was able past the barn and onward (*Tess*, p. 384).

Tess's energies 'returned with the atrophy of his'. A woman who is persistently silenced by men's words is, here, through her direct gaze (the power of her eyes) able to silence and paralyse Alec, just as, through her confession, she is able to paralyse, silence and wither Angel. Increasingly as the book progresses Tess's story gains a power to disturb the moral orthodoxy of her judges (Alec and Angel), not by rational confrontation but by the challenging case-history which forces her men to confront the ways in which they perceive her. Her face, directed powerfully towards this judge, this Pauline moraliser, paralyses and extinguishes his words: 'deliver them he could not as long as she faced him'.

## TWILIGHT

After the opening Cerealia, Tess is rarely described in full light but is most often seen, nebulous and indistinct, in the twilight of dawn (the utopian scenes at Talbothays with Angel) or dusk (the garden scene). The merging of her contours in this light ensures her safety in concealing her from the male gaze which is forever on her. Her self-concealment is so successful in the following passage that our gaze does not even perceive her pregnancy:

> The only exercise that Tess took at this time was after dark; and it was then, when out in the woods, that she seemed least solitary. She knew how to hit to a hair's-breadth that moment of evening when the light and darkness are so evenly balanced that the constraint of days and the suspense of night neutralise each other, leaving absolute mental liberty . . . . She had no fear of shadows; her sole idea seemed to be to shun mankind . . . .
>
> On these lonely hills and dales her quiescent glide was of a piece with the element she moved in. Her flexuous and stealthy figure became an integral part of the scene (*Tess*, p. 134).

Twilight, the moment *between* night and day, gives her absolute mental liberty from the 'constraints' of day and the 'suspense' of night and neutralises the moment. It is almost as if this nebulous light neutralises *her*, by enabling her partial escape from a gaze which seeks always to interpret her, searching her out with its spot-lights. Tess occupies the grey area, the shadow of fissure between moral light and moral darkness where her polarities are dissolved and neutralised. In the descriptions of the early mornings at Talbothays, Angel attempts to decipher the 'ghostly' Tess, a Tess whom he meets in 'that strange and solemn interval, the twilight of the morning'. The 'mixed, singular, luminous gloom' makes him think of Adam and Eve, then of the Resurrection, but 'he little thought that the Magdalen might be at his side', Hardy adds. He can see only the virgin, but not the fallen woman who is also present beside him. Yet the light itself is all things – mixed and yet singular, a luminous gloom, maintaining polarities, dissolving distinctions in a way that Angel cannot in his insistence in making Tess 'a visionary essence of woman – a whole sex condensed into one form' (*Tess*, pp. 186–7).

The animal imagery associated with Tess repeats the active–passive tension of her representation. She is, of course, primarily aligned with images of trapped, hunted and caged animals, but there are other analogies in the text which disturb and undermine these emblems of her victimisation. In the garden scene she is both bird and cat, although it is her cat-like, predatory qualities that are most prominent, reinforced by the imagery of the pigment-stained hunter. On another occasion she is described as staring back at a passing train with the 'suspended attitude of a friendly leopard at pause' (*Tess*, p. 251) and when Angel finds the sleepy Tess stretching herself she is likened to a snake: 'She was yawning, and he saw the red interior of her mouth as if it had been a snake's' (*Tess*, p. 231).

Tess is neither cat nor bird, hunter nor hunted, but like her eyes she bears 'all these shades together, and a hundred others . . . – shade beyond shade – tint beyond tint' (*Tess*, p. 140). Whilst the narrator traces the course of her fatality (and even reads her fatality in terms of biological determinism) he also denies this reading of her as *femme fatale*: 'It was no mature woman with a long dark vista of intrigue behind her who was tormented thus; but a girl of simple life, not yet one-and-twenty, who had been caught during her days of immaturity like a bird in a springe' (*Tess*, p. 261). There seems to be a textual ambiguity *about reading her*, that resists allotting Tess to any fixed stereotypical spaces and this resistance works, paradoxically, by *over*-reading her, by over-playing the stereotype. Victim/sexual aggressor images are often spliced together, as, for instance, in the garden scene, so that they work against each other and draw attention to the process of fixing meaning through language. Sometimes this splicing process works through the juxtaposition of opposing visual images: the scene in which Tess is perceived/read by both Alec and narrative voice as the unveiled *femme fatale* who is able to drain Alec's energy, is prefaced by the stark, brutal image of Tess bent double in the fields of Flintcomb Ash, mid-winter. This returns us to the central question: can we justify taking the narrative disjunctions as a deliberate strategy? John Goode's recent work on Tess insists that we must do just this and cease from looking for or creating textual coherence. He argues that the novel, *Tess*, has a 'polemical design in which discontinuities are seen as properties of the ideological discourses the text articulates'.[35]

## CONSUMERISM AND SELECTION

Mowbray Morris, in his 1892 review of the novel (which he had earlier refused to publish as editor of *Macmillan's Magazine*), objected to Tess's sensuality:

> Poor Tess's sensual qualifications for the part of heroine are paraded over and over again with a persistence like that of a horse-dealer egging on some wavering customer to a deal, or a slave-dealer appraising his wares to some full-blooded pasha.[36]

Hardy parades Tess in the following passage in which we watch her in the fields whilst the voyeuristic authorial presence points out her charms as if they were 'sensual qualifications for the part of heroine':

> This morning the eye returns involuntarily to the girl in the pink cotton jacket, she being the most flexuous and finely-drawn figure of them all. But her bonnet is pulled so far over her brow that none of her face is disclosed while she binds, though her complexion may be guessed from a stray twine or two of dark brown hair which extends below the curtain of her bonnet. Perhaps one reason why she seduces casual attention is that she never courts it, though the other women often gaze around them . . .
> She brings the ends of the sheaf together, and kneels on the sheaf whilst she ties it, beating back her skirts now and then when lifted by the breeze. A bit of her naked arm is visible . . . (*Tess*, p. 138)

John Goode has pointed out, however, that this passage 'is established in terms of the clear gaze of masculine appropriation',[37] a definite invitation to possess the image through the voyeuristic gaze which Tess unsuccessfully tries to resist. Just as Tess holds the corn in an embrace 'like that of a lover', so the gaze holds and fixes her. She is the object for consumption, selected for our delectation just as she is persistently selected by the men in the novel either for sexual or economic exploitation.

W. T. Stead, as I have shown, was similarly aware of the economic causes of the selection and exploitation of young women. He had selected Eliza Armstrong as the subject for his exposé to demonstrate that young women were being selected for the sexual *consumption* of the middle-class male. Thus the method of his exposé was a simulation of the very evil he was denouncing. He was criticised (and imprisoned) for doing so and Hardy has similarly been put on trial by critics for 'violating' his heroine and thus committing the crime he wished to expose: 'The narrator's erotic fantasies of penetration and engulfment enact a pursuit, violation and persecution of Tess in parallel with those she suffers at the hands of her two lovers.'[38] Yet perhaps by forcing us to occupy the position of voyeur and consumer of Tess's 'sensual qualifications' in the above passage, he forces us too, to confront the ways in which any representation of woman (no matter how well-intentioned) enacts a kind of textual exploitation by taking Woman as its text and by inscribing its 'coarse pattern' upon her, reducing her to a passive object denied subjectivity.

Tess is a resistant site for the myriad discourses which are inscribed upon her, a proliferation of signs and readings which allow her escape from signification and endlessly postpone her signification, much as the sign-painter inscribes a moral 'meta-language' on a resistant landscape:

> The old gray wall began to advertise a similar fiery lettering to the first, with a strange and unwonted mien, as if distressed at duties it had never before been called upon to perform (*Tess*, p. 129).

This 'hideous defacement' also offers yet another censorious reading of Tess which violates her: 'But the words entered Tess with accusatory horror. It was as if the man knew her recent history' (*Tess*, p. 128). 'Call me Tess', she asks, refusing to be read by Angel, refusing to be called 'Artemis, Demeter and other fanciful names which she did not like because she did not understand them' (*Tess*, p. 187). Tess does not share the access to literary allusions and figuration that Angel possesses. She refuses to play the naming/inscribing game (although she does idealise Angel). When Alec reads their situation as a replay of the Edenic fall, Tess replies: 'I never said you were Satan, or thought it. I don't think of you in that way at all' (*Tess*, p. 432).

Adrian Poole argues that: 'Hardy is peculiarly sensitive to . . . the efforts of men's words to circumscribe and describe, confine and define woman's bodies.'[39] Hardy's women, he continues, are 'purposively blurred and blurring', refusing 'to be accommodated by these men's words as they cross and re-cross that middle distance between the vague and the coarse'. Tess is read and named (and re-named) infinitely both by the men who desire her and the discursive 'meta-language' that 'defends' and explains her. Yet this discursive

overdetermination ensures, too, a slippage as Tess disappears into
the grey twilight between the polarities of pure woman and prostitute, innocent and guilty, virgin and whore, victim and murderess.
She occupies the twilight spaces *in between* the names, signs and
discourses of textual/sexual appropriation and is finally neutralised
by the multiple and contradictory readings of her which throw each
other into question or cancel each other out.[40]

## THE DEFACEMENT OF TESS/TEXT

*Tess's Lament*[41]

> I would that folk forgot me quite
>             Forget me quite
> I would that I could shrink from sight
>             And no more see the sun . . .
>
> It wears me out to think of it,
>             To think of it;
> I cannot bear my fate as writ
>             I'd have my life unbe
>
> Would turn my memory to a blot,
> Make every relic of me rot,
> My doings be as they were not,
> And gone all trace of me.

Tess in this poem (is this a lament to her maker, her author?) asks to
be unwritten and untraced. Her lament is that her future should be
determined in any form ('I cannot bear my fate as writ') and yet in a
poem entitled 'Heredity'[42] which seems to answer her plea, the 'family face' reminds her that her fate can never be escaped: 'Flesh
perishes, I live on,/ Projecting trait and trace/ To time and times
anon'. Yet it is Tess's beauty that will either be her 'trump-card' or
the means of her persecution:

> [Mother:] 'Well, as one of the genuine stock, she ought to make
> her way with 'en, if she plays her trump card aright. And if her
> don't marry her afore he will after. For that he's all afire wi' love
> for her any eye can see.'

[Father:] 'What's her trump card? Her d'Urberville blood you mean?'

[Mother:] 'No, stupid; her face – as 'twas mine.' (*Tess*, p. 93)

Whilst Tess's father mistakenly believes the 'trump card' to be Tess's noble blood and the marketing of it the saving of the family, her mother knows that Tess has only one card to play, her desirability. Her face is her only market value and now that Prince is dead, the family must send Tess to market, to sell (or gamble) herself for it is Tess's 'comeliness' that will single her out from the other female workers at the Slopes, rather than her noble blood.

Throughout the novel and more particularly in the second half, Tess attempts to deface herself, to *censor* the signs of her desirability, the signs which single her out from the crowd.[43] The novel opens with the self-exhibition of the Cerealia, yet Tess soon learns that such self-exhibition will only attract 'aggressive admiration', and her attempts to disappear become more brutal as the novel progresses. It is not enough to hide her head in a bonnet, for such evasion only increases the persistence of the male (and in this case, the reader's) gaze:

> her bonnet is pulled so far over her brow that none of her face is disclosed while she binds, though her complexion may be guessed from a stray twine or two of dark brown hair which extends below the curtain of her bonnet. Perhaps one reason why she seduces casual attention is that she never courts it, though the other women often gaze around them. (*Tess*, p. 138)

Later, having defaced Angel's image of her through the wedding-night confession, she learns on her journey to Flintcomb Ash that her face draws attention and she resolves 'to run no further risks from her appearance'. By dressing herself in shabby clothes, tying a handkerchief around her face and cutting her eyebrows off she insures herself against 'aggressive admiration'. After her journey to Angel's parents to ask for support she returns angry and humiliated.

> She did, indeed, take sufficient interest in herself to throw up her veil on this return journey, as if to let the world see that she could at least exhibit a face such as Mercy Chant could not show. (*Tess*, p. 378)

Humiliated, she displays her trump-card, a return to the self-exhibition of the opening Cerealia.

Later she makes the mistake of leaving her face exposed when she enters the barn in which Alec d'Urberville is preaching, so that he recognises her. She forgets that she, being unveiled, is left uninsured against aggressive attention, but this passage makes it clear that, as far as Alec is concerned the veil is also there to protect *him* from *her* gaze. He overtakes her as she leaves the barn. Angry, she turns her unveiled gaze upon him:

> 'Don't look at me like that!' he said abruptly. Tess, who had been quite unconscious of her action and mien, instantly withdrew the large dark gaze of her eyes, . . .
>
> 'No, no, Don't beg my pardon. But since you wear a veil to hide your good looks, why don't you keep it down?' She pulled down the veil saying hastily, 'It was mostly to keep off the wind'.
>
> 'It might seem harsh of me to dictate like this', he went on, 'but it is better that I should not look too often on you. It might be dangerous' (*Tess*, p. 388).

There are echoes of *She* here, a novel written only one year before the conception of *Tess*. Ayesha, too, must be constantly veiled to hide her dangerous beauty, for her beauty is a curse upon man ('Beauty is like lightning, it destroys'). It is the man, Hardy emphasises, who protects himself from desire with the censoring veil.

Yet with her defacement Tess has acquired a voice. It is *after* she allows the veil to cover her again that Alec notes that she has acquired a fluency with the atrophy of his: 'I must go away and get strength . . . . How is it that you speak so fluently now?' (*Tess*, p. 389). In defacing herself or covering her face, Tess denies herself as object of desire, she destroys or veils the signs which allow her appropriation. Her attempt is literally to desexualise herself and to disfigure herself (or to designify herself as object). This process gives her increased subjectivity in that she acquires a speaking voice. As she become systematically more defaced (by her own hand and by the text as it increasingly plays down her appearance towards the end of the novel) she becomes more articulate: she challenges Alec's conversion, she writes angry letters to Angel, she becomes increasingly more articulate and bitter about her oppression.

Tess's final effacement is, of course, to relinquish her body entirely after she returns to Alec. Angel recognises this:

his original Tess had spiritually ceased to recognise the body
before him as hers – allowing it to drift, like a corpse upon the
current, in a direction disassociated from its living will. (*Tess*,
p. 467)

Her body, her means of barter, has been finally bought. (In one
version Tells tells Angel 'He has bought me.') It is now Alec who
dresses her. Earlier she had described how, gazing at the stars, she
could release herself from her body in a kind of transcendental
disembodiment ('Our souls can be made to go outside our bodies
when we are alive'). In allowing her body to be bought by Alec she
has achieved a final disembodiment, for her living will is
unpurchasable; it has moved in another direction, severed from her
appropriated body. Tess's various attempts to deface herself have
failed. Her final recourse is to relinquish her body entirely, to cut it
off.

In a novel which is grounded in mutilation, dismemberment and
censorship, Tess's self-disfigurement and defacement can be seen as
attempts at protective self-censorship. Hardy, like Tess, must mutilate the body of his text (*Tess*) in order to avoid aggressive attention.
For Tess this process must end in dis-bodiment; defacement is insuf-
ficient protection against masculine appropriation. She must be finally compromised – she must sell her body (to support her family)
and prostitute herself. Similarly Hardy's decision to mutilate his
novel, rather than to publish in volume form only, was based, he
claims, on economic factors.[44] Hardy's anger at the enforced 'prostitution' of the writer to the monopoly of serial publication and the
subsequent need to destroy the body of his text (*Tess*) for economic
reasons found its most eloquent expression in the text itself which
repeats its own mutilation through its heroine.

## THE FALL AND DEFACEMENT OF THE LAND

Hardy's text is fabricated out of an elaborate system of repetitions
and mirrorings whereby Tess's story is seen to mirror and be mirrored by other patterns of fall and decline. As Hillis Miller has
argued, no pattern echoed by others in this novel has hierarchical
significance, but each part is a node, or point of intersection or focus
'on which converge lines leading from many other passages of the
novel and ultimately including them all'.[45] But it is Tess's story

which stands at the point of intersection of these narratives of fall and decline. Tess's fall and defacement (patterned too in the fall and defacement of the d'Urbervilles, patterned again in the fall of the Hardys) is repeated by the violation and defacement of the land as described in the novel. Once again, the theme of rural decay in its full form, like the heredity material, only entered the novel after November 1889.[46]

In other writings Hardy describes rural decay as a process of attrition and defacement. In the Preface to *Far From the Madding Crowd* Hardy accounts for the 'fatal' break in the continuity of local rural history in terms of migratory labour and in 'The Dorsetshire Labourer' (1883) he laments that labourers:

> are also losing their particularities as a class; hence the humorous simplicity which formerly characterised the men and the unso-phisticated modesty of the women are rapidly disappearing un-der the constant attrition of lives mildly approximating to those of workers in a manufacturing town.[47]

This attrition is paralleled by Tess's gradual inability to resist Alec's pressure, by her weariness caused by the gruelling manual work in the fields of Flintcomb Ash, by the fact that she must be constantly on the move to find work and to escape sexual exploitation.

The socioeconomic perspective of 'The Dorsetshire Labourer' finds its way into *Tess* both as the framework for her tragedy (part of the cause) and as a repetition of it. When Tess finds herself in the Valley of the Great Dairies, for instance, the socioeconomic discourse of the 'fall' of the land is put in evolutionary terms – the *geological* transfor-mation of the land:

> The river had stolen from the higher tracts and brought in parti-cles to the vale all this horizontal land; and now, exhausted, aged, and attenuated, lay serpentining along through the midst of its former spoils (*Tess*, p. 159).

> Thus they all worked on, encompassed by the vast flat mead which extended to either slope of the valley – a level landscape compounded of other landscapes long forgotten, and, no doubt, differing in character very greatly from the landscape they com-posed now. (*Tess*, p. 163).

The river has caused the land to fall from its higher tracts by attrition, so that it is now horizontal, yet it is still compounded of old landscapes long forgotten, differing in character from its past state but still made up of the same material. Tess's family have fallen, have reformed into a different 'landscape' but the family trait and trace are still present, haunting the fate of its descendants. Tess's personal history too has rendered her 'fallen' (also brought down by the attrition of the snake-like Alec), so that she differs in character from the 'innocent' Tess of the opening chapters, yet is still materially the same. Although her personal history will never be forgotten, she, like the land, is in a continual state of flux and transformation.

The alignment of Tess's defacement with the defacement of the land reaches its most stark and explicit expression in the passage which describes Tess working the fields at Flintcomb Ash:

> Each leaf of the vegetable having been consumed, the whole field was in colour a desolate drab; it was a complexion without features, as if a face, from chin to brow, should be only an expanse of skin. The sky wore, in another colour, the same likeness; a white vacuity of countenance with the features gone. So these upper and nether visages confronted each other all day long, the white face looking down at the brown face, without anything standing between them but the two girls crawling over the surface of the former like flies. (*Tess*, p. 360)

Tess, too, has been forced to remove her features, to become a white/drab vacuity of countenance as close to anonymity as is possible. The field has been over-consumed; this has stripped it of its vitality and colour. Likewise Tess has been over-consumed, worn away by work, over-consumption, so that she is left featureless, drab and undistinguished. Tess's violation is repeated, too, in the violation of the land by the reaping machine, and Alec's lust for Tess is figured in the 'insatiable swallower . . . the buzzing red glutton' (the threshing machine) which Tess must 'feed': 'the tyrant that the women had come to serve'.

If rural depopulation is a repetition of Tess's tragedy, it is also enacted in the movement from field to town (depopulation) which is signalled by her change in name from Durbeyfield to d'Urberville. The text first presents Tess in a rural ceremony celebrating fertility and closes with her urban 'prostitution' and urban execution. This is the framework and movement of her decline. She is forced into the town as a result of the eviction of her family, which is itself described as a kind of moral censorship, in its turn connected with Tess's 'fall':

> Ever since the occurrence of the event which had cast such a shadow over Tess's life, the Durbeyfield family (whose descent was not credited) had been tacitly looked on as one which would have to go when their lease ended, if only in the interests of morality. It was, indeed, quite true that the household had not been shining examples either of temperance, soberness or chastity. The father, and even the mother, had got drunk at times, the younger children seldom had gone to church, and the eldest daughter had made queer unions. By some means the village *had to be kept pure*. (*Tess*, p. 436)

Thus the family are expelled – *dis-membered* as members of a community, in the interests of moral purity. Tess and her family's eviction, their censorship, is the means by which the village is to be kept pure.[48] Tess stands at the point of intersection for a series of fatalities in the novel and her story repeats the fall of the d'Urbervilles, the fall of the land and the defacement of an older rural tradition and finally the fate of Hardy's defaced and violated novel which had been censored in the name of 'moral purity'.

### THE UNSPEAKABLE

Tess disappears from the text in agreeing to become Alec's mistress once again. We lose her temporarily until Angel's return to reclaim her back into the text, but dis-embodied, dis-figured, she cannot return. The body that we see cashmere-wrapped and embroidered is not hers, but she does possess a voice, a voice which has *not* been bought by Alec. Her voice hard, her eyes shining unnaturally, she silences Angel ('he could not get on') and tells him to keep away. Tess disappears again, upstairs to Alec and the following scene is absent from the novel, present only in the fragmented words heard by an eavesdropping landlady:

> All that she could at first distinguish of them was one syllable, continually repeated in a low note of moaning, as if it came from a soul bound to some Ixonian wheel –

O – O – O!

Then a silence, then a heavy sigh, and again –

O – O – O!

. . . It was from her lips that came the murmur of unspeakable despair . . . a tone which was a soliloquy rather than an exclamation, and a dirge rather than a soliloquy. (*Tess*, p. 469)

Tess's voice wails its admonishing incantation/dirge. The fragment of reported speech carries the rhythm of music or poetry:

And he is dying – he looks as if he is dying! . . . And my sin will kill him and not kill me! . . . O, you have torn all my life to pieces, . . . made me what I prayed you in pity not to make me again! . . . My own husband will never, never – O God – I can't bear this! – I cannot! (*Tess*, pp. 469–70)

Her life has been torn to pieces and her words are similarly torn, becoming instead a dirge and a *tone*. The words are fragmented, the tone is fluid. Tess's articulation exists between the words, in the unsaid between one word and the next, outside figuration. Her despair is 'unspeakable': that is, it cannot be appropriated by the text, and Mrs Brooks, the voyeuristic agent of the text, cannot 'catch' the words. The fluid tone falls ominously silent, only to be picked up again by the sound of dripping, flowing blood. Earlier Mrs Brooks had noticed that:

The back room was now in silence; but from the drawing room there came sounds . . . one syllable . . . a low note of moaning . . . O – O – O! . . . (*Tess*, p. 468)

Then comes silence until:

She listened. The dead silence within was broken only by a regular beat.

Drip, drip, drip. (*Tess*, p. 471)

The triple 'O' (of Tess's incantation) is converted into the triple 'drip' of Alec's blood which breaks the 'dead silence'. The 'O' (instead of 'Oh') is also a signal of Tess's final encirclement – the circle – and a sign signalling 'nothing' for there is nothing left for her now that Angel is gone (no one to pin her hopes on). The 'O', signalling her worth, is transformed, in the shedding of Alec's blood, to the sign of the Ace of Hearts on the ceiling of the lodging house: the Ace means the *'one'* of cards or dice. She has moved in this act from the zero point (the 'O') to the point of the single unit (the 'one' of the Ace); in the act of murder she has become 'one' again. Tess 'penetrates' Alec with a *knife* and sheds his blood: a sexual role reversal whereby Alec is 'deflowered' which remembers her own violation. It is *his* blood on the sheets and on the ceiling. In the act of violation Alec had traced a coarse pattern upon Tess. Here, figuratively, she traces the Ace of Hearts upon him: her trump-card. Her act purifies her in recovering, through revenge, her lost virginity; a ceremonial act accompanied by the dirge of her incantation, a reversal of the cathartic expulsions enacted upon women in *Dracula* and *She*.

Tess's textual silence (and her sexual passivity) is broken at the point where she 'penetrates' and kills Alec. Earlier she had silenced and paralysed him with her gaze and here she silences him by murdering him with *her voice* as her 'fluid' incantation is translated into the flowing of Alec's blood (it seeps through bed-clothes, bed and ceiling: 'a lot of blood has run down upon the floor'). As there is so much for a woman who has been persistently silenced to articulate, her words, translated into Alec's blood, are boundless. Alec is 'pale, fixed, dead'. Tess has 'fixed' Alec, repeating in this action his fixing of her in the role of fallen woman and courtesan.

I have already stressed Tess's determination (historical, textual, economic and biological) and her impossible attempts to resist such determination. Throughout the novel Tess is hounded and hunted by the aggressive attention of men, by words, labels, by the text, by the authorial voice and by the authorial gaze. Her inevitable appropriation can only be postponed by refusing to tell her story (her reluctance to confess to Angel), by disfiguring and defacing herself (removing the signs for which she will be selected as the appropriated object of aggressive attention), but the threat of appropriation will always be present. Appropriation in the novel is signalled by an encircling motif as she feels her past sorrows as 'gloomy spectres . . . waiting like wolves just outside the circumscribing light', for she knows that 'in the background those shapes of darkness were always spread', waiting 'to touch her' (*Tess*, p. 260) and she can only postpone the moral witch-hunt which demands the sacrifice of her blood as a testament to the moral purity of those who would censor her.

## INSIDE THE STONE CIRCLE

Tess's moral censorship becomes a material reality in the moment of her final encirclement at Stonehenge. The setting is appropriate: a temple of public sacrifice. In an article in *The Times* of October 1908 (a significant year in terms of the debate about censorship), Hardy writes about the history of Maumbury Ring, which had been the site for the execution of a young woman in 1706. The woman, compelled to marry against her will by her parents, had, like Tess, murdered her husband, although the evidence against her was slight. Hardy writes:

> The present writer has examined more than once a report of her trial and can find no distinct evidence that the thoughtless, pleasure-loving creature committed the crime while it contains much to suggest that she did not . . . .
> She conducted her own defence with the greatest ability, and was complimented thereupon by Judge Price, who tried her, but did not extend his compliment to a merciful summing-up. Maybe that he, like Pontius Pilate, was influenced by the desire of the townsfolk to wreak vengeance on somebody right or wrong.[49]

The stress in this passage on the young woman's execution as public sacrifice in the manner of the crucifixion, is important for the context of Tess's execution. This young woman's execution satisfies a public need, a public need for moral censorship, and a need for a sacrificial scapegoat in the search for moral purity. Hardy does not choose Maumbury Ring as the site for Tess's encirclement and capture, but a site with yet clearer sacrificial resonances: Stonehenge, another circle of prehistoric stones.

In an interview with Edmund Blunden Hardy is recorded as saying:

> having decided that she must die, I went purposely to Stonehenge to study the spot. It was a glooming, lowering day, and the skies almost seemed to touch the pillars of that great heathen temple.[50]

Hardy, as high priest, goes to inspect the site of the sacrifice, a site which, as Angel tells Tess, is 'older than the centuries; older than the d'Urbervilles', and as such it evokes a heathen, pagan past before history, before record and figuration. The historical long-view that Hardy gives to this episode repeats Tess's historical figuration for she finds her 'home' amongst all the heathen Others of history who have been sacrificed to satisfy a need for moral purity.

Tess must be removed (censored) as murderess, as sexually illicit object of desire (and as text). She falls asleep upon her pagan altar at night and in the darkness which renders her invisible she is protected from the public gaze which hunts her down. The powerful resignation of her voice echoes out of darkness. Angel has warned her that by daylight the place is visible for miles around, and significantly it is with the rise of the sun and with the return of Tess's visibility that Tess's final reselection takes place. The point of view is of crucial importance here for we remain with Tess and Angel *inside* the stone circle, waiting inside the stone circle, for this is where the authorial presence watches the sleeping Tess and bears witness to her fate. As the night wind dies out and the sun rises in the East,

> something seemed to move on the verge of the dip eastwards – a mere dot. It was the head of a man approaching them from the hollow beyond the Sun-stone . . . . The figure came straight towards the circle of pillars in which they were . . . . Turning, he saw over the prostrate columns another figure; then before he was aware, another was at hand on the right, under a trilithon, and another on the left. The dawn shone full on the front of the man westward, and Clare could discern that he was tall, and walked as if trained. They all closed in with evident purpose . . . .
>
> When they saw where she lay, which they had not done till then, they showed no objection, and stood watching her as still as the pillars around. (*Tess*, p. 486)

Lucy Westenra, the sexualised woman, the 'murderess' (vampire) had been ceremoniously surrounded by the band of men whose duty it had been to stake the illicit sexuality within her, to censor her and to reduce her to pure, dead womanhood. More importantly, Dracula – the great symbol of illicit, anarchic sexuality, had been surrounded and staked by the same band of encircling vampire-hunters, policing the boundaries of moral purity. Our position, as observers, in *Dracula* is with the vampire-hunters. We have travelled with them, hunted with them. Our perspective in the final encirclement of Dracula is, of course, outside the circle watching it converge upon the illicit hunted and censored object (both Lucy and Dracula).

In Hardy's *Tess* the perspective has been reversed. We have moved inside the circle of illicit sexuality and illicit morality (we can also add illicit textuality) and we perceive the wolves of moral censure closing in on *us* with evident purpose.

## 'THE DOLL OF ENGLISH FICTION MUST BE DEMOLISHED'

In describing the process whereby a young woman is forced to deface herself, to become anonymous to insure herself against 'aggressive admiration', and finally to sever self from body in prostituting herself, Hardy remembers the process of mutilation he was forced to suffer upon his own text. Tess dissolves under her own self-defacement (enforced both by her desire to escape from the judgements of others and from her self-judgements) and under the persistent masculine readings of her – her discursive overdetermination. Tess's multiple and dismembered selves violate the unity of character demanded by the nineteenth-century novel[51] yet Hardy's text does not just subvert 'character' as a stable construct, but interrogates the social, sexual and economic processes and discursive practices themselves which construct and dissolve human individuals.

The questioning of unified character construction implicit in *Tess*, needs itself to be seen in terms of Hardy's experimentation with form explored by Penny Boumelha in her fine book, *Thomas Hardy and Women: Sexual Ideology and Narrative Form.*[52] Boumelha argues that the 'liberation of experiment' of the New Fiction, in the last two decades of the nineteenth century, resulted in a profusion of alternative fictional forms: short stories, fantasies, dream stories, essay fiction and impressionistic sketches which constituted a displacement of the 'leisurely and particularised realist narrative'.[53] The New Fiction, she argues, was characterised by an increasing disruption of the circumscribing narrative *voice* – other kinds of voice emerge which throw into question the distance between author and character and unsettle the poise of the distanced, objective narrator. Boumelha concludes that whilst Hardy had experimented with genre and narrative voice from the beginning of his writing career, the practices of many of the lesser-known New Fiction writers 'contextualised' and gave a significant 'contemporaneity' to his experiments. The narrative disjunctions of *Tess*, she argues, mark Hardy's increasing interrogation of his own modes of narration . . . .

The disjunctions in narrative voice, the contradictions of logic, the abrupt shifts of point of view . . . disintegrate the stability of character as a cohering force, they threaten the dominance of the dispassionate and omniscient narrator and so push to its limit the androgynous narrative mode that seeks to represent and explain the woman from within and without.[54]

John Goode, too, argues not dissimilarly that the narrative disjunctions of *Tess* need to be seen as 'properties of the ideological discourses the text articulates'.[55] Other critics, however, have been less confident in Hardy's authorial control: Laura Claridge, for example, argues that the author 'seemed unable to decide what should constitute the norms for ethical sexual conduct'.[56] Bernard Paris has offered a reading of the novel's disunities as 'a confusion of many standards' arising from Hardy's treatment of nature versus convention[57] and Patricia Stubbs proposes that Hardy's moral iconoclasm, his attempt to test the boundaries of Victorian moral absolutes, is undermined by his inability to escape essentially archetypal patterns of character and feeling.[58]

It is notably after the revisions of *Tess* that Hardy wrote to Massingham of his growing conviction that 'the doll of English fiction must be demolished' and *Tess* had already begun this demolition process in its reconstruction of the absent trial of Tess for Tess's character is interrogated so ruthlessly under cross-examination that she begins to diminish under the contradictory judgements of her offered to explain her behaviour (from Angel, Alec and by Hardy himself, her advocate): 'you have torn all my life to pieces'. The novel's 'contradictions', shifting uneasily between readings of Tess as victim and as fatally degenerate sexual being, enact a shifting of positions, a partial movement away from the powerful polarities of sexual typing. It was a shifting of positions towards unanswerable disjunctions that would cause a controversy still reverberating today, a controversy which Hardy addressed in his Preface of 1891:

So densely is the world populated that any shifting of positions, even the best warranted advance, galls somebody's kibe. Such shiftings often begin in sentiment, and such sentiment often begins in the novel.

While Hardy 'shows some awareness of the shaping or constraining force of language upon apprehension'[59] in his presentation of Tess's attempts to escape the moral judgements inscribed endlessly upon her, he is perhaps in the end unable to escape the ideologies of purity built into the very language he was deploying to defend her. From the moment that he appended that dangerous and defiant subtitle – 'pure' – he became caught up in a trial of moral purity from which there was no escape while he argued a case 'whose terms were dictated by the conventional moralists themselves'.[60] This was a trial in which he was himself both defendant (like Tess accused of moral impurity) and defence counsel hopelessly caught up in a language of moral purity beyond his control.

In breaking down the censorious circumscribing discourses of his text, Hardy enacts a breaking-down of the censorious circumscription of *his censored novel*: his own experience of moral censorship. The writing and rewriting of *Tess*, is, in part, a primary expression of that experience: 'I have had enough' states Tess as she approaches her execution and Hardy was himself to say some twenty years or so later, looking back on the controversy caused by his novel which was to trap him again among clamorous and judgemental voices: 'Melius fuerat non scribere'. This was Hardy's penultimate novel. The 'storm of words' which was to break around him after the publication of *Jude the Obscure* was, he said, to cure him of novel-writing altogether.

*Jude the Obscure* portrayed another woman, Sue Bridehead, trying to liberate herself from moral orthodoxy, yet bound by it and finally unable to escape its constraints in her tragic absorption of its false codes. Like *Tess* it suffered mutilation (bowdlerisation) and its publication excited a 'storm of words' a series of 'verdicts from the press' and from the members of the 'morals police' such as Mrs Oliphant who denounced his treatment of marriage in an article entitled 'The Anti-Marriage League' and the Bishop of Wakefield who burned the book in his disgust at its 'insolence and indecency'. But Hardy's decision to abandon fiction was perhaps as much due to his growing realisation of the limitations of language and fictional representation as due to his pain at the public scandal his novel incited. His title-page for this novel was branded with an epigraph which testified to this awareness: 'the letter killeth'.

# Afterwords

I make a point of using the *qualifiers* of sexual difference here to avoid the confusion man/masculine, woman/feminine: for there are some men who do not repress their femininity, some women who, more or less strongly, inscribe their masculinity. Difference is not distributed, of course, on the basis of socially determined 'sexes' . . . . We have to be careful not to lapse smugly or blindly into an essentialist ideological interpretation.[1]

The *femme fatale* does not disappear with the end of the nineteenth century, of course, nor is she a fictional type created solely by male authors during the late nineteenth century. George Egerton (Mary Chavelita Dunne) was one of many avant-garde women writers of this period who were creating new fictional costumes for womanhood, new types of women who challenged the old stereotypes and, like Hardy, exploring new modes of narration which heralded modernism. Egerton's gypsies, fallen women, amazons and witches, draw strongly on the *femme fatale* types of the late nineteenth century, but these are figures who celebrate their Otherness, their sexual difference, rather than challenge it. In 'A Cross Line' Egerton playfully satirises sexual typing in her description of the unnamed 'man with grey eyes' and his 'persistent study' of the 'female animal':

'If a fellow has had much experience of his fellow-man he may divide him into types, and, given a certain number of men and a certain number of circumstances, he is pretty safe on hitting on the line of action each type will strike; t'aint so with woman. You may always look out for the unexpected, she generally upsets a fellow's calculations and you are never safe in laying odds on her. Tell you what, old chappie, we may talk about superior intellect; but, if a woman wasn't handicapped by her affection, or need of it, the cleverest chap in Christendom would be just a bit of putty in her hands. I find them more fascinating as problems than anything going. Never let an opportunity slip by to get new data – never!'[2]

Yet the 'female animal' whom she studies in this short story celebrates her wild and unclassifiable Otherness and lapses into a biological essentialism to rival a Nietzsche or Strindberg:

200

'But few [men] have had the insight to find out the key to our seeming contradictions . . . . They have all overlooked the eternal wildness, the untamed primitive savage temperament that lurks in the mildest, best woman. Deep in through ages of convention this primeval trait burns, an untameable quality that may be concealed but is never eradicated by culture – the keynote of woman's witchcraft and woman's strength. But it is there, sure enough, and each woman is conscious of it in her truth-telling hours of quiet self-scrutiny – and each woman in God's wide world will deny it, and each woman who tells the truth and is not a liar about these things is untrue to her sex and abhorrent to man, for he has fashioned a model on imaginary lines, and he has said, 'so I would have you', and every woman is an unconscious liar, for so man loves her. And when a Strindberg or a Nietzche arises and peers into the recess of her nature and dissects her ruthlessly, the men shriek out louder than the women, because the truth is at all times unpalatable, and the gods they have set up are dear to them . . .'.[3]

The sermons and seances of spiritualism emerging in the late nineteenth century and peopled by figures such as Madame Blavatsky and Annie Besant emphasised, in Sandra Gilbert's words: 'the link between, on the one hand, the alternative historical and theological possibilities propounded by spiritualism and theosophy and, on the other hand, the possibility of disorderly female rule'.[4] Spiritualism, too, created an Other world, a new world colonised by and accessed by women, destabilising and disrupting 'reality', dramatising 'the fragility of the control the rational Western mind had supposedly achieved over a world which might at any moment uncannily assert itself'.[5] Egerton's witches and seers invert the classification of women as savage and unknowable Other by speaking from that imaginary zone, mocking the rational classification of science, yet nonetheless underpinning and maintaining the stereotypes of Otherness.

Lisa Tickner[6] has shown that in the images of the Suffrage Campaigns of the early twentieth century the suffragists presented their demand for enfranchisement as a besiegement from an excluded zone: Mrs Bull hammers on the door of Franchise Villa, a female figure of Justice standing at the door of the House of Commons asks 'I, surely, am not excluded?' (see Plate 8). Yet Tickner demonstrates through the *anti*-suffrage posters that demands for the vote evoked a variety of response amongst those that opposed suffrage and not least a sense of besiegement and a fear of what *else* woman might want if she were granted voting power. An anti-suffrage poster shows a militant suffragette (masculine, strident) shouting from her platform 'we don't know what we want but we'll 'ave it!'. The caption indicates her class origin and her unnaturally large hands signify her voracious and all-consuming demands. Another poster caricatures a group of 'old maid type' suffragettes at a meeting, their placards demanding not only 'Votes for Women' and 'Down with Man' but also 'Husbands for Old Maids' (see Plate 9). The stereotypes confirmed in this poster are significantly informed by criminal anthropology: the speaker in particular has the prominent jaw, teeth, elongated arms and posture of the degenerate and atavistic female as described and documented by Lombroso and Ferrero in *The Female Offender*.[7] In another anti-suffrage poster the demand for the vote is articulated by a caricature of the Suffragette as degenerate hag. She is presented full-face like the female criminals photographed and classified in *The Female Offender* and bears the 'stigmata' of atavistic degeneracy identified in the works of the criminal anthropologists: negroid features (the flat nose, the full lips) reinforced by cross-eyes, a small forehead (and therefore a small cranium). But the focus is on the huge mouth and the three vampiric enlarged and pointed teeth (see Plate 9). It is this mouth that expresses the sense of horror and potential degeneration of the species evoked for some by the idea of extending the franchise to women. This caricature attests to the historical specificity of Otherness: the suffragette is imagined as invader of the franchise, evil and degenerate, bearing criminological and physiological stigmata which identify her as racial outsider, criminal and lunatic, but also the Darwinistic ancestor, the ape.

## PERSONAL DIMENSIONS

Although I acknowledge that '"I" today is perhaps more problematical than it has ever been',[8] nonetheless I have been conscious always of the 'personal dimensions' of this critical project; aware, too, of a writing-out, an expulsion. The following account is no self-portrait and, like all autobiographical accounts, is a self-fiction, but one which has been a meta-narrative in this book. It is a story, an attempt to 'inventory the traces'[9] upon me of making Other as well as being made Other.

I grew up as a member of the last generation of my family to have been called 'Plymouth Brethren',[10] a sect which withdraws from the world as God's chosen people, a withdrawal which, it is believed, ensures protection from the corrupt 'worldliness' of all that lies beyond the safe confines of the 'community'. As children (there were five of us) we were shielded vigilantly from the dangerous emissions of television sets, newspapers and radios and shielded, too, from other children of our own age with whom we came into contact at school whose friendship could corrupt our 'spiritual life'. Especially so as we were the children of a Brethen preacher and the grandchildren of another. Books, too, were carefully screened and there were rituals of book-burning (none that I can remember actually witnessing) that haunted us as children and which increased my own fetishisation of literature. My experience was not unique: for many children growing up in the late twentieth century, including my own son, the world outside the known is understood as a threatening place stalked by mythically monstrous men ('kidnappers' and 'abusers' who are, of course, not confined to the spaces outside the home). But we were told that our community, our haven of spiritual purity, was under constant besiegement from the wickedness and evil of the outside world. We children were, of course, fascinated by this place – this Otherness – perpetually seeking glimpses of it through television sets in shop windows, eavesdropping on the conversations of our school companions who offered us the possibility of alternative ways of living, other fictions. We believed, too, that the 'Rapture' could come at any day: Christ would return in the night and take his people out of iniquity into light and glory. He would discriminate, leaving behind husbands, children, wives, friends who were not 'in faith', leaving us to an apocalyspe-ravaged world.

Then a scandal split the movement and brought my parents 'out', taking us with them through the mirror into the outside world. Most, if not all, of the constraints upon us were lifted, yet for some time I lived in secret fear of worldly contamination and divine punishment. Suddenly, however, those whom we had known 'inside' were termed the 'Jims' (after their leader, Jim Taylor Jr) and represented all that was spiritually fallacious. To them we were fallen, unreclaimable, there would never be (and will never be) a return across the boundary line. My occupation of this outside space has always been ambiguous and my understanding of Otherness tempered by my childhood realisation that I inhabited the spiritual purity of the Brethren community as a secret interloper. Travelling into the outside world did not make me feel less of an interloper or any more 'at home': my Otherness and that of the 'world' is traced upon me indelibly.

There was another story that I was told in my teenage years – a story which was offered to me as an example of the dangerous exclusivity of the Brethren we had abandoned. A man, known to my parents, was deemed to be, for whatever reason, spiritually 'un-healthy' and he suffered the Brethren punishment of being 'shut out' of the community. Confined to his room for an indefinite period, visited only by the spiritual elders as physicians who examined his 'faith' and forbade him any contact with his wife and daughters who occupied the same house, he lost his reason. One nightmare of a day, in a last-ditch attempt to save himself and his family from contami-nation by whatever he had been told possessed him, he took an axe and killed them all, then hanged himself.

In 1974 a Polish refugee took a room in a boarding-house in London. Some time later he was found dead in his room. Bringing with him the superstitions of his heritage and alienated from the Western traditions around him, he enacted a nightly ritual of great complexity in which he sealed the doors and windows of his room with garlic, then sealed his own body by 'plugging' the orifices of his body with cloves of garlic. He choked one night and died, a victim of his Otherness, of his cultural alienation. The inquest recorded a verdict of 'accidental death'.

The AIDS campaigns, too, have been enshrouded with the dis-courses of Otherness as Susan Sontag has shown in her recent book, *AIDS and Its Metaphors*.[11] The disease has been understood, she ar-gues, through a range of metaphors of threat and apocalypse: the disease is imagined always as a foreign 'plague' invading national boundaries, spreading as a moral judgement, a 'model of all the catastrophes privileged populations feel await them'.[12] Sontag's study attests to 'the seductiveness of metaphorical thinking' and she makes the point that it is lack of understanding and primitive fears that provide 'a large-scale occasion for the metaphorizing of illness'.[13] Sontag proposes that the lack of knowledge and understanding of this new disease result in it becoming metaphorically an alien and invading Other (always coming from somewhere else):

> there is a link between imagining disease and imagining foreign-
> ness. It lies perhaps in the very concept of the wrong, which is
> archaically identical with the non-us, the alien. A polluting per-

son is always wrong . . . . The reverse is also true: a person judged to be wrong is regarded as, at least potentially, a source of pollution.[14]


## OUT OF THE STONE CIRCLES OF THE BINARY OPPOSITION

Is it possible to release ourselves from the need to make Other, or to experience difference as Other when our thinking is encoded in the binary oppositions of Western cultures?

I end with an assembly of critical voices:

### Hélène Cixous
Always the same metaphor: we follow it, it carries us, beneath all its figures, wherever discourse is organised. If we read or speak, the same thread or double braid is leading us throughout literature, philosophy, criticism, centuries of representation and reflection. Thought has always worked through opposition.[15]

### Stephen Heath
'Masculine' and 'feminine' – 'male' and 'female' too, in as much as they appear in the same way – are concepts we need to learn to refuse.[16]

### Susan Sontag
But the metaphors cannot be distanced, just by abstaining from them. They have to be exposed, criticised, belaboured, used up.[17]

### Nelly Furman
Although it may be impossible, in the end, to escape the hegemony of patriarchal structures – none the less, by unveiling the prejudices at work in our cultural artefacts, we impugn the universality of man-made models provided to us, and allow for the possibility of side-stepping and subverting their power.[18]

### Terry Eagleton
Woman is not just other in the sense of something beyond his ken, but an other intimately related to him as the image of what he is not, and therefore as an essential reminder of what he is. Man therefore needs this other even as he spurns it, is constrained to give a positive

identity to what he regards as no-thing. Not only is his own being parasitically dependent upon the woman, and upon the act of excluding and subordinating her, but one reason why such exclusion is necessary is because she may not be quite so other after all. Perhaps she stands as a sign of something in man himself which he needs to repress, expel beyond his own being, relegate to a securely alien region beyond his own definitive limits. Perhaps what is outside is also somehow inside, what is alien also intimate – so that man needs to police the absolute frontier between the two realms as vigilantly as he does just because it may always be transgressed, has always been transgressed already, and is much less absolute than it appears .... Such metaphysical thinking, as I have said, cannot be eluded: we cannot catapult ourselves beyond this binary habit of thought into an ultra-metaphysical realm. But by a certain way of operating on texts – whether 'literary' or 'philosophical' – we may begin to unravel these oppositions a little, demonstrate how one term of an antithesis secretly inheres within the other.[19]

### Catherine Clément

The hysteric, metaphor of the petite bougeoisie, is a prisoner; the sorceress, metaphor of the people, is a prisoner. And neither one has liberating powers other than the ability to reread the past, other than mystical effectiveness *now*. Now, they no longer exist. Physically they are no more, neither sorceress nor hysteric; and if someone dresses up as one it is an impersonation. They are old and worn-out figures, awakened only to throw off their shackles. I have dearly loved them but they no longer exist.

Of the mystical bisexuality that gets man immortality which is a far cry from being born of woman, let us keep the bird's wings. Let's keep – it's the same thing – the witch's broom, her taking off, her being swept away, her taking flight. Rather than toward incompatible syntheses and imaginary transitions, let us go toward real transitions and compatible syntheses, a status that is not contradictory. Rather than looking at the spectacle of attacks, let us turn this look, this look that isn't ours, elsewhere, and let it see. Let it see both what it was looking at before and us.[20]

### Frantz Fanon

Come, then comrades; it would be as well to decide at once to change our ways. We must shake off the heavy darkness in which we were plunged, and leave it behind ....

We must leave our dreams and abandon our old beliefs and friendships of the time before life began. Let us waste no time in sterile litanies and nauseating mimicry . . . .

Europe undertook the leadership of the world with ardour, cynicism and violence. Look at how the shadow of her palaces stretched out ever farther! Every one of her movements has burst the bounds of space and thought.

. . . we must find something different. We today can do everything, so long as we do not imitate Europe, so long as we are not obsessed by the desire to catch up with Europe . . . .

It is a question of the Third World starting a new history of Man, a history which will have regard to the sometimes prodigious theses which Europe has put forward, but which will also not forget Europe's crimes, of which the most horrible was committed in the heart of man, and consisted of the pathological tearing apart of his functions and the crumbling away of his unity . . . .

So, comrades, let us not pay tribute to Europe by creating states, institutions and societies which draw their inspiration from her. Humanity is waiting for something other from us than such an imitation, which would be almost an obscene caricature . . . .

For Europe, for ourselves and for humanity, comrades, we must turn over a new leaf, we must work out new concepts, and try to set afoot a new man.[21]

### Hélène Cixous

For me ideology is a kind of vast membrane enveloping everything. We have to know that this skin exists even if it encloses us like a net or like closed eyelids. We have to know that, to change the world, we must constantly try to scratch and tear it. We can never rip the whole thing off, but we must never let it stick or stop being suspicious of it. It grows back and you start again.[22]

### Edward Said

If this book has any future use, it will be as a modest contribution to that challenge, and as a warning: that systems of thought like Orientalism, discourses of power, ideological fictions – mind-forg'd manacles – are all too easily made, applied and guarded. Above all, I hope to have shown my reader that the answer to Orientalism is not Occidentalism . . . . If the knowledge of Orientalism has any meaning, it is in being a reminder of the seductive degradation of knowledge, of any time. Now perhaps more than before.[23]

**Catherine Clément** 'Her laugh keeps a wide gash bleeding in the man's breast.'[24]

**Hélène Cixous** All you have to do to see the Medusa is look her in the face: and she isn't deadly. She is beautiful and she laughs.[25]

# Notes

**Preface**

1. Stephen Heath, *The Sexual Fix* (London: Macmillan, 1982), p. 3.
2. Mrs Lynn Linton, 'The Wild Women as Social Insurgents', *The Nineteenth Century*, 30 (1891), 596–605. This essay is valuable in its representation of what Linton calls the 'wild woman' as both *femme fatale* and New Woman.
3. Mario Praz, *The Romantic Agony* trans. Angus Davidson (The World Publishing Company, Meridian Books, 1956).
4. Ibid., p. 191.
5. Michel Foucault, *The History of Sexuality*, Vol. 1, trans. Robert Hurley (Harmondsworth: Peregrine Books, rpt 1984), p. xii.
6. Ibid., p. 33.
7. Ibid., p. 93.
8. Lynda Nead, *Myths of Sexuality: Representations of Women in Victorian Britain* (Oxford: Blackwell, 1988).
9. Ibid., p. 5.
10. Raymond Williams, *The Long Revolution* (London: Chatto & Windus, 1961), p. 47.
11. Edward Said, *Orientalism* (London: Routledge & Kegan Paul, 1978), p. 21.
12. Roland Barthes, 'The Death of the Author', from *Image/Music/Text*, trans. Stephen Heath (Glasgow: Fontana/Collins, 1977), p. 147.
13. Henrik Ibsen, *Ghosts* in *Ghosts and Two Other Plays* (London and Toronto: J. M. Dent and Sons and New York: E. P. Dutton, 1911, rpt 1926), p. 106.
14. Nelly Furman, 'The Politics of Language: Beyond the Gender Principle', from *Making a Difference: Feminist Literary Criticism*, eds Gayle Green and Coppelia Kahn, New Accents Series (London and New York: Methuen, 1985), p. 64.
15. Gayatri Chakravorty Spivak, 'Feminism and Cultural Theory', in *In Other Worlds: Essays in Cultural Politics* (London and New York: Methuen, 1987), p. 84.
16. Gayatri Chakravorty Spivak, 'Explanation and Culture: Marginalia', in *In Other Worlds: Essays in Cultural Politics* (New York and London: Methuen, 1987), p. 114.
17. Karl Jaspers, from *Psychopathologie Generale*, quoted in Frantz Fanon, *Black Skin, White Masks*, trans. Charles Lam Markmann (London: Paladin, 1970; rpt 1972), pp. 119–20.

**1 Historical Perspectives**

1. Ronald Robinson and John Gallagher, *Africa and the Victorians: The Official Mind of Imperialism* (London: Macmillan and New York: St. Martin's Press, 1961) and 'The Imperialism of Free Trade', *Economic History Review*, 2nd ser., vi (1953), 1–15.

2. Frank Kermode, *The Sense of an Ending: Studies in the Theory of Fiction* (London, Oxford, New York: Oxford University Press, 1966, rpt 1979).
3. Ibid., p. 97.
4. Ibid., p. 96.
5. Ibid., p. 96–7.
6. Ibid., p. 98.
7. Ibid., p. 101.
8. Ronald Robinson and John Gallagher, 'The Imperialism of Free Trade', *Economic History Review*, 2nd ser., vi (1953), 1–15.
9. Heinz Gollwitzer, *Europe in the Age of Imperialism, 1880–1914*, trans. David Adam and Stanley Baron (London: Thames & Hudson, 1969, rpt 1979), p. 54.
10. Disraeli's Crystal Palace Speech of 1872, quoted in Martin Green, *Dreams of Adventure, Deeds of Empire* (London: Routledge & Kegan Paul, 1980), p. 4.
11. For a lucid account of the problems inherent in Robinson and Gallagher's methodology in *Africa and the Victorians* – that of prioritising the 'official mind' or the higher stages of the decision-making process of imperialist policy – see Paul Kennedy, 'Continuity and Discontinuity in British Imperialism 1815–1914' in C. C. Eldridge (ed.), *British Imperialism in the Nineteenth Century*, Problems in Focus Series (London: Macmillan, 1984), pp. 35–6.
12. Ronald Robinson and John Gallagher, *Africa and the Victorians: The Official Mind of Imperialism* (London: Macmillan and New York: St. Martin's Press, 1961).
13. Paul Kennedy, 'Continuity and Discontinuity in British Imperialism 1815–1914', in C. C. Eldridge (ed.), *British Imperialism in the Nineteenth Century* Problems in Focus Series (London: Macmillan, 1984), p. 34.
14. Robinson and Gallagher, op. cit., p. 470.
15. Martin Green, *Dreams of Adventure, Deeds of Empire* (London: Routledge & Kegan Paul, 1980), p. 234.
16. Patrick Brantlinger, *Rule of Darkness: British Literature and Imperialism, 1830–1914* (Ithaca and London: Cornell University Press, 1988), p. 230.
17. Brantlinger, ibid., p. 253.
18. Kennedy, op. cit., p. 37–8.
19. See M. E. Chamberlain's discussion of this issue in 'Imperialism and Social Reform' in C. C. Eldridge (ed.), *British Imperialism in the Nineteenth Century*, Problems in Focus Series (London: Macmillan, 1984), pp. 148–67.
20. See Sturgis's assessment of historical research in this field in James Sturgis, 'Britain and the New Imperialism, C. C. Eldridge (ed.), *British Imperialism in the Nineteenth Century*, Problems in Focus Series (London: Macmillan, 1984), pp. 85–105.
21. Paul Kennedy, 'Continuity and Discontinuity in British Imperialism 1815–1914', in C. C. Eldridge (ed.), *British Imperialism in the Nineteenth Century*, Problems in Focus Series (London: Macmillan, 1984), p. 32.
22. Martin J. Weiner, *English Culture and the Decline of the Industrial Spirit 1850–1980* (Cambridge: Cambridge University Press, 1981), p. 56.
23. John M. Mackenzie, *Propaganda and Empire: the Manipulation of British Public Opinion 1880–1960* (Manchester: Manchester University Press, 1984), p. 45.

24. Patrick Brantlinger, *Rule of Darkness: British Literature and Imperialism, 1830–1914* (Ithaca and London: Cornell University Press, 1988), p. 35.

25. Ronald Robinson and John Gallagher, *Africa and the Victorians: The Official Mind of Imperialism* (London: Macmillan and New York: St. Martin's Press, 1961), p. 161.

26. Ibid., p. 10.

27. Ibid., pp. 71–2.

28. Ibid., p. 120.

29. Ibid., p. 288.

30. James Sturgis, 'Britain and the New Imperialism, C. C. Eldridge (ed.), *British Imperialism in the Nineteenth Century*, Problems in Focus Series (London: Macmillan, 1984), p. 96.

31. John M. Mackenzie, *Propaganda and Empire: the Manipulation of British Public Opinion 1880–1960* (Manchester: Manchester University Press, 1984).

32. See Anna Davin, 'Imperialism and Motherhood', *History Workshop*, 5 (1978), 9–65.

33. Mackenzie, op. cit., p. 204.

34. Lucy Bland, 'The Married Woman, the "New Woman" and the Feminist: Sexual Politics of the 1890s', in *Equal or Different: Women's Politics 1800–1914*, ed. Jane Rendall (Oxford: Blackwell, 1987), pp. 114–64.

35. Ibid., p. 151.

36. Patricia Stubbs, *Women and Fiction: Feminism and the Novel 1880–1920* (London: Methuen, 1981), p. 53.

37. Ibid., p. 55.

38. Ibid., p. 56.

39. Ibid., p. 57.

40. Ibid., p. 57.

41. Ibid., p. 133.

42. Jeffrey Weeks, *Sex, Politics and Society: The Regulation of Sexuality Since 1800* (London: Longman, 1981), p. 92.

43. Stubbs, op. cit., p. 138.

44. J. E. Chamberlin, 'An Anatomy of Cultural Melancholy', *Journal of the History of Ideas*, XLII (1981), 4, p. 691.

45. Rev. Dunbar Heath, 'Anniversary Address', *Journal of the Anthropological Society*, 6 (1868), lxxxvii, quoted in Patrick Brantlinger, *Rule of Darkness: British Literature and Imperialism, 1830–1914* (Ithaca and London: Cornell University Press, 1988), p. 167.

46. James Sturgis, 'Britain and the New Imperialism, in C. C. Eldridge (ed.), *British Imperialism in the Nineteenth Century*, Problems in Focus Series (London: Macmillan, 1984), p. 102.

47. Sturgis, loc. cit.

48. Christine Bolt, 'Race and the Victorians' in C. C. Eldridge (ed.), *British Imperialism in the Nineteenth Century*, Problems in Focus Series (London: Macmillan, 1984), p. 127.

49. Ibid., p. 131.

50. Patrick Brantlinger, *Rule of Darkness: British Literature and Imperialism, 1830–1914* (Ithaca and London: Cornell University Press, 1988), p. 33.

51. J. E. Chamberlin, op. cit., p. 694.

52. W. Greenslade, 'The Concept of Degeneration, 1880–1910' (unpublished doctoral thesis, University of Warwick, 1982).

53. J. E. Chamberlin, 'An Anatomy of Cultural Melancholy', *Journal of the History of Ideas*, XLII (1981), 4, p. 693.
54. E. R. Lankester, *Degeneration: A Chapter in Darwinism* (London: 1880)
55. Quoted in Jenny Bourne Taylor, *In the Secret Theatre of Home: Wilkie Collins, Sensation Narrative and Nineteenth-Century Psychology* (London: Routledge, 1988), p. 67.
56. E. R. Lankester, *Degeneration: A Chapter in Darwinism* (London: 1880), p. 60.
57. Max Nordau, *Degeneration* (first English translation, London: Heinemann, 1895).
58. Penny Boumelha, *Thomas Hardy and Women: Sexual Ideology and Narrative Form* (Brighton: Harvester Press, 1982, rpt 1984), p. 22.
59. Patricia Stubbs, *Women and Fiction: Feminism and the Novel 1880–1920* (London: Methuen, 1981), p. 138.
60. Patrick Brantlinger, *Rule of Darkness: British Literature and Imperialism, 1830–1914* (Ithaca and London: Cornell University Press, 1988), p. 233.
61. Samuel Hynes, *The Edwardian Turn of Mind* (London: Oxford University Press; Princeton: Princeton University Press, 1968).
62. Ibid., p. 34.
63. Brantlinger, op. cit., p. 229.
64. Brantlinger, op. cit., p. 235.
65. Heinz Gollwitzer, *Europe in the Age of Imperialism, 1880–1914*, trans. David Adam and Stanley Baron (London: Thames & Hudson, 1967, rpt 1979), p. 177.
66. Ibid., p. 175.
67. Ibid., p. 176.
68. Paul Kennedy, 'Continuity and Discontinuity in British Imperialism 1815–1914' in C. C. Eldridge (ed.), *British Imperialism in the Nineteenth Century*, Problems in Focus Series (London: Macmillan, 1984), p. 33.
69. J. E. Chamberlin, 'An Anatomy of Cultural Melancholy', *Journal of the History of Ideas*, XLII (1981), 4, p. 691.
70. Ibid., p. 693.
71. Edward Said, *Orientalism* (London: Routledge & Kegan Paul, 1978), p. 207.
72. See Sander L. Gilman, 'Black Bodies, White Bodies: Toward an Iconography of Female Sexuality in Late Nineteenth-Century Art, Medicine and Literature', *Critical Inquiry* Vol. 12 (Autumn 1985), pp. 204–42.
73. See Cynthia Eagle Russett, *Sexual Science: The Victorian Construction of Womanhood* (London and Cambridge, Massachusetts: Harvard University Press, 1989).
74. Joanna de Groot, '"Sex" and "Race": The Construction of Language and Image in the Nineteenth Century', from *Sexuality and Subordination*, ed. Susan Mendus and Jane Rendall (London and New York: Routledge & Kegan Paul, 1989), pp. 89–130.
75. Michel Foucault, *The History of Sexuality*, Vol. 1, trans. Robert Hurley (Harmondsworth: Peregrine Books, rpt 1984), p. 37.
76. Stephen Heath, *The Sexual Fix* (London: Macmillan, 1982).
77. Quoted in Heath, op. cit., p. 7.
78. Ibid., p. 11.

79. Foucault, op. cit., p. 122.
80. Foucault, loc. cit.
81. Gillian Beer, 'Origins and Oblivion in Victorian Narrative' in *Sex, Politics and Science in the Nineteenth-Century Novel*, Selected Papers of the English Institute 1983–84, ed. Ruth Bernard Yeazell (London: Johns Hopkins University Press, 1986), p. 73.
82. Edward Said, *Orientalism* (London: Routledge & Kegan Paul, 1978), p. 8.
83. Ibid., p. 21.
84. Ibid., p. 87.
85. Ronald Robinson and John Gallagher, *Africa and the Victorians: The Official Mind of Imperialism* (London: Macmillan and New York: St. Martin's Press, 1961), p. 472.
86. Patrick Brantlinger, *Rule of Darkness: British Literature and Imperialism, 1830–1914* (Ithaca and London; Cornell University Press, 1988), p. 44.
87. Ibid., p. 234.
88. Said, op. cit., pp. 219–20.
89. Lynda Nead, *Myths of Sexuality: Representations of Women in Victorian Britain* (Oxford: Blackwell, 1975), p. 94.
90. Christine Bolt, 'Race and the Victorians' in C. C. Eldridge (ed.), *British Imperialism in the Nineteenth Century*, Problems in Focus Series (London: Macmillan, 1984), p. 139.

## 2 Theoretical Perspectives

1. Catherine Clément, 'The Guilty One', in Catherine Clément and Hélène Cixous, *The Newly Born Woman*, trans. Betsy Wing, introd. Sandra M. Gilbert, Theory and History of Literature Series, Vol. 24 (Manchester: Manchester University Press, 1986), p. 6.
2. See Sander L. Gilman's, 'What are Stereotypes and Why Use Texts to Study Them?', in Sander L. Gilman, *Difference and Pathology: Stereotypes of Sexuality, Race and Madness* (Ithaca and London: Cornell University Press, 1985), pp. 15–35.
3. Ann Rosalind Jones, 'Inscribing Femininity: French Theories of the Feminine', in *Making a Difference: Feminist Literary Criticism*, eds Gayle Green and Coppelia Kahn, New Accents Series (London and New York: Methuen, 1985), pp. 80–112.
4. Simone de Beauvoir, *The Second Sex*, trans. H. M. Parshley (1949; rpt Harmondsworth: Penguin Books, 1972).
5. Ibid., p. 16.
6. Loc. cit.
7. Ibid., p. 175.
8. Edward Said, *Orientalism* (London and Henley: Routledge & Kegan Paul, 1978), p. 227.
9. Ibid., p. 228.
10. Frantz Fanon, *Black Skin, White Masks*, trans. Charles Lam Markmann (London: Paladin, 1970, rpt 1972), p. 134.
11. Patrick Brantlinger, *Rule of Darkness: British Literature and Imperialism, 1830–1914* (Ithaca and London: Cornell University Press, 1988), p. 179.
12. Frantz Fanon, *The Wretched of the Earth* (Harmondsworth: Penguin, 1967), p. 32.

13. Sander L. Gilman, *Difference and Pathology: Stereotypes of Sexuality, Race and Madness* (Ithaca and London: Cornell University Press, 1985), p. 24.

14. Frantz Fanon, *Black Skin, White Masks*, trans. Charles Lam Markmann (London: Paladin, 1970, rpt 1972), p. 125.

15. Edward Said, *Orientalism* (London: Routledge & Kegan Paul, 1978), p. 190.

16. Joanna de Groot, '"Sex" and "Race": The Construction of Language and Image in the Nineteenth Century', from *Sexuality and Subordination*, eds Susan Mendus and Jane Rendall (London and New York: Routledge & Kegan Paul, 1989), p. 105.

17. Ibid., p. 106.

18. Ibid., p. 89.

19. Loc. cit.

20. C. G. Jung, 'In Memory of Sigmund Freud', in *Collected Works of C. G. Jung*, Vol. XIII (London: Routledge & Kegan Paul, 1966), p. 48.

21. De Groot, op. cit., pp. 92–3.

22. Hélène Cixous, 'Sorties' in Hélène Cixous and Catherine Clément, *The Newly Born Woman* trans. Betsy Wing, introd. Sandra M. Gilbert, Theory and History of Literature Series, Vol. 24 (Manchester: Manchester University Press, 1986), p. 67.

23. Toril Moi, *Sexual/Textual Politics*, New Accents Series (London: Methuen, 1985; reprinted London and New York: Routledge, 1988), p. 167.

24. Max Nordau, *Degeneration* (London: Heinemann, 1895), p. 6.

25. Rosemary Jackson, *Fantasy: The Literature of Subversion*, New Accents Series (London and New York: Methuen, 1981), pp. 121–2.

26. Ibid., p. 23.

27. Frederic Jameson, 'Magical Narratives: Romance as a Genre', *New Literary History*, Vol. 7 (1975), pp. 135–63, repeated in a revised form in *Political Unconscious: Narrative as a Socially Symbolic Act* (London: Methuen, 1981), p. 115.

28. Ibid., p. 140.

29. Frantz Fanon, *Black Skin, White Masks*, trans. Charles Lam Markmann (London: Paladin, 1970, rpt 1972), p. 135.

30. Ibid., p. 33.

31. Edward Said, *Orientalism* (London: Routledge & Kegan Paul, 1978), p. 67.

32. Joanna de Groot, '"Sex" and "Race": The Construction of Language and Image in the Nineteenth Century' from *Sexuality and Subordination*, eds Susan Mendus and Jane Rendall (London and New York: Routledge & Kegan Paul, 1989), pp. 99–100.

33. Ibid., p. 100.

34. Frederic Jameson, *Political Unconscious: Narrative as a Socially Symbolic Act* (Ithaca: Cornell University Press, 1981).

35. Ibid., p. 114.

36. Stephen Heath, *The Sexual Fix* (London: Macmillan, 1982), p. 90.

37. Quoted in Patrick Brantlinger, *Rule of Darkness: British Literature and Imperialism, 1830–1914* (Ithaca and London: Cornell University Press, 1988), p. 194.

38. Loc. cit.

39. General William Booth, *In Darkest England and the Way Out* (London: International Headquarters of the Salvation Army, 1890).
40. Ibid., p. 24.
41. Ibid., pp. 11–12.
42. Lynda Nead, *Myths of Sexuality: Representations of Women in Victorian Britain* (Oxford: Blackwell, 1975), p. 110.
43. General William Booth, op. cit., pp. 13–14.
44. Nead, op. cit., p. 106.
45. Nead, op. cit., p. 113.
46. Toril Moi, *Sexual/Textual Politics*, New Accents Series (London: Methuen, 1985; rpt London and New York: Routledge, 1988), p. 167.
47. Lynda Nead, *Myths of Sexuality: Representations of Women in Victorian Britain* (Oxford: Blackwell, 1975), p. 8.
48. Michel Foucault, *The History of Sexuality*, Vol. 1, trans. Robert Hurley (Harmondsworth: Peregrine Books, rpt 1984).
49. Catherine Clément, 'The Guilty One' in Hélène Cixous and Catherine Clément, *The Newly Born Woman*, trans. Betsy Wing, introd. Sandra M. Gilbert, Theory and History of Literature Series, Vol. 24 (Manchester: Manchester University Press, 1986), p. 14.
50. Ibid., p. 15.
51. Patrick Brantlinger, *Rule of Darkness: British Literature and Imperialism, 1830–1914* (Ithaca and London: Cornell University Press, 1988), p. 179.
52. Stephen Heath, *The Sexual Fix* (London: Macmillan, 1982), p. 120–1.

**3 Dracula: A Social Purity Crusade**

1. G. F. C. Wall, '"Different From Writing": *Dracula* in 1897', *Literature and History*, Vol. 10, no. 1 (Spring 1984), p. 15.
2. Samuel Hynes, *The Edwardian Turn of Mind* (London: Oxford University Press, 1968), p. 34.
3. H. G. Wells, *The War of the Worlds*, 1897; rpt in *Seven Science Fiction Novels* (New York: Dover, n.d.).
4. Ibid., p. 408.
5. Bram Stoker, *Dracula* (first published 1897, reprinted in The World's Classics Series, Oxford: Oxford University Press, 1986), p. 214. All further references will be to this edition and will be incorporated into the text. I have indicated from which account each reference comes, except where this is already evident from the commentary.
6. Joseph Conrad, *Heart of Darkness*, A Norton Critical edition, ed. Robert Kimbrough (New York and London: W. W. Norton & Company, 1988, third edition), p. 13.
7. See Rachel Bowlby's analysis of the etymological roots of 'consumer' and 'consumption' in 'Promoting Dorian Gray', *Colonialism and Other Essays*, *The Oxford Literary Review*, Vol. 9 (1987), p. 153.
8. The Earl of Dunraven, 'The Invasion of the Destitute Aliens', *The Nineteenth Century*, Vol. 31 (June 1892), p. 986.
9. See Charles Blinderman's analysis of transubstantiation and Darwinism in 'Vampurella: Darwin and Count Dracula', *Massachussetts Review*, 21 (1980), 411–28.

10. See *Dracula*, Harker's journal, p. 40.
11. David Seed, 'The Narrative Method of *Dracula'*, *Nineteenth Century Fiction*, Vol. 40 (1985–86), pp. 61–75.
12. Seed, op. cit.
13. See Seward's justification for this group decision in *Dracula*, Seward's diary, p. 256.
14. See Mina Harker's journal, pp. 374–5.
15. Van Helsing refuses to ask the maids for a blood transfusion for Lucy, and explains: 'I fear to trust these women . . .' (*Dracula*; Seward's diary, p. 148).
16. Christopher Craft, '"Kiss Me With Those Red Lips": Gender and Inversion in Bram Stoker's *Dracula'*, *Representations*, Vol. 8 (1984), pp. 123–4.
17. Bram Stoker, 'The Censorship of Fiction', *The Nineteenth Century*, Vol. 64 (September 1908), pp. 477–87. Page references will be given in the text.
18. Censorship became a legal issue after 1857 with the passing of the Obscene Publications Act. Lord Justice Cockburn had provided the legal definition of obscenity in 1868 as that which tended to 'deprave and corrupt those whose minds are *open* to such immoral influences' (emphasis mine). As a result of this Act, and other legislation, the last decades of the nineteenth century saw a series of censorship trials. During all such trials, the Government and the magistrates themselves were under pressure from the National Vigilance Association, formed in 1885 to provide unofficial censorship of literature. The Lord Chamberlain had absolute power over the production of plays. Certain productions could be and were refused a license without explanation, and without power of appeal.
19. The Derby Corporation Act of 1901 had a clause number 171 which stated:

    No person shall return to any Lending Library any book which has been to his knowledge exposed to infection from any infectious disease, but shall at once give notice that it has been exposed to infection to the Medical Officer of Health or to the Inspector of Nuisances, who shall cause the same to be disinfected and then returned to the Librarian. If any person offends against this enactment he shall be liable to a penalty not exceeding forty shillings.

    This warning seems to have been included as a 'special Notice' slipped inside each book in the Lending Library.
20. Geographical frontiers were perceived as having an important role in the censorship issue: French naturalistic fiction and especially Zola were considered to be immoral 'invaders' of British culture as exemplified in the Vizetelly trial for publishing the works of Zola in England. Such works had to be 'kept out' to ensure social and moral purity.
21. See Susan Sontag, *AIDS and its Metaphors* (Penguin, 1989) for her analysis of the apocalyptic fears evoked by the spread of AIDS at the end of our millennium.
22. Stoker is presumably alluding to the writers of New Woman fiction here such as Sarah Grand, Mona Caird and others who were dealing

with controversial subjects such as venereal disease, non-consensual marital sex and the double standard in their fiction.

23. David Punter, *The Literature of Terror* (London: Longman, 1980), p. 259.
24. Ibid., p. 262.
25. Bram Stoker, *The Lair of the White Worm* (1911; rpt Target, London: W. H. Allen, 1986).
26. Stoker gives an interesting account of his first encounter with Sir Henry Irving who was to become his lifelong friend and employer. In this description Stoker experiences a kind of delirium which he later reads as 'hysteria'. See Daniel Farson, *The Man Who Wrote Dracula: A Biography of Bram Stoker* (London: Michael Joseph, 1975), p. 28.
27. Michel Foucault, *The History of Sexuality*, 3 vols (Harmondsworth: Peregrine Books, 1984), pp. 32–3. All further reference to *The History of Sexuality* will be to Volume 1.
28. Loc. cit.
29. This is Foucault's terms which he uses in describing the deployment of confession:

> The motivations and effects it is expected to produce have varied, as have the forms it has taken: interrogations, consultations, autobiographical narratives, letters; they have been recorded, transcribed, assembled into dossiers, published and commented on (*The History of Sexuality*, p. 63).

30. Sheridan Le Fanu, *Carmilla*, reprinted in *Novels of Mystery From The Victorian Age*, introd. by Maurice Richardson (London: Pilot Press, 1945).
31. James B. Twitchell, *The Living Dead: A Study of the Vampire in Romantic Literature* (Durham, North Carolina: Duke University Press, 1949), p. 12.
32. See Corbeck in *The Jewel of the Seven Stars* first published 1912, (reprinted in The Ullerscoft Large Print Series, London: Jarrold's Publishers, n.d.). Like Van Helsing, Corbeck is a jack-of-all-trades with doctorates in law, surgery, science, languages and Egyptology and, like Van Helsing, he speeds up the process of discovery by insisting on collaboration of knowledge. See also Sir Nathaniel de Salis in *The Lair of the White Worm* who remains almost entirely the still centre of the text, working from his study through his team of investigators. Sir Nathaniel's 'special knowledge is of the peak and its caverns'. He is devoted to history, is a local geologist and a natural historian (hence although not a medical man he is a scientist). He functions as the perfect analyst: 'Sir Nathaniel's voice was soft and soothing, nothing of contradiction or overdone curiosity in it – a tone eminently suited to win confidence' (Stoker, *The Lair*, p. 32).
33. Van Helsing is a particular type of scientist, one who might perhaps have been a member of the Society for Psychical Research, set up in London in 1882 and in America in 1885. Nevertheless Van Helsing is evidently a 'modern' and 'unconventional' scientist and a medical man specialising in the treatment of unknown diseases. Sexology, criminology, craniology were similarly 'new' sciences and there are many similarities between Van Helsing and the 'new' scientists, particularly in

their interest in the female body (hysteria, female sexuality, sensitivity to the paranormal). See also Showalter's reading of Van Helsing as a medical 'quack' specialising in the treatment of an unnameable disease (syphilis). See Elaine Showalter, 'Syphilis, Sexuality and the Fiction of the Fin-de-Siècle' in *Sex, Politics and Science in the Nineteenth-Century Novel*, Selected Papers of the English Institute (1983–84), ed. Ruth Bernard Yeazell (Baltimore: Johns Hopkins University Press, 1986), 88–115.

34. Foucault, *The History of Sexuality*, p. 21.
35. Cited in Stephen Marcus, *The Other Victorians* (London: Weidenfeld & Nicolson, 1966), p. 161.
36. Cited in Marcus, ibid., p. 163.
37. See Phillis A. Roth, 'Suddenly Sexual Women in Bram Stoker's *Dracula*', *Literature and Psychology*, Vol. 27 (1977), pp. 113–21 and Carol A. Senf, '*Dracula*: the Unseen Face in the Mirror', *Journal of Narrative Technique*, Vol. 9 (1979), pp. 160–70.
38. Almost half of *Dracula* takes place in a lunatic asylum. Several characters are emotionally unstable: Renfield is a madman; Harker suffers mental breakdown; Lucy shows signs of schizophrenia. Even Seward, a specialist in the treatment of the insane, voices doubts about the group's sanity.
39. Christopher Craft, '"Kiss Me With Those Red Lips": Gender and Inversion in Bram Stoker's *Dracula*', *Representations*, Vol. 8 (1984), pp. 107–33.
40. Foucault, *The History of Sexuality*, p. 72.
41. See Stephen Marcus, *The Other Victorians* (London: Weidenfeld & Nicolson, 1966).
42. See Lombroso and Ferrero's study of the atavism of prostitutes in *The Female Offender* (London: T. Fisher Unwin, 1985).
43. See Josef Breuer and Sigmund Freud, *Studies in Hysteria*, trans. James and Alix Strachey, ed. Angela Richards, Pelican Freud Library, Vol. 3 (Harmondsworth: Penguin, 1974).
44. Richard von Krafft-Ebbing, *Psychopathia Sexualis*, trans. Franklin S. Klaf (rev. edn New York: Bell Publishing Co., 1965).
45. Cesare Lombroso and William Ferrero, *The Female Offender*, introd. W. Douglas Morrison (London: T. Fisher Unwin, 1895), p. 296.
46. See Linda Dowling, 'The Decadent and the New Woman in the 1890s', *Nineteenth Century Fiction*, Vol. 33 (1979), pp. 434–53.
47. Mrs Lynn Linton, 'The Wild Women as Social Insurgents', *The Nineteenth Century*, Vol. 30 (October 1891), p. 603.
48. Lucy Bland, 'The New Woman, the Married Woman and the Feminist: Sexual Politics of the 1890s', in *Equal or Different*, ed. Jane Rendall (Oxford: Blackwell, 1987), pp. 141–64.
49. While I am using some of the discourses of Darwinism and related sciences in this chapter, a larger analysis of the impact of evolutionary theory on late-nineteenth century culture and literature has not been possible. My interest is not so much in the more 'scientific' discoveries of evolutionary theory but in the aspects of this new science which were assimilated into the cultural imagination and which, when adopted by certain writings concerned with the nature of 'woman', justified forms of violence and misogyny.

50. See the Introduction to this book and Jenny Bourne Taylor, *In the Secret Theatre of Home: Wilkie Collins, Sensation Narrative and Nineteenth-Century Psychology* (London: Routledge, 1988) for an analysis of the shaping of a discourse of degeneration in the late nineteenth century. Also W. Greenslade, 'The Concept of Degeneration 1880–1910', Unpublished Doctoral Dissertation, University of Warwick, 1982.

51. David Punter, *The Literature of Terror* (London: Longman, 1980), pp. 234–64.

52. C. S. Blinderman, 'Vampurella: Darwin and Count Dracula', *Massachussetts Review*, Vol. 21 (1980), pp. 411–28.

53. Herbert Spencer, *First Principles* (1862; 6th edn New York: D. Appleton and Co., 1901).

54. Carl Vogt, *Lectures on Man: His Place in Creation and in the History of the Earth*, ed. James Hunt (London: Longman and Green, 1864), p. 8.

55. Ibid., p. 180.

56. Charles Darwin, *The Descent of Man* (1871; 2nd edn, London, 1874), p. 635.

57. Cesare Lombroso and William Ferrero, *The Female Offender*, introd. by W. Douglas Morrison (New York: Appleton, 1899), p. 151.

58. Leonard Woolf, *Annotated Dracula* (New York: Mayflower Books, 1979), p. 300. Stoker was certainly no stranger to the medical profession: three of his four brothers were doctors and one was knighted for his services to the medical science. In addition to Stoker's demonstration of familiarity with the work of Nordau and Lombroso, he makes reference in *Dracula* to Burdon-Sanderson's physiology, Ferrier's brain-knowledge and Charcot's hypnotism. Such specific signals in Stoker's text demonstrate Stoker's familiarity with the science of craniology – the field of Cesare Lombroso. Lombroso's ideas were popularised by Max Nordau's *Degeneration*, translated into English in 1895, two years before the publication of *Dracula*. Nordau would have diagnosed Dracula as an egomaniac, a degenerate type identifiable by an obsession with a fixed idea ('he confines himself to one purpose').

59. See the prevalence of fin-de-siècle images of such women in Bram Dijkstra, *Idols of Perversity: Fantasies of Feminine Evil in Fin-de-Siècle Culture* (New York: Oxford University Press, 1986).

60. Auguste Forel, *The Sexual Question: A Scientific, Psychological, Hygienic and Sociological Study*, 1906, revised edn, trans. C. F. Marshall (New York: Physicians and Surgeons Book Co, 1925), p. 137.

61. The circulation of blood is as follows: Dracula attacks Lucy; her blood is lost and must be replaced; Van Helsing, Arthur, Morris and Seward transfuse their blood into Lucy, enough to make them weak and debilitated; Dracula drains Lucy again, thus acquiring the blood of these four men as well as that of Lucy; finally the last description of blood-sucking we have in the novel is that of Mina sucking Dracula's blood, which contains Lucy's blood and that of the four men. Mina is the last to be seen receiving blood and as such *she* is the final receptacle of all the blood-exchanges of the novel.

62 Christopher Craft suggests another version of the child's genesis which, though suggestive, misses the important textual detail of *Mina* being

the last receptacle of the blood: 'we may say that little Quincey was luridly conceived in the veins of Lucy Westenra and then deftly relocated to the purer body of Mina Harker'. Christopher Craft, '"Kiss Me With Those Red Lips": Gender and Inversion in Bram Stoker's *Dracula*', *Representations*, Vol. 8 (1974), p. 129.

63. Ernest Jones, *On the Nightmare* (London: Hogarth Press, 1949), p. 110, cited in C. F. Bentley, 'The Monster in the Bedroom: Sexual Symbolism in Bram Stoker's *Dracula*', *Literature and Psychology*, Vol. 22 (1972), pp. 27–34.

64. Bentley, ibid.

65. For an analysis of the late nineteenth-century application of an economic principle to sex, see Stephen Marcus, *The Other Victorians* (London: Weidenfeld & Nicolson, 1966) and Stephen Heath, *The Sexual Fix* (London: Macmillan, 1982), pp. 14–18.

66. Peter Gay, *Education of the Senses*, Vol. 1: *The Bourgeois Experience: Victoria to Freud* (Oxford: Oxford University Press, 1984), p. 310.

67. (Nicholas Cooke), *Satan in Society*, 1870 (by 'A Physician'), (rev. edn. Cincinnati: C. F. Vent, 1876), p. 111.

68. Bernard S. Talmey, *Woman: A Treatise on the Normal and Pathological Emotions of Feminine Love* (1904: 6th enl. and rev. edn, New York: Practitioners Publishing Co., 1910).

69. Cesare Lombroso and William Ferrero, *The Female Offender*, introd. W. Douglas Morrison (New York: Appleton, 1899), p. 153.

70. Catherine Clément, 'The Guilty One', in Hélène Cixous and Catherine Clément, *The Newly Born Woman*, trans. Betsy Wing, introduced by Sandra M. Gilbert, Theory and History of Literature Series, Vol. 24 (Manchester: Manchester University Press, 1986), p. 15.

## 4  Rider Haggard's Black Widow

1 Joseph Conrad, *Heart of Darkness* (1899), reprinted in Norton Critical Editions, ed. Robert Kimborough (3rd edn, New York and London: W. W. Norton and Co., 1988), p. 60.

2. Quoted in Hugh Ridley, *Images of Imperial Rule* (London and Canberra: Croom Helm, 1983; New York: St. Martin's Press, 1983), p. 70 and taken from Paul Vigné Octon's *La Gloire du Sabre* (Paris, 1900).

3. Hélène Cixous, 'Sorties' in Hélène Cixous and Catherine Clément, *The Newly Born Woman*, trans. Betsy Wing, introduced by Sandra M. Gilbert, Theory and History of Literature Series, Vol. 24 (Manchester: Manchester University Press, 1986), p. 68.

4. Quoted in General William Booth, *In Darkest England and the Way Out* (London: International Headquarters of the Salvation Army, 1890), p. 9.

5. Philip Curtin, *The Image of Africa* (Madison: University of Wisconsin Press, 1964), p. 319.

6. See Morton Cohen, *Rider Haggard: His Life and Works* (London: Hutchinson, 1960).

7. Richard F. Patterson, '*King Solomon's Mines*: Imperialism and Narrative Structure', *Journal of Narrative Technique*, Vol. 8 (1978), p. 112. See in particular Patteson's account of the recurring plot motifs of this genre. See also Dorothy Hammond and Alta Jablow, *The Africa that Never Was: Four Centuries of British Writings about Africa* (New York, Twayne, 1970)

and Phiefer L. Browne, 'Men and Women, Africa and Civilisation: A Study of the African Stories of Hemingway and the African Novels of Haggard, Greene and Bellow', Unpublished Doctoral Dissertation, Rutgers University, 1979.

8. Lawrence Millman, 'Rider Haggard and the Male Novel, What is Pericles?, Beckett Gags' (Unpublished Doctoral Dissertation, Rutgers University, 1974). To be referred to as 'Rider Haggard and the Male Novel'.

9. H. Rider Haggard, *The Days of My Life*, ed. C. J. Longman, 2 vols (London: Longman, Greene and Co., 1926), Vol. 2, p. 77.

10. H. Rider Haggard, *She*, first published 1887, reprinted in *King Solomon's Mines, She, Allan Quatermain* (London: Octopus, 1979), p. 209. All further references will be given in the text.

11. Captain Richard F. Burton, *Personal Narratives of a Pilgrimage to Al-Madinah and Meccah*, 1855, 2 vols (New York: Dover, 1964), cited in Patrick Brantlinger, *Rule of Darkness: British Literature and Imperialism, 1830–1914* (Ithaca and London: Cornell University Press, 1988), p. 162. On the veil as a symbol of colonial penetration and the harem as a space violated by the colonisers in Algeria, see Malek Alloula, *The Colonial Harem* (Manchester: Manchester University Press, 1987).

12. Brantlinger, op. cit., p. 162.

13. H. Rider Haggard, *Jess* (London: Smith and Elder, 1887), p. 45.

14. H. Rider Haggard, *Ayesha or the Return of She*, first published in serialised form in *The Windsor Magazine* (London: Ward, Lock and Co., 1904–1905), reprinted in Rider Haggard, *The Classic Adventures: Ayesha: The Return of She and Benita: An African Romance* (Poole: New Orchard Editions, 1986). All further references will be to this edition and will be given in the text.

15. H. Rider Haggard, *King Solomon's Mines*, first published 1885, reprinted in *King Solomon's Mines, She, Allan Quatermain* (London: Octopus, 1979), p. 14. All further references will be to this edition.

16. See Anne McClintock's fascinating reading of Haggard's map of *King Solomon's Mines* in 'Maidens, Maps and Mines: *King Solomon's Mines* and the Reinvention of Patriarchy in Colonial South Africa' in *Women and Gender in Southern Africa to 1945*, ed. Cherryl Walker (Claremont, Southern Africa: David Philip Publishers; London: James Currey, 1990), pp. 97–124.

17. Peter Pierce, 'Rider Haggard' (Unpublished Doctoral Dissertion, Oxford University, 1975).

18. I will develop these notions of race-specific sexualities at a later point in this chapter. For recent studies of late nineteenth-century concepts of 'sex' and 'race' see Joanna de Groot, '"Sex" and "Race": The Construction of Language and Image in the Nineteenth Century', from *Sexuality and Subordination*, eds Susan Mendus and Jane Rendall (London and New York: Routledge & Kegan Paul, 1989), pp. 89–130 and Sander L. Gilman, 'Black Bodies, White Bodies: Toward an Iconography of Female Sexuality in Late Nineteenth-Century Art, Medicine and Literature', *Critical Inquiry*, Autumn 1985, pp. 204–42.

19. The text is sprinkled with warnings about penetrating the Unknown which fail to deter the heroes. Here in the underground treasure chamber they pass the petrified bodies of past rulers. There are other pre-

served victims to be found in this body which is Africa. Later, on the breasts themselves, they find the dead Silvestre, preserved in ice: a sad momento of the fate that so often overtakes those who would penetrate into the Unknown (Haggard, *King Solomon's Mines*, p. 64).

20. Graham Greene, *Journey Without Maps* (London: Pan Books, 1948), p. 14.
21. Margaret Atwood, *Survival: A Thematic Guide To Canadian Literature* (Toronto: Anansi Press, 1972), p. 113.
22. Patrick Brantlinger, *Rule of Darkness: British Literature and Imperialism, 1830–1914* (Ithaca and London: Cornell University Press, 1988), p. 194.
23. *Allan Quatermain*, the sequel to *King Solomon's Mines*, has a similar structure and seems to express similar fears about sexually transmitted diseases and devouring female sexuality. Here the adventurers are sucked into an underground tunnel. The rushing subterranean river carries them along for miles through the mountain. They are nearly burned to death as they are carried past the Rose of Fire – a flame shaped like an open flower. Next they are attacked by giant crabs(!): 'a screaming, foaming, stinking mass of monsters'. *Allan Quatermain* first published 1888, reprinted in *King Solomon's Mines, She, Allan Quatermain* (London: Octopus, 1979), p. 513. All further references will be to this edition.
24. Peter Pierce, 'Rider Haggard' (Unpublished Doctoral Dissertion, Oxford University, 1975), p. 23.
25. Steven Marcus gives a satirical account of the landscape of Victorian pornography in *The Other Victorians*. The passage could also be a description or summary of a Haggardian plot outlined above. Thus, the discourses of late nineteenth-century pornography, satirised here by Marcus, contain sublimated fantasies about the exploration and appropriation of a passive landscape which is the female body; imperialist fantasies also plot the movement across and into a foreign landscape which, it is hoped, will receive the penetrator without struggle. See Steven Marcus, *The Other Victorians* (London: Weidenfeld & Nicholson, 1966), pp. 271–2.
26. Phiefer L. Browne, 'Men and Women, Africa and Civilisation: A Study of the African Stories of Hemingway and the African Novels of Haggard, Green and Bellow' (Unpublished Doctoral Dissertation, Rutgers University, 1977), p. 35.
27. 'La Rose D'Amour' from *The Pearl: A Journal of Facetiae and Voluptuous Reading* (rpt Kent: New English Library, 1985), pp. 149–50.
28. Peter Pierce, 'Rider Haggard' (Unpublished Doctoral Dissertation, Oxford University, 1975).
29. See Samuel Hynes, *The Edwardian Turn of Mind* (London: Oxford University Press; Princeton, NJ: Princeton University Press, 1968).
30. See Hugh Ridley, *Images of Imperial Rule* (London and Canberra: Croom Helm, 1983; New York: St. Martin's Press, 1983), pp. 91–2 and Heinz Gollwitzer, *Europe in the Age of Imperialism, 1880–1914*, trans. David Adam and Stanley Baron (London: Thames & Hudson, 1969, rpt 1979), p. 175.
31. Quoted in Hugh Ridley, *Images of Imperial Rule* (London and Canberra, Croom Helm and New York, St. Martin's Press, 1983), p. 91.

32. Ronald Robinson and John Gallagher, *Africa and the Victorians: The Official Mind of Imperialism* (London: Macmillan and New York: St. Martin's Press, 1961).

33. Ibid., pp. 10–11.

34. Patrick Brantlinger, *Rule of Darkness: British Literature and Imperialism, 1830–1914* (Ithaca and London: Cornell University Press, 1988), p. 227.

35. Brian Street, *The Savage in Literature: Representations of 'Primitive' Society in English Fiction, 1858–1920* (London and Boston: Routledge & Kegan Paul, 1975).

36. Ibid., p. 47.

37. Ibid., p. 98.

38. Leo Henkin, *Darwinism in the English Novel, 1860–1910: The Impact of Evolution on Victorian Fiction* (New York: Russell & Russell, 1963), p. 9.

39. Alan Sandison, *The Wheel of Empire: A Study of the Imperial Idea in Some Late Nineteenth and Twentieth Century Fiction* (London: Macmillan, 1967). Sandison argues that of the four writers that he studies – Conrad, Buchan, Kipling and Haggard – Haggard is the writer most responsive to evolutionary theory.

40. Brian Street, *The Savage in Literature: Representations of 'Primitive' Society in English Fiction, 1858–1920* (London and Boston: Routledge & Kegan Paul, 1975).

41. Ibid., p. 41.

42. Leo Henkin, *Darwinism in the English Novel, 1860–1910: The Impact of Evolution on Victorian Fiction* (New York: Russell & Russell, 1963), p. 66.

43. H. Rider Haggard, *Allan Quatermain* first published in 1888, rpt in *King Solomon's Mines, She, Allan Quatermain* (London: Octopus, 1979). All further references will be given in the text.

44. Quoted in Patrick Brantlinger, *Rule of Darkness: British Literature and Imperialism, 1830–1914* (Ithaca and London: Cornell University Press, 1988), p. 230.

45. See Sander L. Gilman, 'Black Bodies, White Bodies: Towards an Iconography of Female Sexuality in Late Nineteenth Century Art, Medicine and Literature', *Critical Inquiry*, Autumn 1985, pp. 204–42 and Cynthia Eagle Russett, *Sexual Science: The Victorian Construction of Womanhood* (London and Cambridge, Massachusetts: Harvard University Press, 1989).

46. Cited in S. J. Gould, *The Mismeasure of Man* (New York and London: N. W. Norton, 1981), p. 86.

47. Cited in Gould, ibid., p. 124.

48. In *The Mismeasure of Man*, Gould demonstrates that the data used by such 'scientists' were consciously or unconsciously manipulated in order to find the results they wanted to find. Sometimes such mismeasurement could be unconscious, for, as Gould points out, 'expectation is a powerful guide to action', but it was also sometimes conscious: a few figures would be altered where results were found to be inconsistent. Gould's point is not that the science of craniology constituted a conscious fraud on the part of a small group of scientists, but that a science such as craniology, based as it was on highly dubious methods of collecting and measuring data, becomes charged with prejudices and expectations of all kinds.

49. Cesare Lombroso and William Ferrero, *The Female Officer* (London: T. Fisher Unwin, 1895).
50. See Gould, op. cit., p. 52.
51. The edition of *The Nineteenth Century* for 1887, the year of the publication of *She*, has a pair of articles debating higher education for women. Both employ evolutionary theory in their arguments: George J. Romanes, 'The Mental Differences between Men and Women' (May Issue, Vol. 21, pp. 654–72)) is answered in the September issue by Edith Simcox's 'The Capacity of Women' (Vol. 22, pp. 391–402).
52. See Leo Henkin, *Darwinism in the English Novel, 1860–1910: The Impact of Evolution on Victorian Fiction* (New York: Russell & Russell, 1963), p. 178.
53. Henkin cites two crucial novels: J. Compton Rickett's *The Quickening of Caliban* (1893) and J. Provand Webster's *The Oracle of Baal* (1896). See also 'Lucas Malet', *Colonel Enderby's Wife* (1885) in which the beautiful young wife of the ageing colonel is diagnosed as a kind of missing link.
54. H. Rider Haggard, *Allan's Wife* (1889) in *Allan's Wife with Hunter Quatermain's Story, A Tale of Three Lions and Long Odds* (London: Macdonald, 1951).
55. Norman Etherington, 'Rider Haggard, Imperialism and the Layered Personality', *Victorian Studies*, Vol. 22 (Autumn 1978), p. 80.
56. S. J. Gould, *The Mismeasure of Man* (New York and London: N. W. Norton, 1981), p. 40.
57. Cited in Gould, loc. cit.
58. See Gillian Beer's *Darwin's Plots: Evolutionary Narrative in Darwin, George Eliot and Nineteenth Century Fiction* (London, Boston and Henley: Routledge & Kegan Paul, 1983), p. 113.
59. Cited in Gould, op. cit., pp. 239–40, emphasis mine.
60. Cited in Lorna Duffin, 'Prisoners of Progress: Women and Evolution' in *The Nineteenth Century Woman: Her Cultural and Physical World*, ed. Delamont and Duffin (London: Croom Helm, 1978; New York: Barnes & Noble, 1978), p. 84.
61. Lawrence Millman, 'Rider Haggard and the Male Novel' (Unpublished Doctoral Dissertation, Rutgers University, 1974), p. 67.
62. See Henry Miller's reaction to this scene in Henry Miller, *The Books in My Life* (London: Peter Owen, 1952), pp. 92–4.
63. Millman, op. cit., p. 55.
64. Sandra Gilbert, 'Rider Haggard's Heart of Darkness', *Partisan Review*, Vol. 50 (1983), p. 448.
65. Ibid., p. 449.
66. Lawrence Millman, 'Rider Haggard and the Male Novel' (Unpublished Doctoral Dissertation, Rutgers University, 1974), p. iii.
67. Sandra Gilbert, op. cit., p. 445.

## 5 The Shadowy Embrace: Conrad

1. Joseph Conrad, *An Outcast of the Islands* (first published 1896, rpt Penguin Modern Classics, 1986). All further references will be to this edition, which will be abbreviated in the text to *An Outcast*.

2.  Joanna de Groot, '"Sex" and "Race": The Construction of Language and Image in the Nineteenth Century' from *Sexuality and Subordination*, eds Susan Mendus and Jane Rendall (London and New York: Routledge & Kegan Paul, 1989), p. 105.
3.  On the importance of deciphering the jungle in Conrad's work, see Ian Watt, *Conrad in the Nineteenth Century* (London: Chatto & Windus, 1980).
4.  Joseph Conrad, *Heart of Darkness* (1899), reprinted in Norton Critical Editions, ed. Robert Kimborough (3rd edn, New York and London: W. W. Norton, 1988), p. 20. All further references will be to this edition.
5.  Another death figure from Conrad's fiction of the 1890s is that of James Wait in *The Nigger of the 'Narcissus'*. Like the savage mistress he is 'calm, cool, towering, superb' and his contours dissolve into darkness as a black mist emanates from him as death itself. As Jimmy deteriorates he becomes more insubstantial: the dying black man dissolves back into darkness.
6.  Joseph Conrad, *Lord Jim* (1900; rpt Edinburgh and London: John Grant, 1925). All further references will be to this edition.
7   On literary impressionism see James Nagel, *Stephen Crane and Literary Impressionism* (University Park and London: The Pennsylvania State University Press, 1980, rpt 1983); for a response to Ian Watt's analysis of Conrad's 'delayed decoding' see Bruce Johnson, 'Conrad's Impressionism and Watt's Delayed Decoding' in *Conrad Revisited: Essays for the Eighties*, ed. Ross C. Murfin (Alabama: Alabama University Press, 1985), pp. 51–70.
8.  For 'delayed decoding' see Ian Watt, *Conrad in the Nineteenth Century* (London: Chatto & Windus, 1980).
9.  See Chinua Achebe's article 'An Image of Africa', *Research in African Literatures*, Vol. 9 (Spring 1978), pp. 1–15 and for a response to Achebe's accusations see Cedric Watts, 'A Bloody Racist: About Achebe's View of Conrad', *Yearbook of English Studies*, Vol. 13 (1983), pp. 196–209; Hunt Hawkins, 'The Issue of Racism in *Heart of Darkness*', *Conradiana*, Vol. 14:3 (1982), pp. 163–71 and Patrick Brantlinger in 'Epilogue: Kurtz's Darkness and Conrad's Heart of Darkness', in *Rule of Darkness: British Literature and Imperialism, 1830–1914* (Ithaca and London: Cornell University Press, 1988).
10. For an almost identical account of Conrad's own obsession with maps see Conrad, *A Personal Record* (London: J. M. Dent, 1945–1955), p. 13.
11. Joseph Conrad, 'Youth' in *Youth: A Narrative and Two Other Stories* (1902: rpt Edinburgh and London: William Blackwood and Sons, 1923). All further references will be to this edition.
12. Ian Watt, *Conrad in the Nineteenth Century* (London: Chatto & Windus, 1980).
13. A. R. Wallace, *The Malay Archipelago: The Land of the Orang-Utan and the Bird of Paradise: a Narrative of Travel with Studies of Man and Nature* (first published Macmillan 1869; rpt New York: Dover, 1962).
14. Joseph Conrad, 'Geography and Some Explorers', in *Last Essays* (London and Toronto: J. M. Dent and Sons, 1926).

15. B. C. Meyer, *Joseph Conrad: A Psychoanalytical Biography* (Princeton: Princeton University Press, 1967).

16. E. H. Visiak, *The Mirror of Conrad* (London: Werner Laurie, 1955), p. 69.

17. Joseph Conrad, *Almayer's Folly* (1895), (rpt Penguin Modern Classics, 1984). All further references will be to this edition and will be cited in the text.

18. Malek Alloula, *The Colonial Harem* (Manchester: Manchester University Press, 1987).

19. Hunt Hawkins makes a similar point in 'Conrad and the Psychology of Imperialism' in *Conrad Revisited: Essays for the Eighties*, ed. Ross C. Murfin (Alabama: Alabama University Press, 1985), pp. 71–5.

20. Joanna de Groot, '"Sex" and "Race": The Construction of Language and Image in the Nineteenth Century', from *Sexuality and Subordination*, eds Susan Mendus and Jane Rendall (London and New York: Routledge & Kegan Paul, 1989), p. 100, emphasis mine.

21. René Rapin (ed.), *Lettres de Joseph Conrad à Marguerite Poradowska* (Geneva: Droz, 1966), p. 166.

22. Ford Madox Ford, *Joseph Conrad: A Personal Remembrance* (London: Duckworth, 1924), p. 214.

23. See Terry Eagleton, *Literary Theory: An Introduction* (Oxford: Basil Blackwell, 1983), p. 128.

24. Martin Ray, 'The Gift of Tongues: The Languages of Joseph Conrad', *Con·adiana*, XV (1983), no. 2, 83–110.

25. George Jean-Aubry, *Joseph Conrad: Life and Letters*, 2 vols (London: Heinemann, 1927), Vol. 1, p. 183.

26. Georges Jean-Aubry, *Joseph Conrad: Life and Letters*, op. cit., Vol. 2, p. 125.

27. Georges Jean-Aubry, *Joseph Conrad; Life and Letters*, op. cit., Vol. 1, p. 183.

28. Conrad, we know, suffered from neurasthenia, a nervous energy which he believed to be a positive creative energy. He wrote to Wells in 1903: 'for me, writing – the only possible writing, is just simply the conversion of nervous forces into phrases . . . . When the nervous force is exhausted the phrases don't come.' Georges Jean-Aubry, *Joseph Conrad; Life and Letters*, op. cit., Vol. 1, p. 321.

29. Patrick Brantlinger, *Rule of Darkness: British Literature and Imperialism, 1830–1914* (Ithaca and London: Cornell University Press, 1988), p. 194.

30. A. R. Wallace, *The Malay Archipelago: The Land of the Orang-Utan and the Bird of Paradise: a Narrative of Travel with Studies of Man and Nature* (first published Macmillan 1869; rpt New York: Dover, 1962).

31. See Cesare Lombroso and William Ferrero, *The Female Offender* (London: T. Fisher Unwin, 1895).

32. Conrad's interest in Nina's choice between two cultures may have been influenced by the choice which he made shortly before writing this, his first novel: a choice between English and French as his artistic medium. He maintained in the Author's Note to *A Personal Record* that he was adopted by the English language: 'it was I who was adopted by the genius of the language, which . . . made me its own so completely that its very idioms I truly believe had a direct action on my temperament and fashioned my still plastic character.' Later in this Author's Note to

*A Personal Record* he reaffirms that English 'was for me neither a matter of choice nor adoption' (p. v) and that it should be regarded properly as 'a matter of discovery and not of inheritance' (p. vi). See Joseph Conrad, Author's Note to *A Personal Record* (London: J. M. Dent, 1949–55).

33. In 'An Outpost of Progress' (1898) Kayerts, marooned like Kurtz in Central Africa, describes his motivation for being there as an attempt to earn a dowry for 'his girl'. Like Kurtz, he is destroyed by Africa. See Joseph Conrad, 'An Outpost of Progress' from *Tales of Unrest* (first published 1898; reprinted in Penguin Modern Classics: Harmondsworth, Penguin, 1985), p. 87.

34. See Bruce Stark's careful analysis of the imagery of this final scene in 'Kurtz's Intended: The Heart of the *Heart of Darkness*', *Texas Studies in Literature and Language*, Vol. 16 (1974), pp. 535–5.

35. B. C. Meyer, *Joseph Conrad: A Psychoanalytical Biography* (Princeton: Princeton University Press, 1967), p. 329.

36. Joanna de Groot, '"Sex" and "Race": The Construction of Language and Image in the Nineteenth Century' from *Sexuality and Subordination*, eds Susan Mendus and Jane Rendall (London and New York: Routledge & Kegan Paul, 1989), p. 106.

37. Georges Jean-Aubry, *Joseph Conrad: Life and Letters*, 2 vols (London: Heinemann, 1927), Vol. 2, p. 83.

38. Joseph Conrad, *The Secret Agent* (first published 1907; rpt Penguin English Library, Harmondsworth: Penguin, 1985). All further references will be to this edition and will be given in the text.

39. Kenneth Inniss, in Conrad's Native Girl: Some Social Questions', *Pacific Coast Philology*, Vol. 5, p. 42, examines the 'dangerous tropical associations' of Conrad's representations of white heroines in *Victory* and 'A Smile of Fortune'. For an analysis of Conrad's portrayal of sensuous women, see also B. C. Meyer, *Joseph Conrad: A Psychoanalytical Biography* (Princeton: Princeton University Press, 1967), p. 109.

40. For the debate on Conrad's use of Lombroso and Nordau, see Robert G. Jacobs, 'Comrade Ossipon's Favourite Saint: Lombroso and Conrad', *Nineteenth Century Fiction*, Vol. 23 (1968–69), pp. 74–84; John Saveson, 'Conrad, Blackwood's and Lombroso', *Conradiana*, Vol. 6 (1974), pp. 57–62; and Martin Ray, 'Conrad, Nordau and Other Degenerates: The Psychology of *The Secret Agent*', *Conradiana*, Vol. 16 (1984), no. 2, pp. 125–41.

41. Allan Hunter, *Joseph Conrad and the Ethics of Darwinism* (London and Canberra: Croom Helm, 1983). See in particular p. 216.

42. Max Nordau, *Degeneration* (first English translation, London: Heinemann, 1895), p. 6.

43. Martin Ray, 'Conrad, Nordau and Other Degenerates: The Psychology of *The Secret Agent*, op. cit.

44. Max Nordau, *Degeneration*, op. cit., p. vii.

45. See, for instance, this description ('reading') of a French female murderess which is accompanied by a photograph of the woman so that the stigmata (facial features) can be read:

> No. 6, aged 36. Of a rich family, with an epileptic mother, and a father addicted to alcohol. She poisoned her husband with arsenic after sixteen years of married life. Nose hollowed out and club-shaped,

large jaws and ears, squint eyes, weak reflex action of left patella. She confessed nothing. Character resolute and devout. Type.

Cesar Lombroso and William Ferrero, *The Female Offender* (London: T. Fisher Unwin, 1899), pp. 90–1.

46. Georges Jean-Aubry, *Joseph Conrad; Life and Letters*, op. cit., Vol. 1, p. 321.)
47. Allan Hunter, op. cit., p. 58.
48. There was a feminist journal published in 1915 entitled *The Free Woman*.
49. Conrad's London underworld shares many of the qualities of primeval darkness which characterise his descriptions of the Otherworld of Africa or the Malayan jungle. By integrating these worlds he draws upon popular representations of London at the turn-of-the-century as the 'nether world' and as 'darkest London'. See Chapter 2.
50. Edward Garnett, *Letters from Joseph Conrad 1895–1924* (London: Nonesuch Press, 1928), p. 82.
51. Sander L. Gilman, 'Black Bodies, White Bodies: Toward an Iconography of Female Sexuality in Late Nineteenth-Century Art, Medicine and Literature', *Critical Inquiry*, Vol. 12 (Autumn 1985), pp. 204–42.
52. 'It was a charnel-house scene, a mass of tissue-fluids and blood, a shovelful of putrid flesh thrown there on the cushion. The pustules had invaded the entire face with the pocks touching each other; and *dissolving* and subsiding with the *greyish look of mud*, there seemed to be already an earthy mouldiness on the *shapeless* muscosity, in which the *features were no longer discernible* . . . . *Venus was decomposing*. It seems as though the virus she had absorbed from the gutters and from the tacitly permitted carrion of humanity, that baneful ferment with which she had poisoned a people, had now risen to her face and putrefied it.' (From Zola's *Nana*, cited in Gilman, 'Black Bodies, White Bodies', p. 235; emphasis mine.)
53. See Kenneth Inniss, 'Conrad's Native Girl: Some Social Questions', *Pacific Coast Philology*, 5, in which Inniss argues that Conrad's representations of native women work comfortably within the cultural Anglo-Saxon stereotypes, and portray a xenophobia complicated by puritanism and late nineteenth-century notions of lesser breeds (p. 44), in contrast to Ian Watt's view that Conrad exposes the internal contradictions of the dominant ideologies of the period. Ian Watt, *Conrad in the Nineteenth Century* (London: Chatto & Windus, 1980), p. 147.
54. Ian Watt, *Conrad in the Nineteenth Century* (London: Chatto & Windus, 1980), p. 147.
55. Georges Jean-Aubry, *Joseph Conrad: Life and Letters* (London: Heinemann, 1927), Vol. 2, p. 25.
56. Georges Jean-Aubry, *Joseph Conrad: Life and Letters*, Vol. 2, p. 125, emphasis mine.
57. Max Nordau, *Degeneration* (first English translation, London: Heinemann, 1895), p. 6.
58. E. Garnett, *Letters from Joseph Conrad, 1895–1924* (London: Nonesuch Press, 1928), p. 153.

## 6 'Something More To Be Said': Hardy's Tess

1. Patricia Stubbs, *Women and Fiction: Feminism and the Novel, 1880–1920* (London: Methuen, 1981), p. 82.
2. Thomas Hardy, *Tess of the d'Urbervilles*, first published in serial form in the *Graphic*, 1891. Because of the many layers and changes made to this text I will be working primarily from the 'definitive' Wessex Edition of 1912 reprinted in Penguin Classics (Harmondsworth: Penguin, rpt 1986), ed. David Skilton. Passages from earlier editions are from J. D. Laird, *The Shaping of Tess of the d'Urbervilles* (Oxford: Clarendon Press, 1975). All further references will be given in the text, abbreviated to *Tess* to draw attention to the parallel between the text (*Tess*) and the woman (Tess) which I will be expanding in this chapter.
3. For an account of the revisions of the text and the history of its production, see J. D. Laird, *The Shaping of Tess of the d'Urbervilles* (Oxford: Clarendon Press, 1975) and Mary Jacobus, 'Tess: The Making of a Pure Woman' from Susan Lipshitz (ed.), *Tearing the Veil: Essays on Femininity* (London, Henley, Boston: Routledge, 1978), pp. 77–92.
4. Tillotson's, a newspaper syndicate, rejected the novel and cancelled the contract in 1889. Hardy then submitted the manuscript to *Murray's Magazine* and to *Macmillan's Magazine*. Both editors – Edward Arnold and Mowbray Morris – rejected the novel, objecting to its 'frequent and detailed reference to immoral situations' and to the novel's 'succulence'. See Laird, op. cit., pp. 10–11.
5. Thomas Hardy, *The Life and Works of Thomas Hardy*, ed. Michael Millgate (London: Macmillan, 1984). I shall be working from this edition as the most recent and comprehensive edition of the text. All further references will be given in the body of the text and will be abbreviated to the *Life*. See the introduction to Millgate's edition for more information about the most recent research on Hardy's *Life* and the curious mixture of biography and autobiography within it. See also Robert Gittings, *Young Thomas Hardy* (Heinemann, 1975; rpt with revisions, Penguin, 1980), pp. 15–16.
6. See Hardy's Preface to *Jude the Obscure* and his article 'Candour in English Fiction' on censorship reprinted in Harold Orel (ed.), *Thomas Hardy: Personal Writings* (London and Melbourne: Macmillan, 1967). The *Life* chapter which describes the revision process of *Jude the Obscure* is entitled 'Another Novel Finished, Mutilated and Restored'.
7. J. D. Laird, *The Shaping of Tess of the d'Urbervilles* (Oxford: Clarendon Press, 1975), p. 106.
8. Tony Tanner, 'Colour and Movement in Hardy's *Tess of the d'Urbervilles*', *Critical Quarterly*, Vol. 10 (1968), pp. 219–39.
9. See Laird, op. cit., p. 191.
10. Thomas Hardy, 'Candour in English Fiction' published in the *New Review* in January 1890 as part of a symposium on censorship, reprinted in Harold Orel (ed.), *Thomas Hardy: Personal Writings* (London and Melbourne: Macmillan, 1967).
11. For Hardy's comments on his sub-title see the 1912 Preface to *Tess* and a letter to his publishers in response to a review in the *Saturday Review*

(16 January 1892) in which he claims that the sub-title is 'absolutely necessary', reprinted in R. L. Purdy, *Thomas Hardy: A Bibliographical Study* (Oxford: Oxford University Press, 1954), p. 75.

12. Tony Tanner, 'Colour and Movement in Hardy's *Tess of the d'Urbervilles*', *Critical Quarterly*, Vol. 10 (1968), pp. 219–39.

13. The *Life* records, for instance, an execution which Hardy witnessed from the top of a hill in his adolescence (just as Angel and Liza-Lu witness Tess's execution from the top of a hill). The physical proximity of murder seems to attract him: see the *Life*, p. 271, p. 223. Hardy also wrote during this time a short story concerned with hanging and hangmen entitled 'The Withered Arm'. See also Robert Gittings' rather spurious speculation about the sexual excitement Hardy found in the hanging of women in *Young Thomas Hardy* (Heinemann, 1975; rpt with revisions, Penguin, 1980), pp. 57–61. Hardy had been a Justice of the Peace in Dorchester in 1884: see Robert Gittings, *The Older Thomas Hardy* (Heinemann, 1978; rpt with revisions, Penguin, 1980), p. 66.

14. David Lodge, 'Tess, Nature and the Voices of Hardy, from *The Language of Fiction: Essays In Criticism and Verbal Analysis of the English Novel* (London: Routledge & Kegan Paul; New York: Columbia University Press, 1966), p. 168.

15. For this material on W. T. Stead I am indebted to M. Pearson's study *Age of Consent: Victorian Prostitution and its Enemies* (Newton Abbot: David and Charles, 1972) which outlines the events leading up to the Stead trial. See also Deborah Gorham, 'The "Maiden Tribute to Modern Babylon" Reexamined: Child Prostitution and the Idea of Childhood in Late Victorian England', *Victorian Studies*, Vol. 21, no. 3 (Spring 1978), pp. 353–79.

16. This speech is quoted in Pearson, ibid., p. 166.

17. Edmund Blunden, 'Hardy Talks About Tess' in *Twentieth Century Interpretations of 'Tess of the d'Urbervilles'*, ed. A. J. Lavalley, (Englewood Cliffs, NJ: Prentice-Hall, 1969), p. 102.

18. After the publication of *Tess*, the *Life* tells us, Hardy was inundated with letters from women with a past such as Tess's or from husbands such as Angel Clare who wrote asking for Hardy's 'counsel' (*Life*, p. 257). These writers were responding to the voice of the novel which defends and judges Tess and finds her 'pure'.

19. H. M. Daleski, '*Tess of the d'Urbervilles*: Mastery and Abandon', *Essays in Criticism*, Vol. 30 (October 1980), p. 330.

20. John Lucas, *The Literature of Change, Studies in the Nineteenth Century Provincial Novel* (Sussex: Harvester; New York: Barnes and Noble, 1977), p. 178.

21. Robert Gittings tells us that in 1891 Hardy was asked by Vizetelly's sons to sign an appeal against his father's imprisonment. Hardy had read at least two of Vizetelly's translations of Zola in the late 1880s. See Robert Gittings, *The Older Hardy* (Heinemann, 1978; rpt with revisions Penguin, 1980), pp. 116–17.

22. Mary Jacobus, 'Tess: The Making of a Pure Woman', in *Tearing the Veil: Essays on Femininity*, ed. Susan Lipshitz (London, Henley and Boston: Routledge, 1978), p. 79.

23. Hardy was obsessed with the 'decline and fall of the Hardys' as he called it: 'so we go down, down, down' he recorded in his notebook in September 1888. See *Life*, p. 224 and Robert Gittings, *Young Thomas Hardy* (Heinemann, 1975; rpt with revisions Penguin, 1980), p. 23. Gittings speculates that Hardy's interest in degeneracy may have been stimulated by the discovery of 'madness' in his wife Emma's family in 1888: see Gittings, *The Older Thomas Hardy* (Heinemann, 1978; rpt with revisions Penguin, 1980), p. 92. Hardy was himself to be labelled 'degenerate' in 1895 with the publication of Jeanette Gilder's attack upon *Jude* in the New York *World* entitled 'Hardy the Degenerate'.

24. J. Hillis Miller, 'Fiction and Repetition: *Tess of the d'Urbervilles*' in *Forms of Modern British Fiction*, ed. Allen Warren Friedman (Austin and London: University of Texas Press, 1975), p. 48.

25. Kathleen Blake, 'Pure Tess: Hardy on Knowing a Woman', *Studies in English Literature*, Vol. 22, no. 4 (Autumn 1982), p. 700.

26. John Lucas, *The Literature of Change: Studies in the Nineteenth Century Provincial Novel* (Sussex: Harvester; New York: Barnes and Noble, 1977), p. 179.

27. Kathleen Blake, op. cit., p. 699.

28. I am grateful to Kaja Silverman's fine article 'History, Figuration and Female Subjectivity in *Tess of the d'Urbervilles*', *Novel*, Vol. 18, no. 1 (Fall, 1984), for this insight.

29. See J. Hillis Miller's article 'Fiction and Repetition: *Tess of the d'Urbervilles*' in *Forms of Modern British Fiction*, ed. Allan Warren Friedman (Austin and London: University of Texas Press, 1975).

30. The *Life* tells us that in the latter part of 1890 Hardy read Weissman's 'Essays on Heredity' and the influence of this on Hardy's *Tess* has been discussed in the articles of Peter Morton and J. R. Ebbatson: Peter Morton, '*Tess of the d'Urbervilles*: A Neo-Darwinian Reading', *Southern Review*, Vol. 7 (1974), pp. 38–50; J. R. Ebbatson, 'The Darwinian View of Tess: A Reply', *Southern Review*, Vol. 8 (1975), pp. 247–53.

31. See Kathleen Blake, op. cit., p. 699.

32. Thomas Hardy, *A Group of Noble Dames* (first published 1891, rpt London: Macmillan, 1952).

33. Ellen Moers, 'Tess as Cultural Stereotype' from *Twentieth Century Interpretations of 'Tess of the d'Urbervilles'*, ed. A. J. Lavalley, (Englewood Cliffs, NJ: Prentice-Hall, 1969), pp. 98–100.

34. Elaine Showalter, 'Syphilis, Sexuality and the Fiction of the Fin-de-Siècle', in *Sex, Politics and Science in the Nineteenth-Century Novel*, Selected Papers of the English Institute (1983–84), ed. Ruth Bernard Yeazell (Baltimore: Johns Hopkins University Press, 1986), p. 107.

35. John Goode, *Thomas Hardy: The Offensive Truth*, Rereading Literature Series, ed. Terry Eagleton (Oxford: Blackwell, 1988), p. 111.

36. Mowbray Morris, 'Culture and Anarchy' (*Quarterly Review*, 1892) reprinted in *Thomas Hardy: The Critical Heritage*, op. cit., p. 214.

37. John Goode, op. cit., p. 128.

38. Penny Boumelha, *Thomas Hardy and Women: Sexual Ideology and Narrative Form* (Brighton: Harvester Press, 1982), p. 127.

39. Adrian Poole, 'Men's Words and Hardy's Women', *Essays in Criticism*, Vol. 31, no. 4 (October 1981), p. 329.

40. Kathleen Blake offers this as a reading of the contradictions in *Jude the Obscure*. See Kathleen Blake, 'Pure Tess: Hardy on Knowing a Woman', *Studies in English Literature*, Vol. 22, no. 4 (Autumn 1982), p. 701.

41. Thomas Hardy, 'Tess's Lament' from *Poems of the Past and the Present* (first published London and New York: Harper Brothers, 1901), reprinted in *The Complete Poetical Works of Thomas Hardy*, ed. Samuel Hynes, Vol. 1 (Oxford: Clarendon Press, 1982), pp. 216–17.

42. Thomas Hardy, 'Heredity' in *Moments of Vision* (London: Macmillan, 1917), reprinted in *The Complete Poetical Works of Thomas Hardy*, Vol. 2, ed. Samuel Hynes (Oxford: Clarendon Press).

43. In one of the stories of *A Group of Noble Dames* a young woman attempts to evade a marriage to a man she does not love by contracting small-pox and thus disfiguring her face. Thomas Hardy, 'The First Countess of Wessex' from *A Group of Noble Dames* (rpt London: Macmillan, 1952).

44. See the *Life*, p. 232.

45. J. Hillis Miller, 'Fiction and Repetition: *Tess of the d'Urbervilles*' in *Forms of Modern British Fiction*, ed. Allan Warren Friedman (Austin and London: University of Texas Press, 1975), p. 58.

46. J. D. Laird, *The Shaping of Tess of the d'Urbervilles* (Oxford: Clarendon Press, 1975), p. 78.

47. Thomas Hardy, 'The Dorsetshire Labourer' (1883), reprinted in *Thomas Hardy: Personal Writings*, ed. H. Orel (London and Melbourne: Macmillan, 1967), p. 180.

48. See 'The Dorsetshire Labourer' in which Hardy also describes eviction as a form of moral censorship: Thomas Hardy, 'The Dorsetshire Labourer' (1883), reprinted in *Thomas Hardy: Personal Writings*, ed. H. Orel, ibid., p. 189.

49. From *Thomas Hardy: Personal Writings*, ed. H. Orel, ibid., p. 229.

50. Edmund Blunden, 'Hardy Talks About Tess', reprinted in *Twentieth Century Interpretations of 'Tess of the d'Urbervilles'*, ed. A. J. Lavalley (Englewood Cliffs, NJ: Prentice-Hall, 1969), p. 102.

51. See Rosemary Jackson on the disruption and deformation of character in fantastic art in *Fantasy: The Literature of Subversion*, New Accents Series (London: Methuen, 1981), p. 82 and pp. 86–7.

52. Penny Boumelha, *Thomas Hardy and Women; Sexual Ideology and Narrative Form* (Brighton: Harvester Press, 1982).

53. Ibid., p. 66.

54. Ibid., p. 132.

55. John Goode, *Thomas Hardy; The Offensive Truth*, Rereading Literature Series, ed. Terry Eagleton (Oxford: Blackwell, 1988), p. 111.

56. Laura Claridge, 'Tess: A Less than Pure Woman Ambivalently Presented', *Texas Studies in Literature and Language*, Vol. 28, no. 3 (1986), p. 325.

57. Bernard Paris, 'A Confusion of Many Standards: Conflicting Value Systems in *Tess of the d'Urbervilles*', *Nineteenth Century Fiction*, Vol. 24 (1969), pp. 57–79.

58. Patricia Stubbs, 'Thomas Hardy, A Study in Contradiction' in *Women and Fiction: Feminism and the Novel, 1880–1920* (London: Methuen, 1981).

59. Kathleen Blake, 'Pure Tess: Hardy on Knowing a Woman', *Studies in English Literature*, Vol. 22, no. 4 (Autumn 1982), p. 700.
60. Mary Jacobus, 'Tess: The Making of a Pure Woman', in *Tearing the Veil: Essays on Femininity*, ed. Susan Lipshitz (London, Henley and Boston: Routledge, 1978), p. 79.

**Afterwords**

1. Hélène Cixous, 'Sorties' in *The Newly Born Woman*, trans. Betsy Wing, introduced by Sandra M. Gilbert, Theory and History of Literature Series, Vol. 24 (Manchester: Manchester University Press, 1986), p. 81.
2. George Egerton, 'A Cross-Line' in *Keynotes and Discords*, first published 1893 and 1894; rpt Virago Modern Classics (London: Virago, 1983), pp. 3–4.
3. Ibid., pp. 22–3.
4. Sandra M. Gilbert, 'Heart of Darkness: The Agon of the Femme Fatale' in *No Man's Land: The Place of the Woman Writer in the Twentieth Century*, Sandra M. Gilbert and Susan Gubar, Vol. 2: *Sexchanges* (New Haven and London: Yale University Press, 1990), p. 29.
5. Loc. cit.
6. Lisa Tickner, *The Spectacle of Women: Imagery of the Suffrage Campaign, 1907–1914* (London: Chatto & Windus, 1987).
7. Cesare Lombroso and William Ferrero, *The Female Offender* (London: T. Fisher Unwin, 1895).
8. See Nicole Ward Jouve, *White Woman Speaks With Forked Tongue: Criticism as Autobiography* (London and New York: Routledge, 1991), p. 102.
9. See Edward Said's use of Gramsci in *Orientalism* (London and New York: Routledge & Kegan Paul, 1978), p. 25.
10. For further information on the Brethren Movement see Roy F. Coad, *A History of the Brethren Movement: Its Origins, its Worldwide Development and its Significance for the Present Day* (Exeter: The Paternoster Press, 1968) and Norman Adams, *Goodbye, Beloved Brethren* (Aberdeen: Impulse Books, 1972). See also Edmund Gosse's account of his childhood amongst Brethren in *Father and Son: A Study of Two Temperaments* (1907).
11. Susan Sontag, *AIDS and its Metaphors* (Harmondsworth: Penguin, 1988).
12. Ibid., p. 84.
13. Ibid., p. 16.
14. Ibid., p. 48.
15. Hélène Cixous, 'Sorties' in *The Newly Born Woman*, trans. Betsy Wing, introduced by Sandra M. Gilbert, Theory and History of Literature Series, Vol. 24 (Manchester: Manchester University Press, 1986), p. 63.
16. Stephen Heath, *The Sexual Fix* (London: Macmillan, 1982), p. 142.
17. Sontag, op. cit., p. 94.
18. Nelly Furman, 'The Politics of Language: Beyond the Gender Principle?' in *Making a Difference: Feminist Literary Criticism*, eds Gayle Green and Copelia Kahn, New Accents Series (London and New York: Methuen, 1985), p. 76.
19. Terry Eagleton, *Literary Theory: An Introduction* (Oxford: Blackwell, 1983), pp. 132–3.

20. Catherine Clément, 'The Guilty One' *The Newly Born Woman*, trans. Betsy Wing, introduced by Sandra M. Gilbert, Theory and History of Literature Series, Vol. 24 (Manchester: Manchester University Press, 1986), pp. 56–7.
21. Frantz Fanon, *The Wretched of the Earth*, trans. Constance Farrington (Harmondsworth: Penguin, 1967; rpt 1969), pp. 251–5.
22. Hélène Cixous, 'Exchange' (with Catherine Clément) in *The Newly Born Woman*, trans. Betsy Wing, introduced by Sandra M. Gilbert, Theory and History of Literature Series, Vol. 24 (Manchester: Manchester University Press, 1986), p. 145.
23. Edward Said, *Orientalism* (London and New York: Routledge & Kegan Paul, 1978), p. 328.
24. Catherine Clément, 'The Guilty One' in *The Newly Born Woman*, trans. Betsy Wing, introduced by Sandra M. Gilbert, Theory and History of Literature Series, Vol. 24 (Manchester: Manchester University Press, 1986), p. 33.
25. Hélène Cixous, 'Sorties' in *The Newly Born Woman*, trans. Betsy Wing, introduced by Sandra M. Gilbert, Theory and History of Literature Series, Vol. 24 (Manchester: Manchester University Press, 1986), p. 69.

# Bibliography

## PRIMARY SOURCES

Conrad, Joseph, *Almayer's Folly* (1895; rpt Harmondsworth: Penguin Modern Classics, 1984).

——, *An Outcast of the Islands* (1896; rpt Harmondsworth: Penguin Modern Classics, 1986).

——, *Heart of Darkness* (1899; rpt Norton Critical Editions, New York and London: W. W. Norton, 1988).

——, *The Secret Agent* (1907; rpt The Penguin English Library, Harmondsworth: Penguin, 1985).

Haggard, H. R., *Allan's Wife* (1889; reprinted in *Allan's Wife, Hunter Quatermain's Story, A Story of Three Lions and Long Odds*, London: MacDonald, 1951).

——, *Ayesha: The Return of She* (1904; reprinted in *Ayesha: The Return of She and Benita: An African Romance*, Poole: New Orchard Editions, 1986).

——, *King Solomon's Mines* (1885; reprinted in *King Solomon's Mines, She, Allan Quatermain*, London: Octopus, 1979).

——, *She* (1887: reprinted in *King Solomon's Mines, She, Allan Quatermain*, London: Octopus, 1979).

Hardy, T. and Hardy, F., *The Life and Works of Thomas Hardy*, ed. Michael Millgate (London: Macmillan, 1984).

Hardy, Thomas, *Tess of the d'Urbervilles*. Penguin Classics Series, ed. David Skilton, Harmondsworth: Penguin, rpt 1986).

Stoker, Bram, *Dracula* (1897; reprinted in The World's Classics Series. Oxford: Oxford University Press, 1986).

——, *The Lair of the White Worm* (1911; reprinted London: Target, 1986).

## SECONDARY SOURCES

Achebe, Chinua, 'An Image of Africa', *Research in African Literatures* 9 (Spring 1978), 1–15.

Adams, Norman, *Goodbye, Beloved Brethren* (Aberdeen: Impulse, 1972).

Alloula, Malek, *The Colonial Harem* (Manchester: Manchester University Press, 1987).

Althusser, L., 'Ideology and Ideological State Apparatuses', in *Lenin and Philosophy and Other Essays*, trans. Ben Brewster (London: NLB, 1971, pp. 121–73).

Astle, Richard, 'Dracula as Totemic Monster: Lacan, Freud, Oedipus and History', *Sub-Stance*, 25 (1980), 98–105.

Atwood, Margaret, 'Superwoman Drawn and Quartered: The Early Forms of *She*', *Alphabet*, 10 (July 1965), 65–82.

——, *Survival: A Thematic Guide to Canadian Literature* (Toronto: Anansi Press, 1972).

Auerbach, Nina, *Woman and the Demon: The Life of a Victorian Myth* (Cambridge, Massachussetts: Harvard University Press, 1982).

——, 'The Rise of the Fallen Woman', *Nineteenth Century Fiction*, 35, no. 1 (June 1980), 29–52.

Barker-Benfield, B., 'The Spermatic Economy: A Nineteenth Century View of Sexuality', *Feminist Studies*, 1 (1972), 45–74.

Barthes, Roland, 'The Death of the Author' in *Image/Music/Text*, trans. Stephen Heath (Glasgow: Fontana/Collins, 1977), 142–8.

Bayley, John, *An Essay on Hardy* (Cambridge: Cambridge University Press, 1978).

Beauvoir, Simone de, *The Second Sex* (trans. H. M. Parshley, 1949; rpt Harmondsworth: Penguin Books, 1972).

Beer, Gillian, *Darwin's Plots: Evolutionary Narrative in Darwin, George Eliot and Nineteenth-Century Fiction* (London, Boston and Henley: Routledge & Kegan Paul, 1983).

——, 'Origins and Oblivion in Victorian Narrative' in *Sex, Politics and Science in the Nineteenth-Century Novel*, Selected Papers of the English Institute 1983–84, ed. Ruth Bernard Yeazell (London: Johns Hopkins University Press, 1986), pp. 63–87.

Belsey, Catherine, *Critical Practice*, New Accents Series (London and New York: Methuen, 1980).

Bentley, C. F., 'The Monster in the Bedroom: Sexual Symbolism in Bram Stoker's *Dracula*', *Literature and Psychology*, 22 (1972), 27–34.

Benzing, Rosemary, 'In Defence of "Tess"', *Contemporary Review*, 218 (1970), 202–4.

Biles, Jack I., 'Winnie Verloc: Agent of Death', *Conradiana*, 13, no. 2 (1981), 101–9.

Blake, Kathleen, 'Pure Tess: Hardy on Knowing a Woman', *Studies in English Literature*, 22, no. 4 (Autumn 1982), 689–705.

Bland, Lucy, 'The New Woman, the Married Woman and the Feminist: Sexual Politics of the 1890s', in *Equal or Different*, ed. Jane Rendall (Oxford: Blackwell, 1987), pp. 141–64.

Blinderman, C. S., 'Vampurella: Darwin and Count Dracula', *Massachussetts Review*, 21 (1980), 411–28.

Blunden, Edmund, 'Hardy Talks About Tess', in *Twentieth Century Interpretations of 'Tess of the d'Urbervilles'*, ed. A. J. Lavalley (Englewood Cliffs, NJ: Prentice-Hall, 1969), pp. 101–2.

Boumelha, Penny, *Thomas Hardy and Woman: Sexual Ideology and Narrative Form* (Brighton: Harvester Press, 1982, rpt 1984).

Bolt, Christine, 'Race and the Victorians' in C. C. Eldridge (ed.), *British Imperialism in the Nineteenth Century*, Problems in Focus Series (London: Macmillan, 1984), pp. 126–147.

Booth, General W., *In Darkest England and the Way Out* (London: International Headquarters of the Salvation Army, 1890).

Bowlby, Rachel, 'Promoting Dorian Gray', in *Colonialism and Other Essays, The Oxford Literary Review*, 9 (1987), 147–162.

Brantlinger, P., *Rule of Darkness* (Ithaca and London: Cornell University Press, 1988).

——, 'Victorians and Africans: The Geneology of the Myth of the Dark Continent', *Critical Inquiry*, 12 (1985), 166–203.

Breuer, J. and Freud S., *Studies on Hysteria*, trans. James and Alix Strachey, ed. Angela Richards, Pelican Freud Library, Vol. 3 (London: Penguin, 1974).

Brodie, Susan, 'Conrad's Feminine Perspective', *Conradiana*, Vol. 16, no. 2 (1984), 141–55.

Browne, P. L., 'Men and Women, Africa and Civilisation: A Study of the African Stories of Hemingway and the African Novels of Haggard, Greene and Bellow' (Unpublished Doctoral Dissertation, Rutgers University, 1979).

Burton, Capt. Richard F., *Personal Narrative of a Pilgrimage to Al-Madinah and Meccah*, 1855, 2 vols (New York: Dover, 1964).

Campbell, H., *Differences in the Nervous Organization of Man and Woman* (London: H. K. Lewis, 1981).

Cash, Joe, *The Treatment of Women Characters in the Complete Works of Joseph Conrad* (Unpublished Doctoral Dissertation, Texas Tech. University, 1972).

Chamberlin, J. E., 'An Anatomy of Cultural Melancholy', *Journal of the History of Ideas*, XLII, no. 4 (1981), 691–705.

Chamberlain, M. E., 'Imperialism and Social Reform' in C. C. Eldridge (ed.), *British Imperialism in the Nineteenth Century*, Problems in Focus Series (London: Macmillan, 1984), pp. 148–67.

Cixous, Hélène, 'Sorties' in Hélène Cixous and Catherine Clément, *The Newly Born Woman*, trans. Betsy Wing, introd. Sandra M.

Gilbert, Theory and History of Literature Series, Vol. 24 (Manchester: Manchester University Press, 1986), pp. 62–132.

Cixous, Hélène and Clément, C., *The Newly Born Woman*, trans. Betsy Wing, introd. Sandra M. Gilbert, Theory and History of Literature Series, Vol. 24 (Manchester: Manchester University Press, 1986).

Clareson, T. D., 'Lost Islands, Lost Races', *Journal of Popular Culture*, 8, no. 4 (1975), 714–23.

Claridge, Laura, 'Tess: A Less Than Pure Woman Ambivalently Presented', *Texas Studies in Literature and Language*, 28, no. 3 (Fall 1986), 324–338.

Clément, Catherine, 'The Guilty One', in Catherine Clément and Hélène Cixous, *The Newly Born Woman*, trans. Betsy Wing, introd. Sandra M. Gilbert, Theory and History of Literature Series, Vol. 24 (Manchester: Manchester University Press, 1986), pp. 3–59.

Clery, T. and Sherwood, T., 'Women in Conrad's Ironical Epic: Virgil, Dante and the *Heart of Darkness*', *Conradiana*, 16, no. 3 (1984), 183–95.

Coad, Roy, F., *A History of the Brethren Movement: Its Origins, its Worldwide Development and its Significance for the Present Day* (Exeter: The Paternoster Press, 1968).

Cohen, Morton, *Rider Haggard: His Life and Works* (London: Hutchinson, 1960).

Conrad, J., *A Personal Record* (London: J. M. Dent, 1949–1955).

——, 'Geography and Some Explorers', from *Last Essays* (London and Toronto: J. M. Dent and Sons, 1926), pp. 1–31.

——, *Lord Jim* (Edinburgh and London: John Grant, 1925).

——, *The Nigger of the 'Narcissus'* (Edinburgh and London: John Grant, 1925).

——, *Tales of Unrest*, Penguin Modern Classics. (Harmondsworth: Penguin, 1985).

Conway, Jill, 'Stereotypes of Femininity in a Theory of Sexual Evolution', *Victorian Studies*, 14 (1970–71), 47–62.

Cooke, Nicolas, *Satan in Society* (1870; rpt Cincinatti: C. F. Vent, 1876).

Cox, R. G. (ed.), *Thomas Hardy: The Critical Heritage* (London: Routledge & Kegan Paul; New York: Barnes & Noble, 1970).

Craft, C., '"Kiss Me With Those Red Lips": Gender and Inversion in Bram Stoker's *Dracula*', *Representations*, 8 (1974), 107–33.

Cunningham, A. R., 'The "New Woman" Fiction of the 1890s', *Victorian Studies*, 17 (1973), 177–86.

Curtin, P., *The Image of Africa* (Madison: University of Wisconsin Press, 1964).

Daleski, H. M., 'Tess of the d'Urbervilles: Mastery and Abandon', *Essays in Criticism*, 30 (October 1980), 326–45.

Darwin, Charles, *The Descent of Man* (1871: 2nd edn London, 1874).

——, *The Origin of Species* (1859; reprinted in Penguin Classics, ed. J. W. Burrow (Harmondsworth: Penguin, rpt. 1986).

Davin, Anna, 'Imperialism and Motherhood', *History Workshop*, 5 (1978), 9–65.

Davis, Eugene, W., 'Tess of the d'Urbervilles: Some Ambiguities About a Pure Woman', *Nineteenth Century Fiction*, 22 (1968), 397–401.

Degler, C., 'What Ought To Be and What Was: Women's Sexuality in the Nineteenth Century', *American Historical Review*, 79 (1974), 467–90.

Demetrakopoulous, S., 'Feminism, Sex-role Exchanges and Other Subliminal Fantasies in Bram Stoker's *Dracula*', *Frontiers*, 2 (1977), 104–13.

Dijkstra, Bram, *Idols of Perversity: Fantasies of Feminine Evil in Fin-de-Siècle Culture* (New York: Oxford University Press, 1986).

Dowling, Linda, 'The Decadent and the New Woman in the 1890s', *Nineteenth Century Fiction*, 33 (1979), 434–53.

Drabble, M. (ed.), *The Genius of Thomas Hardy* (New York: Alfred A. Knopf, 1976).

Dudley, E. and Novak, M. (ed.), *The Wild Man Within* (Pittsburgh: University of Pittsburgh Press, 1972).

Duffin, L., 'Prisoners of Progress: Women and Evolution', in *The Nineteenth-Century Woman: Her Cultural and Physical World*, ed. Sara Delamont and Lorna Duffin (London; Croom Helm, 1978; New York: Barnes & Noble, 1978), 57–91.

Duffin L. and Delamont S. (eds), *The Nineteenth-Century Woman: Her Cultural and Physical World* (London: Croom Helm, 1978; New York: Barnes & Noble, 1978).

Dunraven, Earl of, 'The Invasion of the Destitute Aliens', *The Nineteenth Century*, 31 (June 1892), 985–1000.

Dyhouse, Carol, 'Girls Growing Up in Late Victorian England and Social Darwinistic Ideas in the Development of Women's Education in England, 1880–1920', *History of Education*, 5 (1976), 41–58.

Eagleton, Terry, *Literary Theory: An Introduction* (Oxford: Basil Blackwell, 1983).

——, 'Thomas Hardy: Nature As Language', *Critical Quarterly*, 13, no. 2 (1971), 155–62.

240        *Bibliography*

Ebbatson, J. R., 'The Darwinian View of Tess: A Reply', *Southern Review*, 8 (1975), 247–53.

Egerton, George, *Keynotes and Discords*, first published 1893 and 1894; rpt Virago Modern Classics (London: Virago, 1983).

Eldridge C. C. (ed), *British Imperialism in the Nineteenth Century* (Manchester: Manchester University Press, 1984).

Ellis, Havelock, 'Thomas Hardy's Novels', *Westminster Review*, April 1883. Reprinted in *Thomas Hardy: The Critical Heritage*, ed. R. G. Cox (London: Routledge & Kegan Paul; New York: Barnes & Noble, 1970), pp. 103–32.

——, 'Concerning *Jude the Obscure*', *The Savoy Magazine*, October 1896. Reprinted in *Thomas Hardy: The Critical Heritage*, ed. R. G. Cox (London: Routledge & Kegan Paul; New York: Barnes & Noble, 1970), 214–21.

Ellis, James, 'Kurtz's Voice: The Intended as the "Horror"', *English Literature in Transition*, 19 (1976), 105–10.

Elwin, Verrier, 'The Vagina Dentata Legend', *The British Journal of Medical Psychology*, 19 (1941), 439–53.

Etherington, N., 'Rider Haggard, Imperialism and the Layered Personality', *Victorian Studies*, 22 (Autumn 1978), 71–87.

Fanon, Frantz, *Black Skin, White Masks*, trans. Charles Lam Markmann (London: Paladin, 1970; rpt 1972).

——, *The Wretched of the Earth*, trans. Constance Farrington (Harmondsworth: Penguin, 1967).

Fanu, Sheridan Le, *Carmilla*. Reprinted in *Novels of Mystery From the Victorian Age*, introd. Maurice Richardson (London: Pilot Press, 1945).

Farson, Daniel, *The Man Who Wrote 'Dracula': a Biography of Bram Stoker* (London: Michael Joseph, 1975).

Fletcher, Ian, 'Can Haggard Ride Again?', *Listener*, 86 (1971), 136–8.

Ford, Ford Madox, *Joseph Conrad: A Personal Remembrance* (London: Duckworth, 1924).

Forel, Auguste, *The Sexual Question: A Scientific, Psychological, Hygienic and Sociological Study*, 1906; revised edn. trans. C. F. Marshall (New York: Physicians and Surgeons Book Co., 1925).

Foucault, M., *The History of Sexuality*, Vol. 1, trans. Robert Hurley (London: Peregrine Books, rpt 1984).

Freud, Sigmund, *Totem and Taboo*, ed. James Strachey (London: Routledge & Kegan Paul, 1970).

——, *The Interpretation of Dreams*, in *The Standard Edition of the Complete Psychological Works of Sigmund Freud*, Vol. V, ed. James and Alix Strachey (London: Hogarth Press, 1966).

Friedman, A. W. (ed.), *Forms of Modern British Fiction* (Austin and London: University of Texas Press, 1975).

Fry, Carrol, L., 'Fictional Conventions and Sexuality in *Dracula*', *The Victorian Newsletter*, 42 (Fall 1972), 20–2.

Furman, Nelly, 'The Politics of Language: Beyond the Gender Principle?', in *Making a Difference: Feminist Literary Criticism*, eds Gayle Green and Coppelia Kahn, New Accents Series (London and New York: Methuen, 1985), 59–79.

Garnett, E., *Letters From Joseph Conrad, 1895–1924* (London: Nonesuch Press, 1928).

Gay, Peter, *Education of the Senses*, Vol. 1 of *The Bourgeois Experience: Victoria to Freud* (Oxford University Press, 1984).

Geary, Edward, 'An Ashy Halo: Woman as Symbol in *Heart of Darkness*', *Studies in Short Fiction*, 13 (1976), 499–506.

Gilman, Sander L., 'Black Bodies, White Bodies: Toward an Iconography of Female Sexuality in Late Nineteenth-Century Art, Medicine and Literature', *Critical Inquiry*, 12 (Autumn 1985), 204–42.

——, *Difference and Pathology: Stereotypes of Sexuality, Race and Madness* (Ithaca and London: Cornell University Press, 1985).

Gilbert, Sandra, M., 'Heart of Darkness: The Agon of the Femme Fatale' in Sandra M. Gilbert and Susan Gubar, *No Man's Land: The Place of the Woman Writer in the Twentieth Century*, Vol. 2: *Sexchanges* (New Haven and London: Yale University Press, 1990), pp. 3–46.

——, 'Rider Haggard's Heart of Darkness', *Partisan Review*, 50 (1983), 444–53.

Gollwitzer, H., *Europe In the Age of Imperialism, 1880–1914*, trans. David Adam and Stanley Baron (London: Thames & Hudson, 1967, rpt 1979).

Gittings, Robert, *Young Thomas Hardy* (Heinemann, 1975, rpt with revisions, Penguin, 1980).

——, *The Older Thomas Hardy* (Heinemann, 1978; rpt with revisions, Penguin, 1980).

Goode, John, *Thomas Hardy: The Offensive Truth*, Rereading Literature Series, ed. Terry Eagleton (Oxford: Blackwell, 1988).

——, 'Woman and the Literary Text', in *The Rights and Wrongs of Woman*, ed. Juliet Mitchell and Ann Oakley, Pelican Books (Harmondsworth: Penguin, 1976), 217–55.

Gorham, Deborah, 'The "Maiden Tribute of Modern Babylon" Reexamined: Child Prostitution and the Idea of Childhood in Late Victorian England', *Victorian Studies*, 21, no. 3 (Spring 1978), 353–79.

Gose, Eliot, 'Psychic Evolution: Darwinism and Initiation in *Tess of the d'Urbervilles'*, *Nineteenth Century Fiction*, 18 (1963–64), 261–72.

Gould, S. J., *The Mismeasure of Man* (New York and London: N. W. Norton and Co., 1981).

Green, G. and Kahn, C., 'Feminist Scholarship and the Social Construction of Woman' in *Making a Difference*, eds Green and Kahn, New Accents Series (London and New York: Methuen, 1985), pp. 1–36.

Green, G. and Kahn, C (eds), *Making a Difference*, New Accents Series (London and New York: Methuen, 1985).

Green, Martin, *Dreams of Adventure, Deeds of Empire* (London: Routledge & Kegan Paul, 1980).

Greene, Graham, *Journey Without Maps* (London: Pan, 1948).

——, *The Lost Childhood and Other Essays* (London: Eyre & Spottiswoode, 1951).

Greenslade, W., 'The Concept of Degeneration, 1880–1910' (Unpublished Doctoral Dissertation, University of Warwick, 1982).

Griffin, Gail B., '"Your Girls That You All Love Are Mine": *Dracula* and the Victorian Male Imagination', *International Journal of Women's Studies*, 3 (1980), 454–65.

Groot, Joanna de, '"Sex" and "Race": The Construction of Language and Image in the Nineteenth Century', in *Sexuality and Subordination*, ed. Susan Mendus and Jane Rendall (London and New York: Routledge & Kegan Paul, 1989), pp. 89–130.

Guerard, A. (ed.), *Hardy: A Collection of Critical Essays* (Englewood Cliffs, NJ: Prentice-Hall, 1964).

Gurko, Leo, *Joseph Conrad: Giant in Exile* (London: Collier-Macmillan, 1962).

Haggard, Lilias, *Cloak That I Left: A Biography of H. R. Haggard, K. B. E. By His Daughter* (London: Hodder & Stoughton, 1951).

Haggard, H. R., 'About Fiction', *The Contemporary Review*, 2 (February, 1887), 172–80.

——, *Allan Quatermain*, 1888; reprinted in *King Solomon's Mines, She, Allan Quatermain* (London: Octopus, 1979).

——, *Jess* (London: Smith, Elder and Co., 1887).

——, *The Days of My Life*, ed. C. J. Longman (London: Longmans, Green and Co., 1926).

Hardy, T., *A Group of Noble Dames* (1891; reprinted London: Macmillan, 1952).

——, *Collected Letters of Thomas Hardy*, Vol. 1 (1840–1892), ed. R. L. Purdy and M. Millgate (Oxford: Clarendon Press, 1978).

——, *The Complete Poetical Works of Thomas Hardy*, ed. Samuel Hynes (Oxford: Clarendon Press, 1982).

——, *'Dearest Emmie': The Thomas Hardy's Letters to his First Wife*, ed. Carl Weber (London: Macmillan; New York: St. Martin's Press, 1963).

——, *Thomas Hardy: Personal Writings*, ed. H. Orel (London and Melbourne: Macmillan, 1967).

——, *The Well-Beloved: A Sketch of a Temperament* (reprinted London: Macmillan, 1976).

——, *Jude the Obscure* (1895; reprinted London: Macmillan, 1957).

Harrison, Brian, *Separate Spheres: The Opposition to Women's Suffrage in Britain* (London: Croom Helm, 1978).

Hartman, Mary S., *Victorian Murderesses: A True History of Thirteen French and English Women Accused of Unspeakable Crimes* (New York: Schocken Books, 1977).

Hatlen, Burton, 'The Return of the Repressed/Oppressed in Bram Stoker's *Dracula*', *Minnesota Review*, no. 15, 80–97.

Hawkins Hunt, 'Conrad and the Psychology of Imperialism' in *Conrad Revisited: Essays for the Eighties*, ed. Ross C. Murfin (Alabama: Alabama University Press), 71–5.

——, 'The Issue of Racism in *Heart of Darkness*', *Conradiana* 14, no. 3 (1982), 163–71.

Hay, Eloise, K., *The Political Novels of Joseph Conrad* (Chicago: University of Chicago Press, 1963).

Heath, Rev. Dunbar, 'Anniversary Address', *Journal of the Anthropological Society*, 6 (1868), lxxxvii.

Heath, Stephen, *The Sexual Fix* (London: Macmillan, 1982).

Henkin, Leo, *Darwinism In The English Novel, 1860–1910* (New York: Russell & Russell, 1963).

Hennelly, M., '*Dracula*: The Gnostic Quest and the Victorian Wasteland', *English Literature in Transition, 1880–1920*, 20, 13–26.

Hinz, Evelyn, J., 'Rider Haggard's *She*: An Archetypal History of Adventure', *Studies In The Novel*, 4 (1972), 416–31.

Home, Lewis, B., 'The Darkening Sun of Tess Durbeyfield', *Texas Studies in Language and Literature*, 13 (1971), 299–331.

Humm, Maggie, 'Thomas Hardy and Women: A Psycho-Social Criticism of Tess of the d'Urbervilles and Sue Bridehead', *Massachussetts Studies in English*, 6 (1977), 77–89.

Hunter, Allan, *Joseph Conrad and the Ethics of Darwinism* (London and Canberra: Croom Helm, 1983).

Hynes, Samuel, *The Edwardian Turn of Mind* (London: Oxford University Press: Princeton, NJ: Princeton University Press, 1968).

Ibsen, Henrik, *Ghosts* in *Ghosts and Two Other Plays* (London and Toronto: J. M. Dent & Sons and New York: E. P. Dutton, 1911, rpt 1926), pp. 66–141.

Inniss, Kenneth, 'Conrad's Native Girl: Some Social Questions', *Pacific Coast Philology*, 5 (1970), 39–45.

Irigaray, L., *Speculum of the Other Woman* (Ithaca, NY: Cornell University Press, 1985).

Jackson, Rosemary, *Fantasy: The Literature of Subversion*, New Accents Series (London: Methuen, 1981).

Jacobs, Robert G., 'Comrade Ossipon's Favourite Saint: Lombroso and Conrad', *Nineteenth Century Fiction*, 23 (1968–69), 74–84.

Jacobus, Mary, 'Tess's Purity', *Essays In Criticism*, 26 (1976), 318–38.

——, 'Tess: The Making of a Pure Woman', in *Tearing the Veil: Essays on Femininity*, ed. Susan Lipshitz (London, Henley and Boston: Routledge, 1978), pp. 77–92.

Jameson, F., 'Magical Narratives: Romance as Genre', *New Literary History*, 7 (1975), 135–63.

——, *Political Unconscious: Narrative as a Socially Symbolic Act* (Ithaca: Cornell University Press, 1981).

Jean-Aubry, G., *Joseph Conrad: Life and Letters*, 2 vols (London: Heinemann, 1927).

——, *The Sea-Dreamer: A Definitive Biography of Joseph Conrad*, trans. Helen Sebba (London: Allen & Unwin, 1957).

Jeffreys, Sheila, *The Spinster and her Enemies: Feminism and Sexuality, 1880–1930* (London: Pandora Press, 1985).

Jeffreys, S. (ed.), *The Sexuality Debates*, Women's Source Library (New York and London: Routledge & Kegan Paul, 1987).

Johnson, Alan, 'Bent and Broken Necks: Signs of Design in Stoker's *Dracula*', *The Victorian Newsletter*, 72 (Fall 1987), 17–24.

Johnson, Bruce, 'Conrad's Impressionism and Watt's "Delayed Decoding"', in *Conrad Revisited: Essays for the Eighties*, ed. Ross Murfin (Alabama: Alabama University Press, 1985), 51–70.

Jones, Ann R., 'Inscribing Femininity: French Theories of the Feminine', in *Making a Difference: Feminist Literary Criticism*, eds Gayle Green and Coppelia Kahn, New Accents Series (London and New York: Methuen, 1985, 80–112).

Jones, Ernest, *On the Nightmare* (London: Hogarth Press, 1949).

Jouve, Nicole Ward, *White Woman Speaks With Forked Tongue: Criticism as Autobiography* (London and New York: Routledge, 1991).

Jung, C. J., *The Integration of the Personality* (London: Routledge & Kegan Paul, 1940).

——, 'In Memory of Sigmund Freud' in *Collected Works of C. G. Jung*, Vol. XIII (London: Routledge & Kegan Paul, 1966).

Kappeler, S., *The Pornography of Representation* (Cambridge: Polity Press, 1986).

Katz, Wendy R., 'Rider Haggard and the Empire of the Imagination', *English Literature in Transition*, 23 (1980), 115–24.

Kennedy, Paul, 'Continuity and Discontinuity in British Imperialism 1815–1914' in C. C. Eldridge (ed.), *British Imperialism in the Nineteenth Century*, Problems in Focus Series (London: Macmillan, 1984, 20–38).

Kermode, Frank, *The Sense of an Ending: Studies in the Theory of Fiction* (London, Oxford, New York: Oxford University Press, 1966, rpt 1979).

Kettle, Arnold, 'Hardy the Novelist: A Reconsideration' in *The Nineteenth Century Novel: Critical Essays and Documents* (London: Heinemann, 1972), pp. 262–73.

—— (ed.), *The Nineteenth Century Novel: Critical Essays and Documents* (London: Heinemann, 1972).

Krafft-Ebbing, R., *Psychopathia Sexualis*, trans. Franklin S. S. Klaf (New York: Bell Publishing Co., 1965).

Laird, J. D., *The Shaping of 'Tess of the d'Urbervilles'* (Oxford: Clarendon Press, 1975).

Lankester, E. R., *Degeneration: A Chapter in Darwinism* (London, 1880).

Lavalley, A. J. (ed.), *Twentieth Century Interpretations of 'Tess of the d'Urbervilles* (Englewood Cliffs, NJ: Prentice-Hall, 1969).

Laszowska Gerard, E., 'Transylvanian Superstitions', *The Nineteenth Century*, 18 (July 1885), 130–50.

Lawrence, D. H., *Phoenix: The Posthumous Papers of D. H. Lawrence*, ed. Edward D. McDonald (New York: The Viking Press, 1936), 398–516.

Leavis, F. R., *The Great Tradition* (London: Chatto & Windus, 1948, rpt 1960).

Lederer, Wolfgang, *The Fear of Women* (London: Grune & Stratton, 1970).

Lewis, C. S., *Selected Literary Essays*, ed. Walter Hooper (Cambridge: Cambridge University Press, 1969).

Linton, Mrs. Lynn, 'The Wild Women as Social Insurgents', *The Nineteenth Century*, 30 (1891), 596–605.

Lipshitz, S. (ed.), *Tearing the Veil: Essays on Femininity* (London, Henley and Boston: Routledge, 1978).

Lodge, David, *The Language of Fiction: Essays In Criticism and Verbal Analysis of the English Novel* (London: Routledge & Kegan Paul; New York: Columbia University Press, 1966).

Lombroso, C. and Ferrero, W., *The Female Offender* (London: T. Fisher Unwin, 1895).

Lucas, John, *The Literature of Change, Studies in the Nineteenth-Century Provincial Novel* (Sussex: Harvester Press; New York: Barnes & Noble, 1977).

Luyat, Anne, 'Conrad's Feminine Grotesques', *The Conradian*, 2, no. 1 (1986), 4–15.

MacCormack, C. and Strathern, M. (eds), *Nature, Culture and Gender* (Cambridge: Cambridge University Press, 1980).

MacGillivray, R., '*Dracula*, Bram Stoker's Spoiled Masterpiece', *Queen's Quarterly*, 79 (1972), 518–27.

Mackenzie, John M., *Propaganda and Empire: the Manipulation of British Public Opinion 1880–1960* (Manchester: Manchester University Press, 1984).

Marcus, S., *The Other Victorians* (London: Weidenfeld & Nicolson, 1966).

Marks, E. and Courtivron, I. (eds), *New French Feminisms: An Anthology* (Brighton: Harvester Press, 1981, rpt 1986).

McClintock, Anne, 'Maidens, Maps and Mines: *King Solomon's Mines* and the Reinvention of Patriarchy in Colonial South Africa', in *Women and Gender in Southern Africa to 1945*, ed. Cherryl Walker (Claremont, Southern Africa: David Philip Publishers; London: James Currey, 1990), pp. 97–124.

Meisel, Perry, *Thomas Hardy: The Return of the Repressed – A Study of the Major Fiction* (New Haven and London: Yale University Press, 1972).

Mendus, S. and Rendall, J. (eds), *Sexuality and Subordination* (London and New York: Routledge & Kegan Paul, 1989).

Meyer, B. C., *Joseph Conrad: A Psychoanalytical Biography* (Princeton: Princeton University Press, 1967).

Michael, Leo, *She: An Allegory of the Church* (New York: Frank Lovell and Co., 1889).

Miller, Henry, *The Books In My Life* (London: Peter Owen, 1952).

Miller, J. Hillis, *Thomas Hardy: Distance and Desire* (Cambridge, Massachussetts: Belknap Press, 1970).

——, 'Fiction and Repetition: *Tess of the d'Urbervilles*'. *Forms of Modern British Fiction*, ed. Allen Warren Friedman (London: 1975), 43–71.

Millman, L., 'Rider Haggard and the Male Novel, What Is Pericles?, Beckett Gags' (Unpublished Doctoral Dissertation, Rutgers University, 1974).

Mitchell, J. and Oakley, A. (eds), *The Rights and Wrongs of Women*, Pelican Books (Harmondsworth: Penguin, 1976).

Moers, Ellen, 'Tess as a Cultural Stereotype' in *Twentieth-Century Interpretations of 'Tess of the d'Urbervilles'*, ed. A. J. Lavalley (Englewood Cliffs, NJ: Prentice-Hall, 1969), pp. 98–100.

Moi, Toril, *Sexual/Textual Politics*, New Accents Series (London: Methuen, 1985; reprinted London and New York: Routledge, 1988).

Montag, George, 'Marlow Tells the Truth: The Nature of Evil in *Heart of Darkness*', *Conradiana*, 3, no. 2 (1971–2), 93–7.

Morgan, Rosemarie, *Women and Sexuality in the Novels of Thomas Hardy* (London and New York: Routledge, Chapman & Hall, 1988).

Morretti, F., 'The Dialectic of Fear', *New Left Review*, 136 (1982), 67–85.

Morris, Mowbray, 'Culture and Anarchy', *Quarterly Review* 174 (1892). Reprinted in *Thomas Hardy: The Critical Heritage*, ed. R. G. Cox (London: Routledge & Kegan Paul; New York: Barnes & Noble, 1970), pp. 214–21.

Morse, Peckham, 'Darwinism and Darwinisticism', *Victorian Studies* 3 (1959), 19–40.

Morton, Peter, '*Tess of the d'Urbervilles*: A Neo-Darwinian Reading', *Southern Review*, 7 (1974), 38–50.

Moser, Thomas, *Joseph Conrad: Achievement and Decline* (Hamden, Connecticut: Archon Books, 1966).

Moss, John G., 'Three Motifs in Haggard's *She*', *English Literature in Transition*, 16 (1973), 27–34.

Murfin, Ross (ed.), *Conrad Revisited: Essays for the Eighties* (Alabama: Alabama University Press, 1985).

Nagel, James, *Stephen Crane and Literary Impressionism* (University Park and London: The Pennsylvania State University Press, 1980, rpt 1983).

Najder, Z. (ed.), *Conrad's Polish Background: Letters to and from Polish Friends*, trans. Helina Carroll (London: Oxford University Press, 1964).

Nead, Lynda, *Myths of Sexuality: Representations of Women in Victorian Britain* (Oxford: Blackwell, 1988).

Nettels, Elsa, 'The Grotesque in Conrad's Fiction', *Nineteenth Century Fiction*, 29 (1974), 144–63.

Newton, William B., 'Hardy and the Naturalists: Their Use of Physiology', *Modern Philology*, 49 (1951), 28–41.

Nordau, Max, *Degeneration* (London: Heinemann, 1985).

Nunnally, J. C., 'The Victorian "Femme Fatale": Mirror of the Decadent Temperament'. Unpublished Doctoral Dissertation, Texas Tech., 1968.

O'Connor, Peter, 'The Function of Nina in *Almayer's Folly*', *Conradiana*, 7 (1975), 225–32.

O'Hanlon, R., *Joseph Conrad and Charles Darwin: The Influence of Scientific Thought on Conrad's Fiction* (Edinburgh: Salamander Press, 1984).

Oinas, Felix, 'East European Vampires and Dracula', *Journal of Popular Culture*, 16, no. 1, 108–16.

Orel, Harold (ed.), *Thomas Hardy: Personal Writings* (London and Melbourne: Macmillan, 1967).

Page, N. (ed.), *Thomas Hardy: The Writer and his Background* (London: Bell & Hyman, 1980).

Paris, B. J., 'A Confusion of Many Standards: Conflicting Value Systems in *Tess of the d'Urbervillles*', *Nineteenth Century Fiction*, 24 (1969), 57–79.

Parry, Benita, *Conrad and Imperialism* (London: Macmillan, 1983).

Patteson, R. F., 'King Solomon's Mines: Imperialism and Narrative Structure', *Journal of Narrative Technique*, 8 (1978), 112–23.

——, 'La Rose D'Amour' in *The Pearl: A Journal of Facetiae and Voluptuous Reading* (Reprinted Kent: New English Library, 1985), pp. 82–189.

Pearson, M. *Age of Consent: Victorian Prostitution and its Enemies* (Newton Abbot: David and Charles, 1972).

Philbin, A. I., 'The Literary "Femme Fatale" – A Social Fiction: The Willful Female in the Deterministic Vision of Thomas Hardy and in the Psychological Vision of Henry James' (Unpublished Doctoral Dissertation, Southern Illinois University, 1977).

Pierce, Peter, 'Rider Haggard' (Unpublished Doctoral Dissertation, Oxford University, 1974).

Pittock, M., 'Rider Haggard and *Heart of Darkness*', *Conradiana*, 19, no. 3 (1987), 206–8.

Poole, Adrian, 'Men's Words and Hardy's Women', *Essays in Criticism*, 31, no. 4 (October 1981), 328–45.

Praz, Mario, *The Romantic Agony*, trans. Angus Davidson (The World Publishing Company, Meridian Books, 1956).

Proudhon, P.-J., *La Pornocratie, ou Les Femmes Dans Les Temps Modernes* (Paris: A. Lacroix, 1888).

Punter, David, *The Literature of Terror* (London: Longman, 1980).

Purdy, R. L., *Thomas Hardy: A Bibliographical Study* (Oxford: Oxford University Press, 1954).

Rapin, René (ed.), *Lettres de Joseph Conrad à Marguerite Poradowska* (Geneva: Droz, 1966).

Ray, Martin, 'Conrad, Nordau and Other Degenerates: The Psychology of *The Secret Agent*', *Conradiana*, 16, no. 2 (1984), 125–41.

——, 'The Gift of Tongues: The Languages of Joseph Conrad', *Conradiana*, 15, no. 2 (1983), 83–110.

Rendall, J. (ed.), *Equal or Different* (Oxford: Blackwell, 1987).

Richardson, M., 'The Psychoanalysis of Ghost Stories', *The Twentieth Century*, CLXVI 994 (1959), 426–30.

Ridley, Hugh, *Images of Imperial Rule* (London and Canberra: Croom Helm; New York: St. Martin's Press, 1983).

Robinson, Roger, 'Hardy and Darwin', in *Thomas Hardy: The Writer and his Background*, ed. Norman Page (London: Bell & Hyman, 1980), 128–50.

Robinson, Ronald and Gallagher, J., *Africa and the Victorians: The Official Mind of Imperialism* (London: Macmillan and New York: St. Martin's Press, 1961).

——, 'The Imperialism of Free Trade', *Economic History Review*, 2nd ser., VI (1953), 1–15.

Robinson, W. J., *Married Life and Happiness, Or Love and Comfort in Marriage* (1922: rpt New York: Eugenics Publishing Co., 1933).

Romanes, George J., 'Mental Differences between Men and Women', *The Nineteenth Century*, 21 (May 1887), 654–72.

Roth, Phillis A., 'Suddenly Sexual Women in Bram Stoker's *Dracula*', *Literature and Psychology*, 27 (1977), 113–21.

Said, Edward., *Orientalism* (London: Routledge & Kegan Paul, 1978).

Sandison, Alan, *The Wheel of Empire: A Study of the Imperial Idea in Some Late Nineteenth and Early Twentieth Century Fiction* (London: Macmillan, 1967).

Saveson, John E., 'Conrad, Blackwood's and Lombroso', *Conradiana*, 6 (1974), 57–62.

Seed, David, 'The Narrative Method of *Dracula*', *Nineteenth Century Fiction*, 40 (1985–86), 61–75.

Senf, Carol A., '*Dracula*: Stoker's Response to the New Woman', *Victorian Studies*, 26 (Autumn 1982), 33–50.

——, '*Dracula*: The Unseen Face in the Mirror', *Journal of Narrative Technique*, 9 (1979), 160–70.

Sherry, Norman, *Conrad's Eastern World* (Cambridge: Cambridge University Press, 1966).

——, *Conrad's Western World* (Cambridge: Cambridge University Press, 1971).

Showalter, E., 'Syphilis, Sexuality and the Fiction of the Fin-de-Siècle' in *Sex, Politics and Science in the Nineteenth-Century Novel*. Selected Papers of the English Institute (1983–84), ed. Ruth Bernard Yeazell (Baltimore: Johns Hopkins University Press, 1986), pp. 88–115.

Silverman, Kaja, 'History, Figuration and Female Subjectivity in *Tess of the d'Urbervilles*', *Novel*, 18, no. 1 (Fall 1984), 5–28.

Simcox, Edith, 'The Capacity of Women', *The Nineteenth Century*, 22 (September 1887), 391–402.

Simmons, James C., 'Ambiguities of Tess as Pure Woman', *American Notes and Queries*, 10 (1972), 86–88.

Sizemore, C. W., 'The Small Cardboard Box: A Symbol of the City and of Winnie Verloc in Conrad's *The Secret Agent*', *Modern Fiction Studies*, 24, pp. 23–9.

Smart, Barry, *Michel Foucault*, Key Sociologists Series (Chichester: Ellis Horwood, 1985).

Sontag, Susan, *AIDS and Its Metaphors* (Harmondsworth: Penguin, 1989).

Spencer, H., *First Principles* (New York: A. Appleton and Co., 1901).

Spivak, Gayatri C., 'Feminism and Critical Theory', in *In Other Worlds: Essays in Cultural Politics* (New York and London: Methuen, 1987), pp. 77–92.

——, 'Explanation and Culture: Marginalia', in *In Other Worlds: Essays in Cultural Politics* (New York and London: Methuen, 1987), pp. 103–117.

Stark, Bruce, K., 'Kurtz's Intended: The Heart of *Heart of Darkness*', *Texas Studies in Literature and Language*, 16 (1974), 535–55.

Stoker, Bram, 'The Censorship of Fiction', *The Nineteenth Century*, 64 (September 1908), 477–87.

——, *The Jewel of Seven Stars* (1912; reprinted in The Ullerscroft Large Print Series, London: Jarold's Publishers, n.d.).

Street, Brian V., *The Savage in Literature* (London: Routledge and Kegal Paul, 1975).

Stubbs, Patricia, *Women and Fiction: Feminism and the Novel, 1880–1920* (Brighton: Harvester Press, 1979).

Sturgis, James, 'Britain and the New Imperialism', in *British Imperialism in the Nineteenth Century*, ed. C. C. Eldridge, Problems in Focus Series (London: Macmillan, 1984), 85–105.

Sullivan, Z. T., 'Enclosure, Darkness and the Body: Conrad's Landscape', *The Centennial Review*, 25, no. 1 (Winter 1981), 59–79.

Talmey, B. S., *Woman; A Treatise on the Normal and Pathological Emotions of Feminine Love* (1904; enlarged and revised edn, New York: Practitioners Publishing Co., 1910).

Tanner, Tony, 'Colour and Movement in Hardy's *Tess of the d'Urbervilles*', *Critical Quarterly*, 10 (1968), 219–39.

Taylor, Jenny B., *In the Secret Theatre of Home: Wilkie Collins, Sensation Narrative and Nineteenth-Century Psychology* (London: Routledge, 1988).

Thekkeveetil, B., 'The "Femme Fatale" in the Major Novels of Thomas Hardy' (Unpublished Doctoral Dissertation, St John's University, New York, 1983).

Thompson, Gordon, 'Conrad's Women', *Nineteenth Century Fiction*, 32, no. 4 (1978), 442–63.

Thorslev, Peter Jr., 'The Wild Man's Revenge' in *The Wild Man Within: An Image in Western Thought from the Renaissance to Romanticism*, ed. Edward J. Dudley and M. E. Novak (Pittsburgh: University of Pittsburgh Press, 1973), pp. 281–309.

Thurley, G., *The Psychology of Hardy's Novels: The Nervous and the Statuesque* (Queensland: University of Queensland Press, 1975).

Tickner, Lisa, *The Spectacle of Women: Imagery of the Suffrage Campaign, 1907–1914* (London: Chatto & Windus, 1987).

Trudgill, Eric, *Madonnas and Magdalens: The Origins and Development of Victorian Sexual Attitudes* (London: Heinemann, 1976).

Twitchell, J. B., *The Living Dead; A Study of the Vampire in Romantic Literature* (Durham N C: Duke University Press, 1981).

Van Ghent, D., *The English Novel: Form and Function* (New York: Holt, Rinehart and Winston, 1953).

Vicinus, Martha, *Suffer and Be Still: Women in the Victorian Age* (Bloomington: University of Indiana Press, 1973).

Visiak, E. H., *Mirror of Conrad* (London: Werner Laurie, 1955).

Vogt, Carl, *Lectures on Man: His Place in Creation and in the History of the Earth*, ed. James Hunt (London: Longmans and Green, 1864).

Wall, G. F. C., '"Different From Writing": *Dracula* in 1897', *Literature and History*, 10, no. 1 (Spring, 1984), 15–23.

Wallace, A. R., *The Malay Archipelago: The Land of the Orang-Utan and the Bird of Paradise: A Narrative of Travel with Studies of Man and Nature* (1869, rpt. New York: Dover Publications, 1962).

Walker, Cherryl (ed.), *Women and Gender in South Africa to 1945* (Claremont, Southern Africa: David Philip Publishers; London: James Currey, 1990).

Wallace, Bursey, 'Rider Haggard: A Study in Popular Fiction' (Unpublished Doctoral Dissertation, Memorial University of Newfoundland, 1973).

Watt, Ian, *Conrad in the Nineteenth Century* (London: Chatto & Windus, 1980).

Watts, Cedric, 'A Bloody Racist: About Achebe's View of Conrad', *Yearbook of English Studies* 13 (1983), 196–209.

Weeks, Jeffrey, *Sex, Politics and Society: The Regulation of Sexuality Since 1800* (London: Longman, 1981).

Weiner, Martin J., *English Culture and the Decline of the Industrial Spirit 1850–1980* (Cambridge: Cambridge University Press, 1981).

Weissman, J., 'Women and Vampires: *Dracula* as a Victorian Novel', *Midwest Quarterly*, 18, no. 4 (1977), 392–405.

Wells, H. G. *The War of the Worlds* (1897; reprinted in *Seven Science Fiction Novels*, New York: Dover Press, n.d.).

Williams, Raymond, *The Long Revolution* (London: Chatto & Windus, 1961).

Wilt, Judith, 'The Imperial Mouth: Imperialism, The Gothic and Science-Fiction', *Journal of Popular Fiction*, 14, no. 4 (1980–81), 618–28.

Wolf, L. (ed.), *The Annotated Dracula* (London: New English Library, 1975).

——, *A Dream of Dracula: In Search of the Living Dead* (Boston: Little, Brown, 1972).

Yeazell, R. B. (ed.), *Sex, Politics and Science in the Nineteenth-Century Novel*, Selected Papers of the English Institute (1983–84) (Baltimore: Johns Hopkins University Press, 1986).

# Index